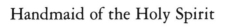

Handmaid of the Holy Spirit

From *Germanies* Desolations, *Rochels* Siege, until *Irelands* Blow, and what since followed; like one waves pursuing another, forerunners of the moments great change and general Iudgement, ~~when persons or Sex; without such respects:~~ even which Passages not unforeshewed by her hand, together with the aforesaid Golden Number of *Nineteen years and a half* to *A*° 1644. extending IRELAND his *January* Account not onely, but the late *Charls* when became a prisoner, *Nazeby*, &c. That day of Iudgement, *A*° 45. current; afterward tasting of the said fatal Moneths cold Cup: as *Buckingbams August* Moneth, him foreshewed, whereupon (boading to that Nation a lash) she wan that

that wager to his smart: The typifying Breeches of the *Sotch* man her Husband, against such wimzes of hers who laid them, as he then termed it, passing not scotfree, &c.

And these with other like, a world not able to contain them : also this for another, 1647. by the same token that Night a bold Star facing the Moon(April. 2.)passed through her Body, at which time served that VVrit, bearing date the second of April : *I send thee to a rebellious house*, &c. *Ezek.* 2. and *cap.* 12. she prefixing *Penticost* ensuing, as when such a mighty rushing wind, to beware them like as when they all assembled, &c. witness *Southwark* : That Mornings ghests unexpected accompanied with such a Thun

Lady Eleanor's notes and corrections on pages from *Appearance*.
Courtesy of the Folger Shakespeare Library.

Handmaid of the Holy Spirit

Dame Eleanor Davies,
Never Soe Mad a Ladie

ESTHER S. COPE

Ann Arbor

THE UNIVERSITY OF MICHIGAN PRESS

1995   1994   1993   1992   4   3   2   1

A CIP catalogue record for this book is available from the British Library.

Library of Congress Cataloging-in-Publication Data

Cope, Esther S., 1942–
    Handmaid of the Holy Spirit : Dame Eleanor Davies, never soe mad a
ladie / Esther S. Cope.
        p.   cm.
    Includes bibliographical references and index.
    ISBN 0-472-10303-2 (alk. paper)
    1. Eleanor, Lady, d. 1652. 2. Prophets—England—Biography.
I. Title.
BR1725.E43C67   1992
274.2'06'092—dc20
[B]   92-26576
                                                                          CIP

Grateful acknowledgment is made to the *Huntington Library Quarterly* for
permission to publish portions of this material which appeared in an earlier
form in my article, "Dame Eleanor Davies Never Soe Mad a Ladie," 50,
no. 2 (1987): 33–44; to the Folger Shakespeare Library for permission to
publish materials D1972.45 Bdw. D2010 and D1980 Bdw. D2010; and
to the Provost and Fellows of Worcester College, Oxford for permission
to publish materials Worc. Coll. AA.1.12(1) Title Page and Worc. Coll.
BB.x.6(1) verso of last page.

For
Elizabeth Read Foster

Acknowledgments

Lady Eleanor's remarkable story has left me indebted to more people than I can possibly mention. I have tried to acknowledge those to whom I owe specific references in the appropriate footnotes. Remaining unnamed are countless others whose response to my topic gave me a new perspective or suggested another point for research. Megan Matschinske and Kate Pahl are among those who have encountered Lady Eleanor through their own work and have shared generously with me in letters or conversation. Librarians and archivists who have been particularly helpful to me as I attempted to trace Lady Eleanor's life and writings include those of the Houghton Library at Harvard; Worcester College, Oxford; Trinity College, Dublin; the Folger Shakespeare Library; the Huntington Library; the Public Record Office; the House of Lords Record Office; and the British Library. Without their willing cooperation and that of many individuals and departments of the University of Nebraska–Lincoln Libraries I would still be at an earlier stage of my research.

Financial aid in the form of a fellowship from the Huntington Library in the summer of 1988, a Maud Hammond Fling Fellowship from the Research Council of the University of Nebraska–Lincoln for the summer of 1989, a grant from the National Endowment for the Humanities for Travel to Collections in the summer of 1989, a leave for research with partial pay from the University of Nebraska–Lincoln during the spring semester of 1989–90, and the Folger Institute's Center for the History of British Political Thought's invitation to conduct an early summer seminar at the Folger Library in 1990 made it possible for me to spend time at critically important archives and to take advantage of invaluable opportunities for interchange with other readers. Those whose time coincided with mine at the Huntington, in England, or at the Folger may be able to identify the fruits of one of our discussions. The members of my Folger seminar and the scholars who visited us deserve special thanks.

I cast my net widely in my efforts to verify and augment the autobiographical information that Lady Eleanor provided in her tracts. Few of my inquiries went unanswered even when the respondent was unable to provide what I had requested. Patricia Demers sent me a copy of her unpublished paper about Jane Lead. The Hon. William R. Benyon of Englefield graciously replied to my letter asking about a previous holder of his estate. The villagers at Englefield responded with similar courtesy when I knocked at their doors one summer's day at dinner time. Canon Keith Walker and the staff at Winchester Cathedral Library welcomed me when I went there to look at the diary of Dean Patrick Young. Patricia Alldridge did the same when I visited the archives at the Bethlem Royal Hospital. Other libraries and archives to whose staffs I turned for help included the Bodleian Library, Oxford; the Corporation of London Records Office; the Institute of Historical Research; Lambeth Palace Library; the National Portrait Gallery; and the National Trust Photographic Library. The members of the UN-L Medieval-Renaissance Studies Group have provided continuing support. They have patiently listened to me talk about Lady Eleanor and have responded to my often not very informed questions about literary matters. The organizers of the November 1990 Conference on Attending to Women in Early Modern England allowed me to discuss Lady Eleanor in a workshop that Margaret Ezell and I facilitated. I have read papers about Lady Eleanor at several meetings: the March 1985 Pacific Coast Conference on British Studies; the November 1988 Mid-Atlantic and North American Conference on British Studies and the November 1990 Southern and North American Conference on British Studies. A revised version of the first of these papers appeared in the *Huntington Library Quarterly* in 1987. I am grateful to the *Quarterly* for permission to draw from that article in my book.

During the long period from conception to birth as a book, I have drawn upon good will of many colleagues, students, and friends. David Sacks and Laetitia Yeandle have each read a part of the manuscript. Barbara Donagan, Barbara Harris, Ellen Macek, and Sears McGee have read the entire manuscript in one of its versions. In addition to reading a draft of the manuscript, Cynthia Herrup sent me a copy of her unpublished paper about the trial of Mervin, second earl of Castlehaven, and shared other findings with me. Anne Cope and Phyllis Mack have each read more than one version of the manuscript. Anne and David eliminated a number of unnecessary or unclear phrases with their editorial pencils, and the staff of the History Department at the University of Nebraska–Lincoln assisted me in printing it out. An invitation from the Women Writers Project to edit some of Lady Eleanor's tracts has enabled me to continue devoting time to her and her prophecies. Many others who did not see the manuscript and whom I have not named have contributed to it by believing in it when I doubted. Their moral support and encouragement deserves more thanks than can be expressed. I hope they will not be disappointed in the result. The final responsibility for what follows is mine.

Contents

Abbreviations

Lady Eleanor's Tracts

Following each abbreviation is the tract's STC number and, where appropriate, a longer title. P&R precedes numbers from Pollard and Redgrave, where she is listed as Eleanor Audeley; D precedes the numbers from Wing, where she is listed as Eleanor Douglas. Dates in parentheses are those shown in the tracts; dates in brackets are supplied from internal or other evidence.

All the Kings of the Earth: P&R 903.5: *All the Kings of the earth shall prayse thee, O Lord, for they have heard the words of thy mouth; yea they shall sing etc. xxviii dayes, 138. Psalme* (1633).

Amend, Amend: D1967: *Amend, Amend; Gods Kingdome is at Hand: Amen, Amen. The proclamation* (1643).

And without Proving: D1968: *And without proving what we say* [1648].

Apoc., chap. 11: D1969: *Apocalyps, Chap. 11. Its accomplishment shewed from the Lady Eleanor* [1648].

Apoc. J.C.: D1970: *Apocalypsis Jesu Christi. Domine Dominus: Psal.8.3* (1644).

Appeal from Court to Camp: [not in STC]: *Her Appeal from the Court to the Camp* (1649).

Appearance: D1972A: *The Appearance or Presence of the Son of Man* (1650).

Arraignment: D1972B: *The Arraignment by the Lady Eleanor* (1650).

As not Unknowne: D1973: *As not unknowne, though hath long beene deferd:* (1645).

Before the Lords Second Coming: D1974: *Before the Lords Second Coming of The last Days To be visited, Signed with the Tyrant Pharoahs Overthrow* (1650).

Benediction: D1975–7 *The Benidiction* [sic]; *The Benediction. From the A:lmighty O:mnipotent* (1651).

Bethelehem: D1978: *Bethlehem, signifying the house of bread or War. Whereof informs, Whoso takes a small Roul to taste cures forthwith Distraction in the Supreamest Nature; with such vertue indu'd* (1652).

Bill of Excommunication: D1979: *The Bill of Excommunication for abolishing henceforth the Sabbath called Sunday or First day.* (1649 [50]).

Blasphemous Charge: D1980–1: *The blasphemous charge against Her; The Blasphemous charge against her* (1649).

Brides Preparation: D1982: *The brides preparation* (1644 [5]).

Crying Charge: D1982A: *The crying charge* (1649).

Day of Judgment: D1983: *The day of Judgments modell* (1646).

Discovery: [not in STC]: *A Discovery unto what Nation the last Day* (1644; 1649). [see *A Sign.*]

Dragons Blasphemous Charge: D1984: *The Dragons Blasphemous Charge against her* (1651).

Elijah the Tishbite: D1985: *Elijah the Tishbite's supplication When was Presented the likeness of a Hand, etc* (1650).

Everlasting Gospel: D1986: *The everlasting gospel* (1649).

Excommunication out of Paradice: D1987: *The excommunication out of paradice* (1647).

Ezekiel, cap. 2: D1988: *Ezekiel, cap. 2* [1647].

Ezekiel the Prophet: D1988A: *Ezekiel the prophet explained* (1647).

For the Blessed Feast: D1989: *For the blessed feast of Easter* (1646).

For Gerbier: D1989B: *For the right noble, Sir Balthazar Gerbier Knight* (1649).

For the States: D1989A: *For the most honorable states sitting at Whitehall* (1649).

For Whitsun: D1990: *For Whitsun Tyds last feast the present, 1645* (1645).

Gatehouse Salutation: D1991A: *The gatehouse salutation* (1646 [7]).

Given to the Elector: D1992–3: *Given to the Elector Prince Charles* [or Charls] *of the Rhyne From the Lady Eleanor, Anno 1633. at her being in Holland or Belgia* (1633 [48]).

Great Brittains Visitation: D1994: *Great Brittains visitation* (1645).

Hells Destruction: D1995: *Hells Destruction* (1651).

Her Appeal (1641): D1971: *The Lady Eleanor her appeal to the High Court of Parliament* (1641).

Her Appeal (1646): D1972: *The Lady Eleanor her appeal. Present this to Mr. mace the Prophet of the most High, his Messenger* (1646).

Her Blessing: D1991: *From the Lady Eleanor, her blessing to her beloved daughter, the right Honorable Lucy, Countesse of Huntingdon. The Prophet Daniels Vision: Chap. 7* (1644).

Her Jubilee: D1996B: *The Lady Eleanor Douglas, dowager, her iubilees Plea or Appeal, Ano & d* [1650].

I am the First: D1996: *I am the first, and the last, the beginning and the ending* (1644 [5]).

Je le tien: D1996A: *Je le tien: The general restitution* (1646).

Mystery of General Redemption: D1996C: *The mystery of general redemption* (1647).

New Jerusalem: D1997: *The new Jerusalem at hand* (1649).

New Proclamation: D1998: *The new proclamation, in answer to a letter* (1649).

Of Errors: D1999: *Of errors ioyned with Gods word* (1645).

Of the Great Days: D1999A: *Of the general great days approach to his Excellency Sir Thomas Fairfax General* (1648).

Of Times: D2000: *Of times and seasons their Mystery* (1651).

Prayer (1644): D2001: *A prayer or petition for peace November 22.1644* (1644); also (1649).

Prayer (1645): D2002–3: *A prayer or petition for peace November 22. 1645* (1645).

Prophesie: D2004: *A Prophesie of the Last Day to be Revealed in the Last Times, And then of the cutting off the Church and of the Redemption out of Hell. The Word of God* (1645).

Prophetia: D2005: *Prophetia de die Novissimo novissimis hisce temporibus manifestando; item de excisione Ecclesiae & Redemptione Ex inferis* (1644).

Reader: D2005A: *Reader, the heavy hour at hand* (1648).

Remonstrance: D2006: *The Lady Eleanor her remonstrance to Great Britain* (1648).

Restitution of Prophecy: D2007: *The restitution of prophecy; that Buried Talent to be revived* (1651 [2]).

Restitution of Reprobates: D2008: *The restitution of reprobates* (1644).

Revelation Interpreted: D2009: *The revelation interpreted* (1646).

Samsons Fall: D2010: *Samsons fall, presented to the House 1642* (1642).

Samsons Legacie: D2011: *Samsons legacie* [1643].

Second Coming: D2012: *The {second} co{ming of Our} Lo{rd} Dedicate{d to} Britt{ain}* (1645).

Serpents Excommunication: D2012A: *The serpents excommunication. In Essex where cutting down a Wood, divers of thesse Sprouts of the Warlike Ash or Branches grew* (1651).

Sign: D2012AA: *A sign given them being entred into the day of Judgment to set their House in order. For the High Court of Parliament assembled* (1644; 1649).

Sions Lamentation: D2012B: *Sions Lamentation, Lord Henry Hastings, his Funerals blessing, by his Grandmother, the Lady Eleanor* (1649).

Star to the Wise: D2013: *The Star to the Wise. 1643. To the high court of Parliament, the honorable House of Commons: the Lady Eleanor her Petition; Shewing cause to have her Book Licensed, being The Revelations Interpretation* (1643).

Strange and Wonderful: D2014: *Strange and wonderful prophesies By the Lady Eleanor Audeley; who is yet alive and lodgeth in White-Hall* (1649).

To the High Court: D2015: *To the most honorable High Court of Parliament assembled, etc* (1643); [see *Samsons Legacie*].

Tobits Book: D2016: *Tobits book: a lesson appointed for Lent* (1652).

Warning to the Dragon: P&R 904: *A Warning to the dragon and all his angels* (1625).

Wherefore to Prove: D2017: *Wherefore to prove the thing* [1648]; [see *And without Proving*].

Woe to the House: 904.5 *Woe to the house* (1633).

Word of God: D2018: *The word of God, to the Citie of London, from the Lady Eleanor: of the Earle of Castle-Haven: Condemn'd, and Beheaded: Aprill 25.1631.etc* (1644 [5]).

Writ of Restitution: D2019: *The writ of restitution* (1648).

Zach. 12: D2020: *Zach{ariah}* 12 (1649) [see *Sions Lamentation*].

Other Abbreviations

Birch, *Charles I:* T. Birch, ed., *The Court and Times of Charles I,* 2 vols (London: Henry Colburn, 1848).

B.L., Add. MS: British Library, Additional Manuscript.

Bodl., MS. Carte: Bodleian Library, Carte Manuscript.

Cal. St. P. Dom: Calendar of State Papers, Domestic Series.

Cal. St. P. Ire: Calendar of State Papers, Ireland.

C.J.: Journal of the House of Commons.

DNB: Dictionary of National Biography.

Folger: Folger Shakespeare Library.

Harvard: Houghton Library, Harvard University.

HEH, Ellesmere MSS: Henry E. Huntington Library, Ellesmere Manuscripts.

HEH, Hastings MSS: Henry E. Huntington Library, Hastings Manuscripts.

Hindle: C. J. Hindle, *A Bibliography of the Printed Pamphlets and Broadsides of Lady Eleanor Douglas, the 17th Century Prophetess* (1934; reprint, Edinburgh, 1936).

HLRO, Main Papers: House of Lords Record Office, Main Papers.

H.M.C.: Historical Manuscripts Commission.

L.J.: Journal of the House of Lords

Pollard and Redgrave: *A Short-Title Catalogue of Books Printed in England, Scotland, and Ireland, And of English Books Printed Abroad,* compiled by A. W. Pollard and G. R. Redgrave (London: Bibliographical Society, 1926).

P.R.O., C: Public Record Office, Chancery.

P.R.O., E: Public Record Office, Exchequer.

P.R.O., PC: Public Record Office, Privy Council.

P.R.O., PROB: Public Record Office, Probate.

P.R.O., SP: State Papers.

S.T.: T. B. Howell, ed., *Complete Collection of State Trials* (London, 1816).

Thomason: George Thomason, *Catalogue of the Pamphlets, Books, Newspapers, and Manuscripts Relating to the Civil War, the Commonwealth, and Restoration, 1640–1661,* 2 vols. (London, 1908).

VCH: Victoria County History.

Wing: *A Short-Title Catalogue of Books printed in England, Scotland, Ireland, Wales, and British America, And of English Books Printed in other countries, 1641–1700*, compiled by Donald Wing (New York: Index Society, 1945).

Worcester College: Library, Worcester College, Oxford.

Introduction

I first met the woman I shall call Lady Eleanor when I was doing research for my book on the politics of the 1630s. She was virtually the only woman among the individuals summoned to answer in the courts of Star Chamber and High Commission for political and religious criticism of the Caroline regime. My interest in her grew with the discovery that she had claimed to be a prophet, that she had not only been imprisoned but also confined to Bedlam, and that many in her day as well as later believed that, if she was not mad, she was the prototypical rebellious woman whom the pamphleteers lampooned.[1] Although I tried to put her aside, I was unable to forget her. I had misgivings about moving from the seemingly solid foundations of parliamentary history to the controversial and shadowy world of women, prophecy, and madness, but my fascination compelled me to persist even though my experience confirmed my apprehensions.

Writing about madness in the seventeenth century is challenging in itself. Men and, especially, women who violated social conventions and expressed political or religious dissent might be called mad. Lady Eleanor was mad by these standards. Her determined pursuit of her goals and her vehement denunciations of those who impeded her exhibited the fanaticism that, both in her own era and since, have frequently been equated with madness. Her claim to be a prophet and her candor in questioning established authority make her contact with reality appear tenuous, but, in recognizing inconsistencies and irrationalities in the world in which she lived, she sometimes saw what many of her contemporaries refused to see. A diagnosis of her condition using modern criteria is neither possible nor appropriate for a historical study. Readers may wish to speculate about this for themselves.

Having repeatedly struggled to sort out and identify the ingredients among Lady Eleanor's veritable puree of biblical, historical, personal, and prophetic references and to untangle her life from my own, I eventually admitted that I could not write the straightforward biography that I had anticipated. Unless I were to abandon history for the novel that well-meaning friends had assumed I was writing when they heard about my topic, I had to deal with what my sources revealed. The result is a book that focuses upon her interpretation of her experiences, an interpretation that has its basis in religious belief. Like people who, over the centuries, have seen inspiration to free themselves from bondage in the Bible, Lady Eleanor found a message that spoke to her condition in its texts. She put her own idiosyncratic stamp upon it.

If Lady Eleanor had regarded herself only as a prophet after she began writing in 1625, her biography would necessarily begin with a description of the experience in July of that year that led her take up prophecy. A prophet ordinarily gave up her or his own identity to be a vessel for another, greater power; Lady Eleanor did not. She took her responsibilities as prophet very seriously. Modeling herself on such biblical examples as Daniel, Elijah, and St. John the Evangelist, she identified herself with the British Isles, saw her personal struggles in public conflicts, and devoted herself to correcting and annotating her tracts. Maintaining, at the same time, that her traditionally female roles were crucial to her prophetic work, she continued to act as wife, mother, and aristocratic woman. She defended her honor with a self-importance that we see among others of her class and era. Her "vision" raised questions about who she was, and it belongs within the larger context of her life. Although she concentrated upon the period after she had become a prophet in her tracts, she did not make it the sole focus of her attention.

Lady Eleanor published most of her tracts during the 1640s, when increasing numbers of women and men of all ranks were speaking publicly, preaching and prophesying, and having their words printed. Like these activist contemporaries, Lady Eleanor challenged ideas, institutions, and individuals in authority, but she began speaking out in the 1620s and 1630s when few other women did. A baron's daughter, she aspired to make a figure in society. Aristocratic attitudes continued to infuse her life and prophecies after the outbreak of civil war and even after the king's execution in 1649. In her tenacity in seeking to recover property that she believed was hers, she followed a course similar to that of Anne Clifford, Countess of Dorset and later of Pembroke.[2] Lady Eleanor nevertheless stood apart both from other aristocratic women and from women who were, at the same time, pointing out the evils around them and predicting that Judgment was imminent. Unlike some of the women who prophesied, she never attracted followers.

Lady Eleanor's intellect, rank, and reputation for being outspoken invite comparisons with Margaret Cavendish, Duchess of Newcastle, who likewise remained a solitary figure. Both women probably grew up apart from siblings, both married older men with unfulfilled ambitions for recognition, and both felt ostracized at court and in society even before their publications had marked them as different. They also took their writing seriously; they referred to their books as their children. Although both lamented some of the restrictions imposed upon them as women, they dealt with these in very different ways. Lady Eleanor, whose husbands burned her books, lashed out at the evils of the world in her prophecies, whereas the Duchess of Newcastle expressed herself more gently in letters, plays, and essays. She even wrote an admiring life of her husband, and he contributed a poem of commendation at the beginning of her *Sociable Letters*.[3]

Lady Eleanor was an early feminist, although both the language she used and her focus upon the wrongs she herself had suffered were different from those of more recent advocates for women. Rather than the secular idiom of social change or revolution, she employed words and phrases from the Bible, and her language was that of apocalyptic expectation. As prophet, she represented herself as a figure or symbol for all of God's people, for her own country, and particularly for women, and, in her complaints about her own experiences, she raised fundamental questions about the position of women in early Stuart Britain. Like the women of the next generation whom Hilda Smith has called "reason's disciples," Lady Eleanor identified a host of irrationalities in English law and society with regard to women.[4] Recent developments in women's studies suggest new ways of looking at her life. Rather than simply seeing her as a flawed prophet or third-rate political critic based upon a male model, we need to examine her in her own right and as a woman. Her prophecies were at once unique and characteristic of women's autobiographical writings of the era.[5] In many instances she employed the words of scholars, but she told what it was like to be a woman in a patriarchal world. Covered by the clothing of her prophecies, which were often in the style of conversion stories or romancelike tales and adorned with examples from paintings on alehouse walls, the world of nature, the seasons, the weather, and other features of everyday life, were her own mundane experiences as daughter, wife, mother, and widow.

Through Lady Eleanor we can, in addition to learning about her and her mission, explore what Sara Mendelson has called "the mental world of Stuart Women." We can also delve into social, cultural, political, and religious issues of her times—the debates about church government, discipline, and doctrine and the conflicts of civil war and revolution. Her own awareness of the "Great Brittaines foure Crownes or Kingdomes" that had "married" or "united" contrasts with the Anglocentricism of many historians.[6] Readers less interested in the seventeenth-century historical context may wish to compare and contrast Lady Eleanor's experiences with those of the medieval women visionaries whose development Elizabeth Petroff has studied. Petroff's model for the personal spiritual journeys of women, such as the Beguines and Catherine of Siena, can be used to examine the course of Lady Eleanor's prophetic life.[7] Others may choose to juxtapose her with recent crusaders for equal rights. Through her life we confront questions about women, class, property, family, and law.

The evidence for a study of Lady Eleanor falls into two categories: material about her from public and private records, especially from family papers among the Hastings Manuscripts at the Huntington Library, and her own prophetic tracts, many of which appear in a volume that probably belonged to her daughter and is now in the Folger Library. The sixty-odd tracts that she published between 1625 and her death in 1652 are most important. Many of these she corrected and annotated in her own hand. Varying in length from a broadsheet to one hundred pages, her texts are cumbersome and delphic even for a genre noted for enigma. She ordinarily wrote in the third rather than the first person, strung phrases together, often omitted subjects or verbs, shifted abruptly from the biblical to the historical or personal, and so packed the tracts with anagrams, puns, and complex images that their seemingly inscrutable message demonstrated graphically how the unbeliever could not understand the wisdom of the prophet. At the same time that she consciously veiled her message, she also made attempts to win the attention and sympathy of readers by using forms and techniques that might be familiar to them. Whether she or her printer was responsible for the capitalizations and italics that emphasize particular words and phrases, these contribute to the unique character of her texts. Contemporaries who read copies of the tracts would have seen them, and I have attempted to reproduce these in my quotations. Even when not quoting, I have placed her anagrams entirely in capitals.

Rather than providing a clear narrative of her life, Lady Eleanor's tracts created a multidimensional world of truth and time that seemed to defy my efforts to impose an analytical framework upon it. None of her own writings, and only a few references in other sources, survive from the years before 1625, when she took up prophecy. One body of material telling little about Lady Eleanor but contributing to her image as an exotic concerns her brother, Mervin Touchet, Lord Audeley and second earl of Castlehaven, whose trial and execution for rape and sodomy in 1631 shocked and disturbed contemporaries.

I have chosen to call my subject Lady Eleanor. This is a slightly abbreviated version of "The Lady Eleanor," the signature she herself adopted on the title page of many of her tracts. The various sobriquets that she assumed in the course of prophesying were part of her effort to convince her contemporaries to heed her message. To address her by the surname of her father or, subsequently, her husband deprives her of part of the new identity she assumed when she became a prophet.

The language that Lady Eleanor used in referring to herself suggests that she recognized the difficulty of finding the right words to describe her role. In becoming a "Handmaid to the Holy Spirit," whom she saw as neither traditionally masculine nor feminine, she too had become androgynous. Sometimes she called herself a *prophet* and sometimes a *prophetess*. Time and again she noted the significance of the fact that she, a woman, was bearing the word of the Second Coming. The Bible itself explained why the mission she had assumed was appropriate for one of her sex and why she should not be reprimanded for defying conventions concerning women's conduct by publishing books inter-preting the will of God for England. In order to emphasize the tension between others' expectations and her prophetic activities, I have re-frained from using the term *prophetess*. She was a prophet.

Lady Eleanor based her examination of her own life and of history in general upon the Word of God, the Bible. She was sufficiently familiar with the Bible in both the King James and Geneva versions that she drew from it without necessarily indicating that she was doing so or citing the source of her text. For the benefit of readers who, like me, may be less well versed in scripture, I have added some parenthetical biblical references.

From the Bible, Lady Eleanor took the chronological framework that she, as prophet, made her particular concern. Even though her reckonings of the application of divine time to terrestial life seem to make no sense by our standards, she recorded the dates that specific events occurred. The beginning of the year on 25 March, according to the Julian calendar then used in England, was important to her because that day was Lady Day, the Feast of the Annunciation. I have nevertheless decided that, although giving dates in the old style, I should for purposes of clarity make the year begin 1 January.

The narrative of Lady Eleanor's development as a prophet during a critical period in British history provides the foundation for analysis of the content of her message. It also offers an opportunity to examine her contemporaries' notions about women, prophecy, madness, obedience, and order. From this basis, readers may compare and contrast her experience with that of women and dissidents in her own era and at other times, both before and since.

CHAPTER I

The Lady Eleanor

At her birth in 1590, Lady Eleanor entered a world in which gender mattered more than class. The experience of the Queen herself illustrated the overwhelming importance of gender. Elizabeth I, who sat upon the throne until 1603, was, by virtue of being queen, freed from the restrictions of class, and because she remained unmarried, she escaped the bondage to a husband that defined the lives of most women. The image that she projected emphasized the extraordinary and compensated for what would, in other women, be regarded as feminine inadequacies: her unmarried and childless state and her not being a man. She took the role of the divinely appointed deliverer, the virgin who would bring new life to her kingdom, and that of a ruler whose strength and courage could match that of any king.

Queen Elizabeth was exceptional, but she was not unique in not conforming to the legal, theological, and cultural paradigms of gender in her era. What women said and did in their daily lives provided a wealth of examples of how the models might be confirmed, rejected, or altered. The well-known controversy about women's nature was only one facet of tension that expressed itself in various arenas from the theater and the printed page to the courts of law, the hearth, and the home. The woman who, at marriage, exchanged her father's rule for her husband's and who accepted the injunction to be silent, chaste, and obedient was no more real than her opposite, who created havoc by violating all precepts. Yet their images exercised considerable influence.

Early modern English works about women draw upon three conceptual frameworks. Examples of each include both substantive studies and more superficial treatments. Underlying many discussions was the bipolar scheme that, on the basis of the Bible, divided women into Eves and Marys, Sinners and Saints. Included here are sermons and conduct books that exhorted women to behave properly and the morality tales about particular women who reaped the rewards of goodness or suffered the consequences of badness. A second, more complex arrangement grouped women around types, such as the muses whom Thomas Heywood used for his *Gunaikeion or Nine Books of Various History concerning Women* (1624). By taking particular historical contexts for its basis, the third structure made possible, although not necessary, a more thorough examination of the personality and experience of individual women. Some authors combined one or more of the schemes. John Foxe, in his *Book of Martyrs,* described specific women at moments when they confronted circumstances requiring them to demonstrate their religious commitment. Not all were able to stand firm in the face of persecution; some went farther than others in following in the footsteps of saints.

Within the parameters that gender set for women's behavior, social status provided a more detailed prescription of how the devout woman or the dutiful wife would be expected to conduct herself—where she might go, what she might wear, how she would speak, and what she might do. Lady Eleanor, as the fifth daughter of George Touchet, eleventh Baron Audeley, created earl of Castlehaven in 1616, and his wife, Lucy, daughter of Sir James Mervin of Fonthill Gifford, Wiltshire, claimed certain privileges, yet social boundaries, like those of gender, did not so completely form women's lives so as to prevent Lady Eleanor or others from developing patterns of their own.[1]

Though not among the most wealthy and powerful of the aristocracy, Lady Eleanor took pride in a heritage from "antiquity." When she became a prophet, she did not abandon that, but, by virtue of her new understanding, she reinterpreted her previous self to add credentials that could remedy weaknesses. The baronage of Audeley, she asserted, predated the Norman Conquest and thus did not stand upon the "yoke" of tyranny that her contemporaries believed the Normans had imposed. Her family's was "no created Peership" but, literally translated, the title was *"Audleigh,* or *Oldfield* in the *Saxon* tongue." The letters *A* and *O,* Audleigh and Oldfield, Alpha and Omega, the first and the last, proclaimed at once its ancient origins and the end that she anticipated.[2]

In presenting herself in terms of her paternity, Lady Eleanor conformed to a practice used by others of her class.[3] Like them, she expected the patriarchal world in which she lived to accord her the recognition that was her due from birth and complained when it did not. Using phrases that her father himself may have used, she bragged about her family's pedigree and described him as "no inferior peer" and the first Baron.[4] In 1613, in a letter to the Lord Deputy of Ireland, he pointed out "that having taken place firste and before all the barrons of Englande at his Majesties first coming to the Crowne," he found the order of precedence for the forthcoming Irish Parliament "unfitting."[5] From his aristocratic sensitivity about rank she drew justification for her own assertions to be first and last. She also pointed out ties that linked her family to the kingdoms claimed by the House of Stuart, whose title made them rulers of Great Britain, France, and Ireland. Her birth made her English, the Touchets connected her with France, Castlehaven, her father's earldom, added Ireland, and Douglas, her second husband, brought Scotland.[6] The vicissitudes that befell her family foreshadowed those that Britain would experience, but within her were the seeds of a new and Protestant unity that would heal the divisions that sin had caused. Her family's motto, *Je le tien* which she used as the title for a tract of 1646 and translated as "Hold fast till I come" (Revelation 2:25) signified the faith that was essential.[7]

As a prophet, Lady Eleanor extended the claims she had expressed as Audeley's daughter. No longer forced to accept judgments about her position that others derived from the law, she made her own determinations on the basis of the gospel. Much as the College of Arms scrutinized genealogies brought there by would-be gentry, she examined lineages to point out how the House of Stuart or her own family's violations of the bonds of matrimony had brought divine wrath upon their descendants. She reinterpreted the heraldic devices with which the elite proclaimed their rank and ancestry in order to manifest how tainted were those, like the House of Derby, who challenged her. Prophecy gave her an escape much as the duchess of Newcastle's literary life provided some compensation for a family history that was stained with indiscretion and embarrassment. Lady Eleanor contrasted the defects in her blood with the dishonor of others and with the legitimacy of her inspiration that made her work "no spurious *off-spring* of *Davids.*"[8] As prophet, she could surmount, too, the constraints that her society imposed upon women.

Gender prevented Lady Eleanor from pursuing the legal or clerical profession that would have seemed appropriate for one of her intellect and education. Like the aristocratic lineage that would also have counted for more if she had been a man, she may have acquired her taste for learning from her father. The Latin letters that Lord Audeley wrote to Lord Burghley in 1572 from Oxford (where he was a fellow at Magdalen College) and are almost the only evidence we have about his education suggest that he had taken that seriously.[9] We know even less about what provisions he may have made for the instruction of his seven children. His frequent absence from home during Lady Eleanor's early years makes it seem unlikely that he personally devoted much time to teaching his youngest daughter, even if he recognized how able she was. The role of Lady Eleanor's mother, Lucy, Lady Audeley, is likewise difficult to discern. She probably was able to write in English but not in Latin.[10] If Lady Eleanor had the advantage of a tutor like Samuel Daniel, who taught Lady Anne Clifford, neither she nor he have acknowledged this though the subsequent course of her life would have given anyone who had been responsible for her upbringing some cause for concealing that information.[11] Like others of her contemporaries, she may have shared a teacher with her brothers, Mervin and Ferdinando, who were both younger and close to her in age, but she was not the only one of the sisters to have Latin. Maria, the third, twelve years older than Eleanor, also had Latin and wrote well.[12]

Although some of Lady Eleanor's Latin involved common words and phrases that one might pick up without formally studying the language or biblical verses that one might copy, she also incorporated some longer passages in her writings and she probably composed the Latin text of her tract *Prophetia* (1644), of which an English edition was published the following year.[13] In the *Mystery of General Redemption* (1647), she argued that, by rendering the Latin *secula* into English as "for ever" instead of "ages," biblical translators had distorted the meaning of passages and contributed to the misunderstanding of God's mercy. An examination of the texts in question corroborates her.[14] Her knowledge, if any, of Greek and Hebrew was cursory, but she nevertheless discussed versions in those languages along with the English and Latin in *The Mystery of General Redemption*.[15] She was probably either using a polyglot Bible or relying upon the assistance of her daughter Lucy, who did know both Greek and Hebrew in addition to Latin, French, and Spanish. In *New Proclamation* (1649), she printed

Lucy's response to her query about the translation from the Greek and the interpretation of Philippians 2:6, concerning the trinity.

Both the form and content of Lady Eleanor's tracts illustrate, in addition to her facility with language and her scholarship, her familiarity with the subject matter of a traditional education in the liberal arts. She referred to the differences between sufficient and efficient causes and other elements of medieval schoolmen's arguments. She also knew the commonplaces of rhetoric—"a pleasing Theame . . . makes a good Orator"—and she consciously eschewed them. The standard "ornaments" and the "endlesse Figures" that some writers "borrowed out of old Orators Bookes" were, she said, not necessary to make her points.[16] She only occasionally referred explicitly to authors, either classical (Ovid, Seneca) or Christian (Origen or Tertullian), but, in accord with her own style and purpose, she incorporated a vast amount of ancient and modern learning in what she wrote. In a note to one of her tracts, she associated "the admirable arte of Navigation and Printing" with the end of time when prophecy would be fulfilled.[17] Although no records have survived of books belonging to her father, her husbands, or to her, she was surely a prodigious reader whose memory supplied her with material when she had no access to a good library.

Lady Eleanor's output suggests that she wrote easily and often took up her pen when particular events or incidents moved her to do so. Caught up in her emotions, she sought, through her writing, revenge against those who stood in her way and opposed prophecy. Hers was no uncontrolled torrent of words; her passion unleashed her intellect and energy to create a finely wrought piece. Even such brief works as the *Benediction* to Cromwell or her eight-page *Remonstrance,* which she could have dashed off without the references that she probably relied on when preparing the fifty-two pages of *Restitution of Prophecy* or the thirty-two pages of *Mystery of General Redemption,* bear the marks of her craft. For *Blasphemous Charge,* where she printed an account of her appearance before the High Commission in 1633, or *Crying Charge,* which included the trial of her brother, Mervin, in 1631, she artfully introduced transcripts of the proceedings themselves from among her papers.[18]

Using the Italic script that was common for women, Lady Eleanor wrote in a firm, bold hand that reveals both practice and confidence. Not for her were apologies like that of the duchess of Newcastle concerning illegibility or those that aristocrats sometimes made for relying upon a secretary.[19] The clarity of many of her letters contrasts dramatically with the unusual grammar and syntax that is characteristic of the majority of her tracts. Obfuscation suited her purpose when, as a prophet, she was interpreting what most individuals could not understand. She compared her prophecies to the ciphers or hieroglyphics that fascinated some of her contemporaries but were incomprehensible to the vast majority.[20] Through her writings she inverted order and claimed wisdom and power for herself instead of those who were currently ruling and neglecting true religion.

Anagrams, which were popular in cultured society at the time, allowed her to employ her intellect and amuse herself while accomplishing her mission. Her prophecy was, she said in 1625, "a salve to annoint and open the eyes of the blinde . . . a true looking-glasse, a large houre-glasse," and she illustrated how her message would act as a clarifying mirror by printing her own name, Eleanor Audeley, backward and her anagram of it, REVEALE O DANIEL forward.[21] By watching her printers like a hawk and by making handwritten corrections on printed copies of her tracts, she varied her spelling in order to have the letters she needed for the anagrams. The Babylonian king who ordinarily appeared in her texts as Belchazzar became BELCHASER when she wanted to create CHARLES BE.[22] Although there are times when irregularities slip through, she took pride in her work and intended that it be done right.

Lady Eleanor approached religion, her fundamental concern, with a seriousness similar to that which she gave to her writing. In the absence of evidence either about household devotional practices or about clergy associated with her family, it appears unlikely that she grew up amid puritanism.[23] Her mother's family, the Mervins, seem conventional in contrast to the more committed Protestantism of their Wiltshire rivals, the Thynnes and Knyvetts.[24] Although the Crown counted her father among the Protestants when it granted him the Irish earldom of Castlehaven in 1616, each of her brothers, Mervin and Ferdinando, flirted with Catholicism during his life.[25] Their popery and that of others she encountered in Ireland may have played a part in leading her to her own vehemently antipapist stance. Whether her spiritual journey began when she was a child or later, her tracts show that she was very familiar with the Bible, with biblical typology on which she made her own variations, and with a range of issues in regard to belief and practice.[26] She never described her own routine, but, like Lady Grace Mildmay, she may have systematically read several chapters of the Bible each day.[27] For the innumerable biblical citations that she only sometimes identified by book, chapter, and verse, she relied heavily upon the preference of puritans, the Geneva Bible and its commentary as well as the Authorized Version of 1611. She probably also consulted the Latin Bible of Beza and Junius. Sir John Davies, in contrast, used the Henrician "Great Bible" in his work on the Psalms.[28] Although her rigorous defiance of episcopal authority and her familiarity with the Bible make it tempting to call her a puritan during the 1630s and a sectarian in the following decade, she was generally orthodox in doctrine. Her rhetoric has more in common with that of Lancelot Andrewes than that of John Cotton and, like Andrewes, she focused upon the feasts of the liturgical calendar. She did not conform to or fit within the patterns of community that emphasized the godly household and the congregation. She could accept neither the notion of a gathered church nor radical redefinitions of the sacraments. If she indulged in the kind of spiritual self-examination, fasting, or devotional practices that we have come to associate with puritans and sectarians, or if she enjoyed a close relationship with one or more members of the clergy, she does not say so.[29] Although she denounced abuse of the sabbath, drinking, gaming, and idolatry, she had little to say about sermons. The form and language of her tracts owed more to the prophetic models in the Bible and the liturgy than it did to sermons, though she was certainly exhorting and instructing her readers. As a prophet, she focused upon the interpretation of history and the condition of Britain, not the state of her own soul.[30] Preoccupying herself with the Second Coming, she offered only hints of other aspects of her own beliefs. These, for the most part, were conventional.

Apart from her education and religion, Lady Eleanor's tracts provide us with only a few clues about her childhood and youth. Justifying her prophecies, not biography, was her focus. Unlike Lady Anne Clifford, who was also born in 1590, Lady Eleanor left no diary.[31] In accord with the patriarchal culture of her day she invoked her father in setting forth her lineage. Although she omitted all direct references to her mother, she may have drawn inspiration from Lady Audeley for some of the multitude of feminine images that she employed. Lady Audeley, for whom Lady Eleanor had apparently named her own daughter Lucy, played an active role in family affairs; she, not her husband, took part in the controversial secret marriage between Lady Eleanor's sister, Maria, and Thomas Thynne.[32]

Lady Eleanor's four sisters, Anne (Amy), Elizabeth, Mary (Maria), and Christian, were, like her mother, virtually absent from her tracts. They were all older than she, and the differences in their ages may have meant that they grew up separately although they had occasional contacts as adults.[33] Without additional evidence, we can only speculate about the relationships among Lord Audeley's children and the apparent similarities between Lady Eleanor's experience and that of the duchess of Newcastle, who grew up separately from much older siblings. Lady Eleanor's silence about her youth may reflect unhappiness that could have led her to turn toward religion, but her purpose and priorities can also account for the content of her writing. There is little to warrant the conclusions that have been sometimes drawn that childhood in a dysfunctional family can explain her conduct in adulthood.[34]

Lord Audeley's military career, which the public records tell us took him to the Netherlands and France and then to Ireland, thus, like the naval profession of Lady Anne Clifford's father, separated him from his family.[35] Lucy, Lady Audeley and her children probably saw more of her father, their grandfather, Sir James Mervin. Stalbridge, their home in Dorset, was not far from Mervin's at Fonthill Gifford, Wiltshire.[36] He, in contrast to his son-in-law, lived as a prototypical country gentleman. He was active in county business in addition to managing his estate.[37] Lacking sons, he arranged for the marriage of Lady Eleanor's sister Christian, his granddaughter, to a kinsman, Henry Mervin, and for them to inherit Fonthill so it would remain in the hands of Mervins.[38]

The house at Fonthill Gifford that Lady Eleanor would have known as a child was one her grandfather had modernized through additions and other changes to an earlier, sixteenth-century structure. The painting that provides our principal source of information about Fonthill Gifford shows a Tudor house, much as we might imagine it, with large mullioned and transomed windows, gabeled fronts on three sides, a one-story cloister, a forecourt crossed by a bridged canal, and, beyond, a barbican, gardens, and fishponds.[39] The site was a prominent one. William Beckford, the late eighteenth- and early nineteenth-century eccentric who built Fonthill Abbey there, retired to Lansdowne Hill near Bath because it afforded him a view of Fonthill.[40]

Lady Eleanor invoked Fonthill in *Woe to the House,* published in 1633, bewailing her brother Mervin's condemnation two years earlier. From Fonthill during her childhood she may have made the relatively short journey to Bath and, like Beckford, looked back upon the house from Lansdowne. Later she used Bath's boiling waters as a metaphor for those of Babylon and mentioned Lansdowne along with other "mountains" surrounding Bath to represent the seven hills of Rome and those of Revelation 17:9.[41] While staying in Wiltshire, Lady Eleanor probably also visited Stonehenge. In *Before the Lords Second Coming* (1650), she referred to the monument to illustrate a point. Frustrated at people's deafness to her repeated warnings and the testimony that supported her exhortations to prepare for judgment, she declared them as hard as the pillar of salt that was Lot's wife or "Wyldshires stoneage wonder" that, she added, was "proper for Pharoahs of these days."[42]

Sometime between her tenth and fifteenth birthday, Lady Eleanor and her mother went to Ireland to join her father. Having commanded troops at Kells in 1599, Lord Audeley took part in the siege of Kinsale, where he was wounded two years later.[43] Even before that he had apparently decided to settle in Ireland. He obtained permission to return to England in 1600 to deal with his estate and to press a suit with the Queen for land in Munster.[44] In this he encountered obstacles, some of which may have arisen from the fact that, as he put it, he had once been "much devoted to the earl of Essex" though he was far enough removed from the earl at the time of the latter's rebellion to respond to charges of complicity with a statement that he had no knowledge of the "conspiracies."[45] Not until 1605 was Audeley successful in obtaining land in Ireland, but over the next years he built up sizeable holdings there, some of which he acquired as an undertaker in the schemes for developing Ulster.

Evidence about the family's life in Ireland and even how much time they spent there is sketchy. It is tempting to draw a picture of an isolated existence, not unlike that of the duchess of Newcastle's childhood, in which the adolescent Lady Eleanor turned inward and laid the foundations for her later prophetic career. In a letter that he wrote to his future wife's sister, Maria, in June 1607, John Davies mentioned his regret that her mother, Lady Audeley, was "so distasted" with Ireland. He thought that she would have been much more positive if she had seen Dublin, where there was "loving conversation" and "good company in as civil a fashion as any in Christendom."[46] In 1609, the year that Lady Eleanor and Davies married, Lord Chichester reported to Salisbury that Lord Audeley kept to himself rather than offering the hospitality expected of someone in his position.[47] A survey taken of the undertakers and servitors in Ulster in 1612, by which time Audeley had been widowed and remarried, gives a similar impression. Only he, his second wife, and his servants were living on the 11,000 acres he, his sons, and son-in-law had undertaken.[48] Yet, Audeley himself did not remain constantly on his Irish estates, and Lady Eleanor and her mother may not have either. Records of attendance in the *Journals* of the House of Lords show that Audeley was in England and present there at the beginning of the session in 1604 and again in the spring and early summer of 1610, even though he gave his proxy to Northampton, with whom he had family ties.[49] In 1608 he wrote to the earl of Salisbury from lodgings in Clerkenwell.[50]

Scholars have assumed that the foundations for Lady Eleanor's marriage with Sir John Davies, who had been appointed King's Solicitor in Ireland in 1603 and became Attorney there in 1606, were laid in that kingdom when both he and her family were there, perhaps during his circuit in Munster in 1606.[51] Davies, who was thirty-six in 1606, was well past the age when young men ordinarily married for the first time. Will Ravenscroft wrote him from Lincoln's Inn in March 1607 to recommend a "deare and near cosen," Mistress Bagnall, but we do not know whether Davies considered that advice seriously.[52] Nor do we know when he and Lord Audeley began to negotiate the marriage that actually occurred two years later, in the spring of 1609. Connections between them predate their Irish residence. Davies, a Wiltshire man, had been born in Tisbury parish, not far from Fonthill. He had visited the Mervin house and even written a poem to the "Ladyes of Fonthill," presumably Lady Audeley and her daughters.[53] By June 1607 when he wrote to Maria, he was in touch with several members of the family.[54] Lord Audeley's occasional visits to the Middle Temple, where Davies was a member, gave them another opportunity to meet and talk.[55]

Lady Audeley may have played as much a role in the marriage negotiations as her husband did. In 1610 she claimed that Davies had had "no more but my word for his wife's marriage portion," a claim that may explain the absence of documents regarding the same.[56] References to the terms of the contract in later litigation assert that

Lord Audeley had provided his daughter with an ample portion: £6,000 in money, land, and "a good quantity of household stuff amountinge to a greate value"; in return, Davies had promised to settle on her "as much land as was answerable to . . . [her] portion, birth, and quality," though no specific figure is mentioned.[57] In purchasing the manor and rectory of Pirton in Hertfordshire at about that time, Davies probably intended to fulfill the obligations he had assumed.[58] Neither he nor Audeley was likely to make an agreement that did not appear advantageous.[59] Davies's connections at court presumably enabled him to gain social benefits from marrying the daughter of a peer, while Audeley bargained that he would be able to obtain far more in Irish lands through Davies than he granted to conclude the match. The two were indeed associated as undertakers in Ulster soon after.[60] Whether either considered Lady Eleanor's feelings about the arrangements we do not know. A brief reference in one of John Chamberlain's letters suggests that the marriage occurred in March 1609, but the absence of information about the exact date, place, ceremonies, or festivities accompanying the wedding makes it difficult even to speculate what the occasion may have been like for her.[61]

Nineteen at the time she married Davies, Lady Eleanor was hardly a child bride. Attractive and bright, she may have found herself drawn into a marriage by love that prevented her from seeing that she was accepting thralldom to a man twice as old as she who had little but wit, money, and connections to recommend him.[62] However much age and experience had by 1609 moderated the strident tone, coarseness, and offensive behavior that had caused Davies to be expelled from the Middle Temple in 1598, he remained a man whose primary asset was his brain, not his personality or his appearance.[63] Regardless of their truth, unflattering descriptions stuck to Davies. Sir Benjamin Rudyerd described him as "pock-marked and clumsy," one who waddled "with his arse out behinde," and the earl of Tyrone, who was hardly an unbiased witness, complained to James I that Davies was "more fit to be a stage player than a counsaill to your highness."[64] Davies' reputation for being quarrelsome and difficult would not have made him easy to live with, even for someone, like Lady Eleanor, who could appreciate his intellect.

Davies, whom John Donne once playfully proposed as the author of *Vacation Exercises . . . on the Art of forming Anagrams approximately true and Posies to engrave on Rings,* and Lady Eleanor, who in her tracts proved herself skilled in such crafts, could have shared the pleasures of word games.[65] Lady Eleanor was a woman with whom Davies could also have talked about professional matters. The multitude of legal terms and images that appear in her writings show clearly that she could speak the language of the law and knew not merely that which had become part of contemporary culture. Writs, sessions, and judges suited her topic, the Day of Judgment, and she made the most of them.[66] Ezekiel's roll, a favorite image among prophets over the centuries, she described as her writ or commission.[67] In *Bill of Excommunication*, she compared messages recorded in the Book of Revelation to the angels of the churches to her writs to "Westminsters Church," the Gatehouse, the courts of justice, Parliament, and others whom she warned to cleanse and reform all within their authority. If Davies did not discuss his official business with her, she must have made the most of her opportunities to hear him talking with others about the law and to browse in his books and papers.

Sir Isaac Oliver's portrait miniature, dated ca. 1610 and identified as Lady Eleanor, presents a woman of considerable beauty whose blue eyes and delicate face communicate sensitivity.[68] The nose and eyes resemble those of her sister Maria and of her daughter Lucy.[69] Evidence about Sir John Davies's appearance and age make it likely that those differences were one of the factors that led Lady Eleanor to compare herself to Jane Shore in 1647.[70] Her experiences with marriage, prophecy, and royal disfavor provided other grounds for that allusion. Shore, whose story became a well-known part of English history during the sixteenth century, had been married while very young to a London goldsmith whom she never loved. She left this husband to become the mistress of King Edward IV. The "respect of his royalty, the hope of gay apparel, ease, pleasure, and other wanton wealth" appealed to her "soft tender heart" and led her to accept his desire to have her as his mistress.[71] After Edward's death, Shore became mistress to Lord Hastings, and when he fell, Richard III deprived her of all she had, accused her of witchcraft, imprisoned her, and forced her to do public penance. Like Shore, Lady Eleanor may have been captivated by men other than Davies, and she may have been drawing literally as well as figuratively from her own experience when, in her 1625 tract *Warning to the Dragon*, she compared the divine command to have no other gods to a husband's injunction "after his Marriage to a young Virgin" that, though he would not keep her in a "Cloister," she must not forget her

"Covenant to be subject" to his "desires." Such a husband might warn his wife, that

many strangers will strive to bee your Servants, not all for your beautie but some for malice and envie to me; Though your intent be good in all things, yet because I am very jealous of mine honor, entertain none in that manner; though they be silent for a time, and conceale themselves, in the end they will draw your affection from me; Besides, much resort though shee be never so chaste, is dalliance the marke of a knowne Harlot, which sort of women I would have you differ from. [72]

The stern authoritarianism of the admonition fits what we know about Davies as well as Lady Eleanor's desire that Charles I inhibit his wife's popery.

With her marriage to Sir John Davies in the spring of 1609, Lady Eleanor entered a social circle in Ireland that included the key figures among the English officials there. She witnessed how her husband and his associates failed to take a principled and uncompromising stand when they faced resistance from the old English settlers who, like the Irish, had continued to adhere to Catholicism. In an apparent effort to soothe the ire of the Catholics after the parliamentary conflicts in 1613, Davies actually entertained some of them at his home. Lady Eleanor may have performed her domestic duties on this occasion, but when she became a prophet, she pointed out how those who thought they might deal with the papists had fallen victim to the Serpent's wiles. [73] Those who ignored religion or reduced it to political loyalty endangered the kingdom. When, in tracts written after what she would refer to as the "massacre" of 1641, Lady Eleanor invoked *"Irelands* green plantation," which had been "by the rootes pluck'd up," she was probably expressing both her prophetic lamentation for the division of the kingdoms and for the sufferings that evil had unleashed upon the land and also her personal regret for her own loss of income from estates there, rather than nostalgia for the scenes where she had spent an earlier era in her life. [74] Whatever her experience in Ireland as Audeley's daughter or Davies's wife, she had no sympathy either for popery or for "the wrathfull *Irish*." [75] In introducing *Amend, Amend* in 1643, she included "Dubylon" as well as London with Babylon.

Davies's intention that his years in Ireland should assist him in building his career in England meant that he became increasingly restive as time passed.[76] While attempting to profit as much as he could from his Irish office, he also spent much time seeking English opportunities. Fionnuala Byrne believes that, after 1612 when he started wearing his serjeant's robes, he was probably practicing law in London as well as Dublin.[77] The controversy surrounding his selection as speaker in 1613, his incurring the king's displeasure in 1615 for allegedly repeating in Ireland what James had said to him in England, and the replacement in the following year of lord deputy Chichester with whom he had worked so closely for so long were blows to Davies's aspirations to rise above his position as King's attorney. In addition to contributing to domestic tensions, Davies's frustrations probably provided Lady Eleanor with object lessons about the ephemerality of faction and favor at court.[78]

Occasionally, evidence about Davies's professional activities sheds more direct light on Lady Eleanor's life. Despite his earlier attempt to convince Lady Audeley that she would be happier in the city than elsewhere in Ireland, Davies did not make Dublin his sole residence. Following his marriage, he turned to the land he had undertaken in the north and built Castle Curlews and Castlederg in County Tyrone. In contrast to the relative simplicity of Castlederg, the "elegance and regard for amenities" D. M. Waterman of the Archaeological Survey of Northern Ireland found even in the ruins of Castle Curlews suggests that Sir John meant this for a country home.[79] Determining how much time he spent there is difficult; establishing the same for Lady Eleanor is virtually impossible. We know that they, like other husbands and wives in that period, were not always together. Both made prolonged journeys to England. In December 1609, Lady Eleanor did so in the company of her father. Lord Audeley reported to Davies that they had had a good passage and promised he would not leave her until he had "brought her to her desyred place of reste."[80] She was apparently in England without her husband again in 1617 but, perhaps because of pregnancy and childbirth, seems not to have joined him when official business took him to London in 1612 and 1614.[81]

The death of Lady Eleanor's father on 20 February 1617 brought evidence of the significance of the paternity that she later cited on so many occasions, for Lord Audeley made her, his youngest daughter, along with her husband, administrator of his estate. The position entitled the Davies to his personal estate in return for paying his debts.[82] Davies's legal skill, his prominence in Dublin, and his involvement with Lord Audeley in Ulster certainly made him particularly suited for this position. Neither Audeley's two sons nor their sisters challenged the grant of administration. The clear interest of the Davies, the relatively small size of the personal estate, and the existence of some debts may have deterred them. Audeley's widow, his third wife, did dispute Lady Eleanor and Sir John's claim to some of the land.[83]

Lady Eleanor took advantage of her role in settling her father's affairs to acquire some of her family's furniture, tapestries, and linens. A decade later, after Davies died, she insisted that these heirlooms, including eighty-eight yards of tapestry forest work, other tapestry forest work amounting to fifty-five yards and forty-eight yards, two turkey carpets, a drawing table, five shovels, two pairs of pothangers, a brass kettle, and three pewter candlesticks, should be hers and not part of her late husband's estate.[84] Although she exhibited the same possessiveness about land and money, she had a sensitivity to the visual that may have deepened her appreciation of tapestries. Among the many scenes described in her tracts are those from the Armada tapestry in the House of Lords and the fruits and flowers shown on hangings in the House of Commons.[85]

Matters arising from her father's death may explain Lady Eleanor's trip to England in 1617. By then, much of her energy was taken up with motherhood. Her daughter, Lucy, who lived to be the heir of both her parents, had been born in Dublin on 20 January 1613.[86] Lady Eleanor also gave birth to two sons: Richard, who died in infancy and about whom so little is known that some sources only refer to his brother, Jack, who is mentioned in a letter that the Irish solicitor general, Sir Robert Jacob, wrote Davies on 13 May 1617 when Lady Eleanor and Jack were in London.[87] Jacob's report indicates their common concern about Jack who, he noted, "is wonderfully amended in his understanding of late, for he understands any thing that is spoken to him, without making any signs, so as it is certein he hath his hearing, and then the defect must be in his tongue." Though recognizing that "yr Lady no doubt will use all the meanes she may to recover him," the solicitor suggested that if Jack were "putt into the hands of a skillful man he might be brought to speak."[88] Without other evidence, we can only speculate about the nature of his problem. Whether it was autism, as one physician has suggested, or something else, Jack placed special demands on Lady Eleanor and Sir John and, undoubtedly, aroused questions about how best to care for him, doubts about the efficacy of the course taken, and the guilt that belief in a judging God imposed upon those who experienced misfortune.[89] Jack's drowning in Ireland not too long after that put an end to his suffering but deprived his parents of the male heir that their society valued so highly.[90]

Although Lady Eleanor never explicitly mentioned the two sons of her body in her tracts, she emphasized the significance of her maternal role in prophesying. Her writings, which brought life to the world, replaced the children who had died, and she poured her love and care upon them. Years later on two occasions when Lucy lost a son, Lady Eleanor's immediate and heartfelt response manifested her own experience of similar pain. She wrote knowingly about maternal grief and anguish and sought to comfort Lucy with hope of the new Jerusalem that would follow the time of Lamentation and Judgment. In 1639, when Lucy suffered her first loss, Lady Eleanor, who was then in the Tower of London, counselled her daughter "not to thinke any paine heretofore too much or worse bestowed in bearing him then it bestowed upon the rest of his brothers and sisters." She recounted her sad dream that very morning, before receiving Lucy's letter, of a "childs head cut off" and women trying to comfort the "head that cryed."[91] Ten years later, when Lucy lost a second son, Lady Eleanor made his funeral the subject of her tract *Sions Lamentation.*

The two brief Latin tributes to his children that Davies left among his papers suggest that Davies, too, felt the emotions of parenthood. For Lucy, who became his principal heir, he constructed an anagram, "LUCIDA VIS oculos teneri perstrinxit amantis, / Nec tamen erravit, nam VIA DULCIS erat" [Her brilliant power dazzled the eyes of her tender lover, but he still did not wander for the road was pleasant]. For a deceased son, he wrote an epitaph, "Qui iacet hic fuit ille aliquid, fuit et nihil ille. / Spe fuit ille aliquid, re fuit ille nihil" [He who lies here was something and he was nothing. I hope he was something—in fact he was nothing].[92] The form and language that may seem emotionless to modern readers were an appropriate expression of feelings for one of Davies's learning. Grief over the loss of his boys may also have played a part in leading him to write his *Psalms* in 1624, when Lucy's marriage the preceding year had also reminded him of his own advancing age. The serious tone of the *Psalms* contrasts with Davies's earlier literary efforts and with the legal and political works upon which he had concentrated during the previous two decades.[93]

Notwithstanding the contrary arguments of some sociologists and historians, the Davies were not unusual in their era if they struggled as a result of the loss of their children.[94] Among the patients of physician-astrologer-clergyman Richard Napier, bereavement was the "third most common stress," and many of those bereaved were mothers whose babies or children had died.[95] Elizabeth Countess of Bridgewater, whose son Henry died when he was twenty-nine days old, wrote that no joy nor pleasure could relieve her grief for him. She tried to submit to God in her prayers on that occasion and on the death of her daughter Kate of smallpox just before the age of two. During her pregnancies, the countess prayed that the child she was then bearing would be born without deformity.[96]

The writings of Lady Eleanor and Sir John Davies make it appear that they struggled alone with their grief, and they may have done so. They seem to have functioned as a nuclear family with relatively little contact with their siblings or parents. Lucy, Lady Audeley, Lady Eleanor's mother had died soon after her daughter's marriage. Lord Audeley had lived on, but his death in February 1617 preceded that of his grandson. It seems likely that the burdens of parenthood aggravated other potential sources of strain in the Davies' marriage. The circumstances could explain Lady Eleanor's turn to religion and prophecy, but because we cannot firmly establish when the boys died and because our information about her and Sir John between 1617 and 1625 is so limited, any account of the years immediately preceding her becoming a prophet must remain frustratingly tentative. Three events seem significant: the Davies' return to England in 1619; Lucy's marriage in 1623; and Lady Eleanor's encounter with George Carr in 1625.

When King James finally relieved Sir John Davies of his official responsibilities on 31 October 1619, he did so without rewarding his longtime Irish Attorney with a new appointment in England. Davies's unfulfilled professional ambitions and the demands of the English practice he had been nurturing meant that his wife and daughter were probably under pressure to conduct themselves in ways that would be advantageous to him at a time when they themselves were facing the challenges of adjustment to a new life. The family settled in London, not on the Hertfordshire manor of Pirton that Davies had purchased in 1609 as a jointure for Lady Eleanor.[97] Amid the competition, gossip, and politics of others who were seeking favors from the court, the Davies were seeing firsthand the kind of goings-on that had held sway over their lives when they were in Ireland and seeing these at a time when, thanks to the rise of George Villiers, Marquis and later Duke of Buckingham, corruption seemed to be replacing traditional patronage. Although Lady Eleanor may have derived some pleasure from being at the center of society and politics, she, like the duchess of Newcastle during her days at court, may have found herself an outsider. Her sharp criticism of Buckingham in her tracts may owe its vehemence to her blaming him, both for her own discomfort and for the unsavory atmosphere around the court.[98]

Lady Eleanor became directly involved in the kind of quarrels that critics associated with Buckingham's ascendancy in her dispute with Lady Jacob, a dispute that moved into the Star Chamber in 1622. John Chamberlain reported to Carleton that the suit was about "womanish brabbes," and indexes to the court's records provide no evidence either to confirm or to deny this. In view of the numbers of suits in Star Chamber at the time, we can hardly draw conclusions about Lady Eleanor's personality as a result of this.[99] Chamberlain's account in the same letter of "an uncivill scurrilous letter" written to Lady Eleanor by Kit Brooke in the aftermath of some heated exchanges between her and his wife may be another clash of a common type. The two copies of what Brooke allegedly wrote that appear among the Conway Papers in the Domestic State Papers fit Chamberlain's description. Accusing Lady Eleanor of having abused his wife and "that innocent childe" and comparing her to Lady Wouldbe in Jonson's *Volpone*, Brooke, more than a month before "Midsummer moone" 1622 addressed her with a series of offensive epithets: "Lady Tryfle, . . . an incorrigible Malkyn, . . . abominable stinking greate Symnell faced excrement, . . . a notable sluttish ornament of Bedlam, . . . Hecate, Medusa, Legion, clovenfooted Gorgon." He described her features in most unflattering terms, "scurvy contracted purse mouth . . . black patches of ugly deformitie . . . the eyes of thy body are allwayes hoodwynkt and clouded with cypres and vales and mercury clowes most filelily putt on."[100]

Is the conjunction of Brooke's invective and Lady Eleanor's quarrel with Lady Jacob significant? How seriously would we take either if we did not know that Lady Eleanor was confined to Bedlam in 1637? Contemporaries used some of the same terms Brooke had when they accused other women, such as those who petitioned the parliament in the 1640s, of behavior inappropriate for their gender.[101] However uncomplimentary he was, Brooke did not ascribe to Lady Eleanor the physical deformities by which, according to Dalton, magistrates might identify witches.[102] If, by 1622, she bore the marks of smallpox, she was far from unique in that and probably, like other survivors among her contemporaries, tried to conceal her scars with makeup. The evidence in her tracts confounds his taunt that she would have to depend upon her husband to translate the Latin verses that he incorporated in his blast against her. Brooke was angry, and he wrote with a force similar to that Lady Eleanor herself used when she became a prophet. It is not difficult to imagine her during later years provoking a response such as his, but, in the absence of more information about this incident, we cannot judge the case. The letter's inclusion among the Conway papers may indicate that either Lady Eleanor or Davies thought that Brooke's statement was chargeable and submitted it to the authorities.

The disputes and rumors that pervaded court life may have encouraged Davies to look for a satisfactory country seat. At the time, King James was exhorting nobles and gentlemen to return to the country to provide hospitality for their "neighbors" and to perform their traditional roles as local leaders. By remaining in London and about the court, Sir John risked incurring the displeasure of the ruler he wanted to grant him a post, and without a country house he and Lady Eleanor were hard pressed to live in accord with their ambitions and pretensions. An estate could confirm the social advantages of his marriage and acknowledge Lady Eleanor's pride in her aristocratic heritage. If she were away from the more active social life of city and court, she would be less likely to embarass him in his quest for advancement. The example of Lady Hatton, whose outspoken opposition to the marriage Sir Edward Coke had arranged for their daughter to the Viscount Purbeck, brother to the Duke of Buckingham, may have made Davies particularly anxious.[103]

Eventually Davies found the manor of Englefield in Berkshire, not far from Reading, on the road to Newbury, and arranged to buy the estate from Londoner Sir Peter Vanlore who had himself just purchased Englefield from the earl of Kellie.[104] Easily reached from London, Englefield provided a home where Lady Eleanor and Lucy frequently stayed and where Sir John came when business permitted him to leave the city. They may have had plans for improving their new estate from the beginning, but it was not until April 1626 that they contracted together with one Guy Hopkins for £1,000 to "pulldowne a great part of the house and build it againe."[105]

Despite the expenses of purchasing Englefield and those arising from life at court and pursuit of place, Davies was apparently well enough off financially in 1623 so that, in addition to buying his country estate, he could conclude a marriage for Lucy, who was not yet eleven years old, with Ferdinando, son and heir of Henry Hastings, fifth earl of Huntingdon. Sir John provided his daughter with a dowry of £6,500.[106] While the match was expensive, it linked Lucy with the heir to a noble, albeit impoverished, title. For the Hastings, Davies's money, his prominence as a serjeant-at-law, and Lady Eleanor's parentage were attractions. More than a decade earlier, in 1612, Davies had purchased the manor of Aller in Somerset from the earl of Huntingdon, and it seems likely that the two men had had other business dealings prior to the marriage of their children.[107] In 1624, Davies took pains to keep his daughter's father-in-law, who was not attending parliament, informed about proceedings there. In that same year a union, not mentioned in the correspondence concerning the former marriage and one that proved to be unfortunate for all concerned, occurred between Lady Eleanor's brother, Mervin, Lord Audeley and second earl of Castlehaven, and the countess of Huntingdon's sister, Anne, widow of Lord Chandos.[108]

Lucy Davies' youth—she was not yet eleven—at the time of her marriage to Ferdinando Hastings in the summer of 1623 has led to speculation that Sir John meant to get her away from a mother who was mentally ill.[109] Lady Eleanor had not yet taken up prophecy in 1623, and evidence from two disputes in which she was involved in 1622 is not sufficient to prove her unstable. Like other couples who married early, Lucy and Ferdinando did not reside together but remained with their parents. At least part of that time, Lucy was with Lady Eleanor at Englefield while Sir John Davies was in London.[110] The Hastings's desire to alleviate their own fiscal problems by conclusion of the contract was probably more important in its timing than was Lady Eleanor's mental condition. According to Ferdinando's not disinterested testimony in the litigation following Sir John Davies's death, Lady Eleanor was herself a "principall actor and mover" in the marriage agreement.[111]

The concern that both families had to protect their interests makes it curious that no one had obtained the license for the union that Lucy's youth made necessary. Archbishop Abbot, who had previously exchanged words with the earl of Huntingdon about the latter's protection of suspended ministers and may have suspected that the earl was once again defying ecclesiastical authority, complained about the apparent oversight and threatened excommunication.[112] Rather than repeating the ceremony that had occurred on 7 July 1623 at Harefield, the home of Ferdinando's maternal grandmother, Alice, Dowager Countess of Derby, the family arranged a second ceremony a month later, this time conducted by the parson (with the proper license) in the parish church at Englefield.[113]

Although Lady Eleanor did not face immediate separation from her daughter in 1623, the event served to remind her that her days of active motherhood were numbered. Henceforth she would have to share her daughter, her only remaining child, with the Hastings, who made a fuss over their son's new wife. Lucy's mother-in-law, Elizabeth, Countess of Huntingdon, was a woman who would express her opinions and expect to be heard. She, like her mother, the dowager Countess of Derby, was protective of her family and would make the most of the legal claim upon Lucy that the marriage gave them. Troubled by the debts of her husband, she wrote to the family's solicitor, consulted some of her own male relatives, and persisted until she thought the provisions for herself and her children were adequate.[114] Her letters in the months following the wedding made her colors manifest.[115] She addressed these to Sir John Davies, not to Lady Eleanor. In doing this she was acknowledging Davies's position as father and as the signatory of the legal agreements for the marriage. Although she did not hesitate to meddle in family business, the countess realized where utlimate authority lay. She may also, from the very beginning, have feared that Lady Eleanor saw through and would oppose her schemes for advancing her family's interests that, as we shall see, became evident after Sir John Davies's death. It is possible that an attempt by Lady Eleanor to warn her brother about his new wife, the countess of Huntingdon's sister, also contributed to tension between the two women. Although the countess expressed appropriate sentiments about my lady's health in her letters, she did nothing more to cultivate relations between them. Davies himself may have found her behavior trying. He directed his responses to the earl, not to her, and wrote about "our," not "my," wishes concerning Lucy.[116]

Neither Lady Eleanor nor Lucy left evidence about their relationship or feelings at that time, but it seems likely that they had already established the close bonds that they maintained, despite many vicissitudes, until Lady Eleanor's death. Like her mother, Lucy was bright, classically educated, and interested in religion. She was probably responsible for collecting the unique copies of Lady Eleanor's tracts, a number of them annotated by the author herself, that are now in a volume in the Folger Library.[117] In the months when they were together after Lucy's wedding until she joined the Hastings at Easter 1625, they probably strengthened their ties and shared their devotional and spiritual interests.[118]

The Hastings, having finally sent Ferdinando to Cambridge in January 1625, were able to welcome Lucy in the following April without worrying about the young people's premature consummation of their marriage.[119] The two families had previously agreed upon this course of action, and there is no evidence that reports that spring of Lady Eleanor's intense interest in a young boy who was something of a religious phenomenon hastened Lucy's departure. Indeed, both mother and daughter may have welcomed the lad's presence in the household while they were anticipating their own separation. Tension tinged the letters exchanged between the Davies and Hastings when an apparent misunderstanding left Lucy initially without a woman servant.[120] The Countess of Huntingdon indicated that Lady Eleanor behaved graciously in this instance, but she went to some lengths to explain herself and to seek assurance that she was acting in her daughter-in-law's best interests. On 21 July, three months after Lucy's leaving home and just a week before Lady Eleanor's vision, Sir John Davies wrote to the earl of Huntingdon to arrange for Lucy to return for a visit.[121]

Chronology makes it possible to interpret Lady Eleanor's prophetic career as a consequence of a midlife crisis that followed the marriage of her daughter and the deaths of her sons. In the course of contemplating her past and future, she could have had the kind of purgative experience that Petroff identified as the first stage for medieval women visionaries.[122] In her prophecies, Lady Eleanor endorsed the contemporary wisdom that interpreted the deaths of children as indications of divine displeasure. It seems likely that, in searching for answers to her spiritual questions, she found herself applying her intellect to study and writing. When, a few days before the death of King James and just a few weeks before Lucy left home, Lady Eleanor took in George Carr, she gained a substitute for the children she mourned, a way to combine her maternal role with that of religious seeker, an opportunity to test her faith, and a mode of demonstrating that she was a great lady

who performed charitable works for those in need and that her household was a place where young people could be trained. Carr also
provided her with a pretext for challenging the power of the men who
ruled in church and kingdom.

Carr, a thirteen-year-old Scot known as "the dumb Boy or Fortune-
teller," was attracting a great deal of attention around London. Seeking
to determine whether he was an impostor, people tested him by opening a Bible or chronicle and asking him to act out its contents without
looking at the passage, by making loud noises to see if he would jump,
or or by having him guess the number of items in a bag or box. [123]
When Carr gradually became able to speak while staying with the
Davies and during the same period "the Spirit of Prophesie" fell upon
Lady Eleanor, both he and she became the focus of speculation, talk
about witchcraft, and demands that he no longer be "harbored" in
their home. Who was responsible for these occurrences, God or the
devil? Was Carr another Friar Rush, the devil who disguised himself
as a friar and, in a multitude of exploits recounted in popular literature
of the time, led both women and men astray? [124]

In protecting Carr, Lady Eleanor too became a phenomonen, an
example of the violation of order. Even though she had taken the
womanly part and nurtured the lad, she had erred in the eyes of the
authorities. She adhered to her own conviction about Carr rather than
joining the JPs and "church-men" in their disbelief and suspicion, and
in contrast to some of the "chief Divines of the City" who gave him
"a shilling" after he had demonstrated his abilities, she believed that
his knowledge was priceless. Faced with a choice between two courses
that both seemed incompatible with what her society termed appropriate for women, she made her own decision.

Lady Eleanor's choice may have been easier because she sensed some
similarities between Carr's condition when she first met him and and
that of her son Jack even though Carr, at age thirteen, would have
been several years older than Jack was at the time of his death. If this
is true, her experience with Jack may have enabled her to provide Carr
with the love and attention that paved the way for his development.
Although she must have been familiar with the story of the Bilson
Boy, an impostor whose much publicized case had come up at the
Staffordshire assizes when Sir John Davies was on circuit there a few
years earlier, she seems to have believed from the outset that Carr was
legitimate. [125] By the time she encountered him in the spring of 1625,

she had already been studying the book of Daniel and she may have reached what Petroff calls a second, or psychic, visionary stage. This condition, characterized by concern about the spiritual welfare of others and by the hearing of voices, left her open to the possibility of receiving instruction from one such as Carr. [126]

The earliest of Lady Eleanor's extant writings about her experiences with the Scottish boy date from 1633. By then she viewed him as a "saint" because in his "numbering [which] foretold all things" he exhibited the "gifts of the Holy Ghost." [127] Carr played for her the role that Daniel played for Nebuchadnezzar (Daniel 1–2); he offered an interpretation of the visions and dreams that troubled her, and that the divines, wisemen, of her day could not understand. His influence confirmed her in her study of the Bible and in her resistance to domestic, ecclesiastical, and political patriarchy. She says she laid "aside Household cares all," conversed with "no one," and focused her attention upon the Book of Daniel, particularly Daniel 8:13, where one saint asks another, "How long *shall* be the vision *concerning* the daily *sacrifice, and the transgression of desolation,* to give both the sanctuary and the host to be trodden under foot?", or as the Genevan commentary puts it, how long shall Christ's religion and people be suppressed? [128]

Thus, as a result of her experience with Carr, Lady Eleanor moved even farther away from the society whose conventions she had challenged when she initially accepted him in her home. She, whom her culture denied a public voice, began to find that voice through giving nurture to one, like her son Jack, whom the world ostracized for his silence. She also felt the consequences of her action. When Carr, "being terrified" (presumably from the crowds who gaped and tested him) "and provoked to speak, lost the wonderfull gife [*sic*] [of prophecy] for that time and after went beyond sea," Lady Eleanor was left alone with her spiritual struggles. [129] In the spring of 1625, Sir John Davies was caught up in the transition following the death of King James and the accession of Charles I. He wrote the earl of Huntingdon that, immediately upon hearing of King James's death, he left Englefield for London to kiss the new king's hand and renew his serjeant's patent. If he played his cards properly, he might secure the appointment as a judge for which he had been waiting. [130] Anxious about his future and probably also sorry to see Lucy leaving, he was hardly likely to offer Lady Eleanor any support. Davies's preoccupation with his career as a public servant probably meant that he, like many of those Lady Eleanor encountered, was more interested in figuring out how to work with King Charles than about preserving Protestantism in the face of the monarch's marriage with a papist princess, Henrietta Maria of France. The wrongheadedness of these priorities deepened the distance that separated his personal religious path from Lady Eleanor's. The verses into which Davies had put the psalms he had published in 1624 were models of technique, the process a means of directing his energy, and the result a reassuring structure, a bulwark against the unsettling questions she was asking and the perhaps even more troubling answers she was receiving.[131]

Like the medieval visionaries whom Petroff describes in the third stage as unconsciously absorbing doctrine, Lady Eleanor, with her concentration upon the Bible in the spring and early summer of 1625, laid the foundations for a transition and for the "emergence of a new and powerful identity" that came with her early morning experience on 28 July 1625.[132] That vision confirmed her in the independence she had asserted in defending George Carr. It gave her a voice and changed her life and marriage.

CHAPTER 2

Singing a New Song

Lady Eleanor was at Englefield, the Davies's Berkshire estate, early in the morning on 28 July 1625 when, "Awakened by a voyce from HEAVEN," she heard the words, "There is Ninteene yeares and a halfe to the day of Judgement and you as the meek Virgin."[1] She described that experience again and again in her tracts, and, although the words she quoted vary slightly, the basic facts are consistent. The message was clear; it came from Daniel and disclosed the information that he had been told would be sealed until "the time of the end" (Daniel 12:4). Suddenly she understood the meaning of verses she had been puzzling over, and, fortified by the event, she began singing "a new Song."[2]

That moment at Englefield in the summer of 1625, when she became convinced that she should be the vessel for Daniel's message, served as the foundation for Lady Eleanor's writings. It explained why she, a woman, should venture to publish tracts about matters that were both esoteric and of overwhelming importance to the king and kingdom. In contrast to the epoch it marked for her, subsequent occurrences seem inconsequential. Yet, in the last years of her life, she spoke with a confidence and an authority of her own that she did not have when she began prophesying. She recognized that such events as her being ordered to appear before the High Commission and Laud's burning of her books in 1633, his execution in 1645, and King Charles's execution in 1649 were additional signs of her prophetic role.

We can divide the twenty-seven years of her prophetic activity into three periods. This chapter concentrates on the era between July 1625 and her summons before the High Commission in October 1633, a time during which she discovered that, although she attracted some

33

public attention, her message was welcome neither at home nor at court. The visions and struggles that ensued upon her visit from Daniel inaugurated an epoch in her life that resembles what Petroff defined as the fourth stage of development for medieval visionaries.[3]

The opposition of the authorities who tried and imprisoned Lady Eleanor in 1633, confined her to Bedlam in 1636, and subsequently committed her to the Tower of London characterizes the second phase of her life as a prophet. Their response dramatized the dimensions of the task she had assumed. The significance of these years in shaping her thought is evident during the third era, the time between 1640, when she was released from the Tower, until her death in 1652. During this twelve-year period she wrote most of her tracts.

From the morning of 28 July 1625, religion, that is prophecy, became Lady Eleanor's priority. She incorporated her personal life into her public office of prophet, and, during the years that followed, she continued prophesying in both senses of the term then common. She foretold specific events regarding individuals. Sometimes she did this in response to requests; sometimes she offered unsolicited forecasts. An even more important aspect of her work was a second kind of prophecy, the explication of divine intentions within history. For her, this meant interpreting the Bible as it applied to England's experience. Although she also drew upon astrology, natural, and customary means of understanding events, she used them within a general biblical frame-work. Particularly important for her were the texts of Daniel and the Book of Revelation. In construing their meaning, Lady Eleanor's approach was scholarly. She employed her knowledge of fields such as Latin, the Church Fathers, and law, which were considered inappropriate for women's study, but, unlike some of other prophets of the era, she took no explicit notice of Joachimism or other prophetic traditions of the late Middle Ages or Renaissance.[4] Lady Eleanor compounded the offense she caused by her scholarship and by her prophecies by criticizing, as no subject should, the actions of king, bishops, Parliament, and local officials. She also prophesied in defiance of her husband. By doing so and by publishing her pronouncements on matters of religion and government, she challenged early Stuart patriarchy both within her own family and within the kingdom.[5]

Englefield assumed a special significance for her. Unlike Fonthill which had been an important part of her childhood, Ireland where she had spent much of her adolescence, or Pirton, the Hertfordshire manor Davies had purchased soon after their marriage as her jointure, Englefield was relatively new to Lady Eleanor in 1625. The family had taken up residence at Englefield soon after Davies bought it in 1623, and, in the following summer, the parish church there was the scene of Lucy's marriage with Ferdinando.

Englefield was a place where, as Lady Eleanor stated repeatedly in her tracts, events demonstrated the presence of the spirit, though some of the evidence she cited to prove her claim may seem delphic to anyone not able to follow her line of thought. Located in Berkshire, "the first of the Shires," Englefield was where she, the daughter of the first peer or baron (as we have seen Lord Audeley called himself), in the first year of the king's reign, had heard Daniel who told her about the last days. Englefield was England, a place of the angel.[6] Although she might have been able to interpret King Ethelwulf's rout of the Danes at Englefield, centuries earlier, to serve her purpose, she failed to mention that.[7] Her subsequent choice of lodgings at the Angel in Lichfield and again in Kensington was probably no accident. Under the Long Gallery at Englefield where she had heard Daniel's voice was the "Western Road," and "a Mile or two distant" from Englefield was "a place called Hell of old" where "such decrepid with age, and their Associates blinde and halt" would beg for relief beside the highway.[8] After the outbreak of the civil war, she declared that her experience at Englefield in July 1625 had presaged "Englands bloody field," and, indeed, in May 1643, the armies had been fighting within a "boweshot" of the house itself.[9] The second battle of Newbury, which again brought the war close to Englefield, occurred in late October 1644, the anniversary of her hearing before the court of High Commission eleven years earlier.[10] Such "blows" showed the consequence of the king's failure to heed her prophecy.

Lady Eleanor tells us little more about the house at Englefield than that she was "under the Gallery" when she was awakened on 28 July 1625.[11] Other sources indicate that the house was built in the sixteenth century. The date on the roof timber of the Long Gallery is 1558; other parts may have been enlarged and improved during the Elizabethan or early Jacobean era.[12] No evidence seems to remain concerning what the Davies had planned when they contracted with Guy Hopkins in April 1626 to "pulle downe a greate parte" of Englefield and rebuild it.[13] How much work he had completed at the time of Sir John Davies's death is also unclear. Lady Eleanor maintained that she had paid Hopkins £700, but Lord Hastings challenged that.[14] Accounts in the Hastings MSS show that they made some payments in 1629 and 1630 for minor improvements and repairs of the entire estate, but not for major rennovations of the house.[15]

About the circumstances in which she received the revelation Lady Eleanor says not much more than she does about the setting. The voice spoke "as through a trumpet," a phrase, common to prophecies and probably emanating from her familiarity with Revelation 1:10 ("I was in the Spirit on the Lord's day, and heard behind me a great voice as of a trumpet"). It added a warning "to take heed of pride."[16] Although she never described seeing anything specific while hearing these words, she sometimes referred to the event as a vision and called it a "magnified morning Star," another conventional image that she adopted and adapted for herself.[17] In 1643, making reference to the star that guided the wise men to Bethlehem to see the Christ child, she named her twenty-page petition to parliament *Star to the Wise*.

Both the timing and the content of Lady Eleanor's experience in 1625 bear some similarity to the more fully described voices heard and sights beheld by Grace Cary, the "prophetess," whose following of King Charles in 1639 Lady Eleanor cited in the gloss on her 1648 edition of *Given to the Elector*,[18] Theophilus Toxander's publication, in 1646, of an account, ostensibly by someone else, of Cary's "strange and wonderfull visions and propheticall revelations," probably brought her to Lady Eleanor's attention. Not only did Cary's message to the king help to demonstrate the accuracy of the prophecy to the Elector that Lady Eleanor had originally published in 1633, but the consequences of Cary's devotion to prayer to overcome worldliness and a temptation toward "popish superstition" showed what King Charles should have done. In contrast to the two groups of women whom Lady Eleanor passes over in silence, those who in increasing numbers had taken up prophecy by the 1650s and those, such as Katherine Chidley, who had published polemical works about religion during the 1640s, Cary, by 1648, was no longer active and thus not a potential rival whose recognition might diminish the significance of Lady Eleanor's own mission. Early one Sunday morning "before she was full awake," at the time she customarily prayed and meditated, Cary, a widow, felt a "celestiall extasie of joy." After hearing voices crying out and seeing terrible scenes of bloody violence on several subsequent occasions, she wrote down the information she had received. Like the classic seeker, she found that her successful quest left her with a burden she did not want. Unable to free herself from the obligation through her own prayer and fasting or through the prayers of various clergymen whom she consulted, she finally went to the king.[19]

Lady Eleanor, on the other hand, gave no indication that she hesitated before accepting the legitimacy of Daniel's call and assuming the difficult errand he imposed upon her. She responded immediately because Daniel brought her an answer she had been seeking. When remembering the event in 1633, she noted that the words she heard on 28 July had dissolved "within three dayes" the "ambiguity" in Daniel's visions that she had begun "to understand" six months earlier. She specified that, in her effort to comprehend them, she had eaten "no pleasant bread, was mourning full three moneths," probably the period between when, during Carr's stay in her home, the "spirit of Prophesie" fell upon her and the moment she heard Daniel speaking to her in late July.[20] That morning's experience enabled Lady Eleanor to comprehend her encounter with George Carr and to interpret Daniel 8:13–14, upon which Carr and current events had focused her attention. As the weeks had passed since the end of March when King Charles had succeeded his father on the throne, reality had begun to undermine the hopes for change with which people had greeted his accession. The Duke of Buckingham continued to wield power; in May, Charles, who had previously won such praise when he had broken the negotiations for a Spanish marriage, married another popish princess, Henrietta Maria of France; rather than making the joyful entry with his wife that Londoners anticipated, the king had rendered the City's preparation futile; he had postponed meeting a Parliament and holding his coronation. Finally, toward the end of June, even though the outbreak of plague grew more serious, he assembled an anxious Parliament at Westminster, where it quickly became evident that his expectations clashed with those of some of his leading subjects. They were uneasy about Charles's assertion of his financial needs and worried about toleration of popery. Apprehension mounted when he adjourned the session in mid-July and, breaking with the tradition of several centuries that parliaments met at Westminster, called another for Oxford in early August. As Lady Eleanor meditated about these happenings during her period of abstinence from conversing "with any but the Word of God," she paved the way for hearing Daniel's message that morning of 28 July.[21]

In the critical period between April and July, Lady Eleanor, although she never discussed her practices in conventional terms, seems to have departed from her previous patterns by following the disciplines of the devotional life that frequently characterized the stories of religious persons and often preceded their significant spiritual experiences. She does not say whether she continued these observances or subsequently took occasional retreats. Nor does she hint of links between her prophecies and her own condition of godliness. Unlike her contemporaries, Sarah Wight and Anna Trapnel, she seems not to have prophesied from a trancelike state during long periods of fasting.[22] Believing that she was following in the footsteps of the prophets of the Old Testament, Lady Eleanor gave priority to publicizing the knowledge imparted. In the course of doing this she nevertheless reveals that she herself was touched by the divine spirit, whose message she bore.

Lady Eleanor's personal religious experience remained an element within her prophecy rather than transforming it into mysticism or enthusiasm. Her approach to prophecy was relatively traditional.[23] She saw herself as the vessel chosen for a divine message. Like the monarch who exercised divinely ordained authority, the prophet who bore a message from God was not bound by the limitations that affected other people. Women who were prophets could venture into such realms as preaching, writing, and discussing public affairs that otherwise belonged exclusively to men. Proof of the authenticity of their inspiration was essential. The very characteristics that made women susceptible to powers beyond themselves also made them likely targets for evil. The substantial part of Lady Eleanor's message, which was unexceptional in its content, did not conceal the unusual in its content, style, or the fact of her gender. Her contemporaries had few doubts about the dangers of religious or political heterodoxy. Prophecy, whether practiced by men or women, posed special problems in an age when freedom of expression was strictly limited, dissenters were suspected of fomenting sedition if not treason, and those who stubbornly clung to aberrant views were deemed mad.[24] The importance of spiritual experience and prophecy intensified concern about impostors. The Bible warned against "false prophets which come to you in sheep's clothing, but inwardly they are ravening wolves" (Matthew 7:15); parliaments enacted statutes against false prophecy and witchcraft.[25] Feminine sensitivity made women likely vessels for powers, whether good or evil, beyond themsleves and thus justified patriarchy, which in turn made it difficult for women to attain the independence from the restrictions and institutions of society that being a true prophet required. Although women in Jacobean and Caroline Britain moved between the domestic and public spheres, their freedom was limited. Many positions were denied to them, and they were subject to the authority of their fathers and husbands. Even the influence women exercised depended upon their place within a family to a considerable extent.[26] Whether they encountered only skepticism of their claims of spiritual experience or were condemned as witches and burned, women suffered as a result of their world's beliefs about gender and evil.

Lady Eleanor repeatedly declared by what authority she prophesied. In the General Epistle with which she opened the tract she published in the year of her vision, she explained that she had written because "no age so weake, nor sex excusing: when the Lord shall send and will put his words in their Mouth."[27] In one of her later tracts she described herself as a "secretary," an image illustrated by the hand holding a pen that appears on the title page of one of the 1648 editions of *Given to the Elector,* and one similar to that of the pen or pencil to which Mary Cary, another contemporary, compared herself.[28]

St. Teresa described words she heard, not with her "corporall eares, but . . . understood much more playnly," implying a power that could not be ignored.[29] Such seemed to be true for Lady Eleanor. Her experiences in the months preceding July made her receptive to the message, and she proceeded immediately to act upon it. The fulfillment, several weeks later, of Daniel's promise that the plague that had driven parliament and many individuals from London would promptly abate confirmed the authenticity of her experience, but she did not wait for that proof to begin her own work of prophecy.[30] In her subsequent tracts, she took advantage of the events of the summer to draw a parallel between the word of the Second Coming that she, "the meek virgin," received at Englefield and the Virgin Mary's giving birth to Christ. Just as the wise men and others from the east had travelled to Bethlehem to see the baby Jesus, Parliament had fled from the plague west to Oxford, and the law courts were keeping the term in Reading, also west of London, and, like Oxford, near Englefield.[31] Although Protestants condemned the cult of the virgin, women from Queen

Elizabeth herself to the radical women of the mid-seventeenth century cited her. Some, much as Lady Eleanor did, claimed to be the virgin who would bear the second Messiah.[32]

Immediately after Lady Eleanor heard Daniel's voice that morning, she set to work to prepare a text that she personally delivered, a few days later, to Archbishop Abbot of Canterbury at Oxford where he was attending Parliament. This text probably formed the basis of *Warning to the Dragon,* a hundred-page commentary upon chapters 7 through 12 of Daniel and the only one of her extant tracts dated 1625.[33] Although her text showed little originality, it was independent. Its apparently quick composition was not because it was derived from one of the better known contemporary expositions of Daniel and Revelation.[34] The prophecies of Daniel were familiar to Lady Eleanor. She later tells us that she had been studying and, in fact, preparing a brief introduction and marginal commentary for the Geneva Bible's text of these five chapters during the period immediately preceding her vision.[35] She had intended to present this work to King James, but his death on 27 March 1625 had prevented that. Inspired by her vision of 28 July, she incorporated her marginal notes into a much fuller commentary, which became the text she gave the Archbishop. Her subsequent productivity suggests that words flowed from her pen. The impetus of her vision would have lent special intensity to her work immediately afterward. The very fluency of *Warning to the Dragon* may indicate that she did not labor over it to introduce the figures that often weigh down her later tracts and emphasize the recondite nature of her message.

At the core of Lady Eleanor's prophecies were the visions related by Daniel. To each of the four great beasts he described in chapter 7, she, like other commentators, equated a kingdom that had power for a time. The first, the lion with eagle's wings, was the lion of Judah.[36] The second beast, the bear "that had three ribbes in the Mouth," represented the "Heathen" Roman Empire whose "devouring Raigne" had lasted three hundred years. The third beast, which "was like a Leopard or halfe a Lyon," showed the divison of that Empire. The fourth beast, which had ten horns, was the devil, "the Antichrist Pope of Rome."[37] Having discussed those beasts, she continued through Daniel, chapter by chapter, interpreting the contents to show the need for repentance and preparation. (At this point in her life, she seems to have subscribed to a Calvinistic belief in predestination that she would later reject.)[38] She believed that she was writing during the moment in history when the twelfth chapter of Daniel began. Martyrdom, such as those of John Wycliff and John Hus, would not be necessary in her day; the world stood ready for Michael, "the great Prince that defends the Faith," and Charles must be Michael.[39] To help persuade him to act before it was too late and to warn him not to permit his wife to serve the popish idols of her heritage, Lady Eleanor hailed him with an anagram of his name, Charles Stuart, "AL TRUTHS CESAR."[40] By showing him truth he could not deny, truth concealed within those letters that spelled his identity, she performed her prophetic function and demonstrated the limits of his authority. She, as the "meek virgin," had knowledge to present to him, the monarch. His failure to respond and assume the part she had designated for him led her subsequently to revise her message.

In taking her book to Archbishop Abbot, Lady Eleanor was not only appealing to the English primate and the man whose position made him most directly concerned with her information about impending Judgment, but she was also looking to a religious leader whose evangelical Calvinism and intense opposition to Rome should make him sympathetic to what she said. While Abbot's relations with the new king were tenuous, his apprehension about popery made him a strong candidate for persuading Charles to listen to her warning. The archbishop's history of active participation in Parliament also meant that he might bring the news to that body.[41] Because Parliament had fled from Westminster to Oxford to avoid the plague, she did not have to travel far from Englefield to find him.[42]

To prove the validity of her message, Lady Eleanor told the prelate that the plague, which that week took a toll of 5,000 in London, would soon abate. The failure of either Abbot or Parliament to heed her made less difference to her at that particular moment than the fact that the plague moderated shortly afterward. This offered confirmation of the accuracy of her prediction, but she quickly discovered that the truth of her prophecies did not protect her from the anger of those who did not want to hear and who sought to silence her.[43]

For Sir John Davies, who was in London on 28 July, Lady Eleanor's decision to publish her beliefs seemed to place another obstacle between him and the attainment of his professional objectives. While she had called upon Charles to guide his wife away from false religion, she was defying the authority of her own husband in the same regard. Would

the king appoint as judge a man who appeared to be unable to control
his household, a man whose wife went to the archbishop and Parliament with prophecies that suggested the reign would end in Judgment? Lady Eleanor does not tell us when and how Sir John learned
about her new career. If neither she nor any of the servants had told him
previously, he undoubtedly heard when she took the public step of
carrying her prophecy to Oxford and delivering it to Abbot. Davies
himself may have been in Oxford; in a letter of 21 July to the earl of
Huntingdon, he had proposed meeting Lucy there and bringing her
home for a visit. [44]

Davies responded unequivocally when he learned what Lady Eleanor
had done; he burned the book that she had written. He probably did
not stop to consider how best to deal with her. If he hoped that his
action would intimidate her, he had seriously misjudged her. [45] Having
turned to books from childhood, she, like many women of her day, had
become a student of the Bible and other devotional literature that
provided her with both a basis for assessing what she saw around her
and with an authority that could contest that of the men who ruled her
life. [46] Rather than play the wifely part and submit, she interpreted her
husband's opposition as another indication of the validity of her message. Using an anagram of his name, JOHN DAVES, JOVES HAND,
she told Davies that he himself would die within three years and began
wearing mourning. [47] Thus she denied him the power he had attempted
to reclaim by consigning her words to the flames. She separated herself
from him, not by a commitment to chastity as medieval visionaries
often had done, but by announcing the divine judgment that would
fall upon him because he had rejected the new life to which she wished
to introduce him. [48] No longer was she merely wife and mother; she
was Daniel's handmaid, a vessel for the Word of God. [49] In so demonstrating her freedom from Davies, she warned Archbishop Abbot and
King Charles that they should take her seriously. By persisting, she
would threaten order, not only in the family, but also in the church
and kingdom. With her example, she showed Charles what could be
the consequences if he failed to govern his wife.

Later sources suggest that Sir John did not accept Lady Eleanor's
revolt against his authority and that the two had a further exchange of
angry words. Although we cannot prove that this occurred, we can
postulate a scenario where Sir John accused her of wanting him dead
in order to marry someone else—he may have suspected that she and

Douglas, who later became her husband, were attracted to each other, she responded by vowing that, if he died, she would remain a widow, and he, determined to hold her to her promise, made it a condition of her inheritance. Although evidence suggests that widows were becoming less likely to remarry and that husbands were more frequently making inheritance dependent upon continuing widowhood, Lady Eleanor had particular reasons for eschewing remarriage.[50] Remaining a widow enabled her at once to claim fidelity to him and to appropriate, for herself, the life-style of a prophet who, unlike a wife, could serve no earthly authority. One can only imagine what life in the Davies household was like after Lady Eleanor's vision. Neither Lady Eleanor nor Sir John was inclined to compromise. She spent much of her time at Englefield, while he occupied himself with legal matters in London, yet, unlike Viscount and Lady Falkland, whose quarrels brought separation and vendettas, the Davies did not part completely.[51] In a deposition taken in connection with litigation following Davies's death, one witness described a scene when the family was at supper. Sir John suddenly invited their daughter, Lucy, to come with him and see the papers concerning "my ladies jointure."[52] Years later, Lucy's son, Theophilus, claimed that Davies, provoked by something Lady Eleanor had said, had revoked her jointure and made her another, which was conditional upon her remaining a widow.[53]

Late in November 1626, when word came that Sir John, who had just written a treatise on the royal prerogative, would become Chief Justice, the tension between husband and wife may have eased.[54] They were together at dinner with friends early in December 1626 when Lady Eleanor started weeping. Davies did not recognize the significance of her tears. Unlike Jesus, who forgave the sins of the woman who washed his feet with her tears, Davies told his wife, "I pray weep not while I am alive, and I will give you leave to laugh when I am dead."[55] Three days later, on 7 December, he was dead.

Sir John Davies's death shocked London. Although people had heard reports of Lady Eleanor's earlier prediction that her husband would die within three years, few seem to have believed it. Apparently well when he had supped at the lord keeper's that evening, Davies died during the night at his house in the Strand.[56] Lady Eleanor and Lucy, who were at Englefield, came to London when they heard the news.[57] So too did Ferdinando Hastings and as many other representatives of his family as could be mobilized. His maternal grandmother, the virtual matriarch of the family, the dowager Countess of Derby, promptly pointed out that his marriage with Lucy must be consummated, so that no question could arise about the legitimacy of the family's claims to the inheritance and to the wardship necessitated by Lucy's youth.[58] Eager to make sure that their interests in Davies's estate were protected, the Hastings confronted Lady Eleanor immediately with demands to see Sir John's papers and to administer the estate.[59] On the very day of his burial at St. Martin's-in-the-Fields, London, they took possession of Englefield.[60] No source comparable to the Hastings' correspondence survives to present, from Lady Eleanor's side, her position at the time. Their letters and the evidence from the later litigation suggest that, despite her prediction, she was caught unprepared for her husband's death and responded by frantic scheming.

In the ensuing legal disputes, both she and the Hastings recounted the events that directly followed Davies's death to substantiate their claims to his estate. She described herself as struggling to deal with her own grief while they pressed for action. They, in turn, maintained that she was single-mindedly trying to undermine her late husband's disposition of his property. A few comments that she made in later writings suggest that, whatever her immediate emotions, she came to regard the years of her first marriage with some nostalgia.[61] The implications of Sir John's death, in confirmation of her prophecy, could have given her pause. It demonstrated the awesomeness of the knowledge given her and the gravity of her task. No longer wife even in name, she was alone and responsible to God for performance of the duties laid upon her. Sir John's distaste for her prophetic office had led him, while he lived, neither to prevent her from pursuing her calling nor to abandon her. She saw to it that he had a funeral that cost £500, a sum that the Countess of Huntingdon thought too high and a sign of Lady Eleanor's "improvidence," even though it was about half what the funeral of the fourth earl of Huntingdon had cost in 1604.[62] According to the genealogical notes made by Davies's grandson, John Donne preached at the funeral. Donne, Dean of St. Paul's and one of the best-known preachers of the day, was probably an acquaintance of Lady Eleanor as well as Sir John, but we know neither who arranged for his sermon nor what Donne may have said.[63]

For Lady Eleanor, widowhood also meant the loss of Englefield. The Hastings' prompt seizure of the manor and the contents of the house deprived her both of the estate that she had at the time of her husband's death counted on for her jointure and of many possessions that she treasured.[64] Quite apart from any considerations of comfort or money, Englefield had a value to her that Pirton, the manor Davies had purchased at the time of their marriage to serve as her jointure, would not satisfy. She tried to claim both manors, but it was Englefield that mattered most to her. The emotion with which she sought possession of the Berkshire estate was disproportionate to the reasons she stated in the course of the litigation. Neither the encumbrances upon Pirton nor the plans then in progress for building at Englefield can explain her insistence upon having the latter, but her recognition (in her tracts) of its prophetic importance can.[65] Her attorney cited the role she apparently took in managing that estate to argue that it should be hers, but, like her, he did not mention in court what happened there on 28 July 1625.[66] In the eyes of the law, she was a woman, a widow, limited by the decisions her husband had made, not a prophet who maintained that the existing order must be changed.[67]

The Countess of Huntingdon, who could hardly be expected to look favorably upon Lady Eleanor's attempts to claim Englefield may also have been put off by conduct based upon prophetic rather than conventional standards. In January, the month following Davies' death, the countess wrote to her husband in exasperation,, "I have had to do with such an irisolute woman that tis impossible to drawe sartin conclusions from soe fantasticall a cretuer." Rather than agreeing to the terms the Hastings wanted concerning Davies's estate, Lady Eleanor claimed "she had other matters to thinke of."[68] Quite apart from prophecy, she probably did have much to do in the aftermath of her husband's death and little desire to accept a settlement proposed by her daughter's grasping in-laws. Compounding the countess's impatience was Lucy's show of independence. Lucy, then fourteen, was talking the "language of a free woman," declaring that she had an estate of her own and would not live "under" her mother-in-law. Finally, the Countess reported, "she sayd if her lord went downe to live with us she must," but if he did not, she would not either.[69] Lucy probably guessed that, in view of the disputes about Englefield, complying with her mother-in-law would mean virtual estrangement from her mother. When writing to Lucy in January 1629, Lady Eleanor showed that she was aware that her daughter's position was difficult. She bemoaned the "division in our estates," declared her sorrow at not being able to come to terms with Ferdinando about them, and made it clear that she believed Lucy was "neither cause nor party" to the disputes. The villain of the piece was Ferdinando's mother, the Countess of Huntingdon.[70]

Despite her subsequent efforts to reassure Lucy, Lady Eleanor may, in the wake of Davies's death, have appeared to be pressing her daughter to resist the countess's plans. Sir John's passing confronted the still very young woman with the loss of a parent at the very time when she was being expected to begin to assume the duties of a wife, but, in a Hastings household dominated by Ferdinando's mother and grandmother, she would have little of the power normally associated with her new role. Whether or not Lucy's reluctance to fall in with her in-laws arose from an understanding of the legal issues, she gave Lady Eleanor additional reason to obstruct the settlement of Sir John's estate.

Lady Eleanor introduced another element to the already contentious situation when she married Sir Archibald Douglas sometime before the end of April 1627, probably in March, only three months after Davies's death.[71] Amid the conflicting claims expressed in the legal papers and the restropective account of the events of this period in her life that Lady Eleanor gave in her prophetic writings, truth is elusive. Her own admission that she had vowed not to remarry and the evidence that suggests she was familiar enough with Sir John's papers to realize that, if she married again, she would impair her claim to his property, may seem proof of her emotional instability if not outright irrationality, but she herself accounted for her conduct by citing her commitment to prophecy. The events that had occurred during the two years since Charles I had assumed the throne showed that he had not responded to her appeal to act as Michael. Daniel's message to her concerning the prospect of Judgment seemed likely to be fulfilled, and she needed to do what she had been bidden.

Douglas, a Scot, was a man she had most likely encountered at court during the preceding years. He had been knighted at Whitehall, Christmastime 1624.[72] Although in 1628, when he petitioned to be a free denizen, he simply said that he was "borne in Scotland about the time your Majesties father . . . came to England," Lady Eleanor maintained that he claimed to be heir to the earldoms of Morton and Douglas and to the throne of Great Britain, by virtue of his birth, a few months before Prince Charles, to King James by the daughter of James's tutor, Sir Peter Young.[73] Shortly before he died, James, despite the opposition of the Duke of Buckingham, had allegedly granted Sir Archibald an annuity of £10,000, but the king's death, which frustrated Douglas's hopes for further preferment, may also have prevented his receipt of the pension.[74] Douglas's views about religion were much closer to Lady Eleanor's than Davies's had been. She later published letters questioning points such as kneeling for communion that Sir Archibald had written to Dr. James Sibbald.[75] Douglas also could easily have been more physically attractive than Sir John Davies. The only extant description of Douglas merely mentions his clothing. A messenger who had gone to his house at St. James stated in a deposition that he had spoken with a gentleman in a velvet-lined cloak who identified himself as Sir Archibald.[76] As a professional soldier, Douglas may have reminded Lady Eleanor of her father. If she had stopped to weigh the pros and cons of remarriage, she probably realized that any decision had both advantages and disadvantages. Countering legal and economic costs were social benefits and, thanks to the long absences that were common for soldiers, he would leave her free to pursue her prophetic career.

In her own writing, Lady Eleanor emphasized Douglas's alleged proximity to the throne rather than other attributes. If God had sent him to be an instrument whereby she could fulfill her prophetic mission, she might have cause to break the vow she had made to remain a widow and to discount any awareness that remarriage would probably complicate her efforts to retain Davies's property.[77] The Hastings argued that Davies, if he had at one point granted Englefield to Lady Eleanor, had revoked that and replaced it with a provision that the manor should be hers only during her widowhood. Her marriage with Douglas, they claimed, thus insured that the estate should go to Lucy.[78] The Hastings' interests, like those of Lady Eleanor, should make us wary of unquestioningly accepting their arguments. If Sir John intended to make Lady Eleanor's inheritance contingent upon her remaining a widow, he seems to have died before translating his wishes into directions that would stand up in court. Although professional expertise should have enabled him to avoid this, he, like many others, may have postponed his own business in favor of that of clients.[79] In the litigation, the parties produced contradictory evidence. The Hastings argued, and Davies's inquisition post mortem accordingly states, that, at the time of Lucy's marriage to Ferdinando, Sir John had agreed that Pirton and all his lands in Ireland should go to Lucy's benefit at his death.[80] They denied the validity of an earlier deed found in Davies's chambers at Serjeants' Inn after his death which designated

Pirton as Lady Eleanor's jointure. They also challenged a "writing" giving Englefield to Lady Eleanor during her widowhood and a deed bestowing the house in the Strand upon her. They threw doubt upon the documents by charging that she had put the first two of these items in her pocket at the time when she and they had gone through his chambers and later had produced the third from her pocket.[81] Of greater import to the Hastings' stance were Davies's notes in preparation for making a will in which, although he did not mention her jointure, he made his bequest of jewels, plate, and hangings to Lady Eleanor for only so long as she did not remarry.[82] She, on the other hand, claimed that Davies had died intestate, just as the earl of Huntingdon had feared she would.[83] Without a will, the Hastings would have to postpone their hopes of obtaining Davies's property until after her death and try to convince her to let them share in the administration of the estate, whereby they might have access to his goods. While they succeeded in getting letters of administration and asserted that they had done so with her complicity, she denied this.[84] Whether she was too distraught to be decisive or whether, in her desire to cooperate with Lucy, she misjudged the Hastings is not clear from the accounts of her conduct that appear in later depositions.

During the spring of 1627, soon after Lady Eleanor married Douglas, she began the legal campaign to recover what she believed was hers. In the eyes of the law, her authority as a prophet meant nothing. Having remarried, she was a *feme covert* who must act through Douglas to challenge what others maintained her late husband, Sir John Davies, had done. The process, which eventually involved cases in the Courts of Wards, Chancery, Exchequer Chamber, and King's Bench and also at the assizes, was fraught with special frustration. Douglas was ordered to leave England with troops for Denmark.[85] As a Scot, he also faced obstacles in trying to use the English courts. These moved him, in September 1628, to appeal to King Charles for letters of denization, which Charles granted.[86]

The disputes remained unresolved in May 1630, and Douglas took matters into his own hands. He went to Englefield with four or five armed men. They cut some grass and threatened Lord Hastings's servants in the house that they would not desist until they had taken that too. This action, predictably, brought cries of protest and more litigation.[87] Finally after three years of acrimonious charges and countercharges, Lady Eleanor regained both Pirton and Englefield, but her victory was both limited and shortlived.[88] Soon afterward, during her imprisonment, she lost both manors and would not recover them until more than a decade had passed. Her claims to possession of the jewels and hangings proved even less successful. Her attorneys argued in vain that she was entitled to the jewels, which she had apparently taken, because she wore them, because they were "convenient for her degree" as the daughter of a noble, and because the custom of London dictated the wife should have half her late husband's goods.[89]

Lady Eleanor, like some other aristocratic women of her day, poured time and energy into her efforts to claim what she believed was her inheritance. Neither her persistence nor the seeming flimsiness of her case was unique. In court, she refrained from drawing upon prophetic arguments, but, in her tracts, most of which she wrote during the 1640s, she interpreted her struggles to hold on to the estates within the larger framework of upheavals that preceded the Second Coming. In this context, she could rail against the chains with which the law bound women. They were one aspect of the anti-Christian regime that held Britain's monarch and church in thrall.

During the years immediately following Davies's death, at the same time that she was seeking legal recourse for her losses, Lady Eleanor had seen little evidence that Charles I would be *AL TRUTHS CESAR,* and live up to the anagram she had made from his name shortly after his accession.[90] She continued to hang around the court and approached the queen, whose loyalty to popery had been worrying her. Although she may have hoped to reach the king through his wife, Lady Eleanor's decision to turn to Henrietta Maria was in accord with what was later her pronounced emphasis upon women's power, whether they used it for evil or for good. In 1642 and 1643 in *Samsons Fall* and *Samsons Legacie,* she accused the queen of taking the part of Delilah, who stripped Samson of his power, and, in 1651 in *Restitution of Prophecie,* she called her Jezebel.

Lady Eleanor's background and experience reinforced the cultural factors that made the court the natural place for her to turn for support for the mission she had received from Daniel. Later, when she wrote about this brief time in her life, she, like many contemporaries who recorded in letters and diaries their experiences and observations from Whitehall and Westminster, proudly recounted the details of particular incidents and named those, both men and women, who were present (although she rarely gave dates). The conventions of such descriptions make it difficult to determine how far, as in the group who gathered around her a few years later at Lichfield, women played an especially important role. She told how she had waited upon the queen "as shee came from Masse or Evening Service," on All-Saints Day in 1627. When her chance arose, she asked the queen "what service shee pleased to command." Henrietta Maria, who knew of Lady Eleanor's reputation as a prophet, inquired "when she should be with child" and then "what success the Duke would have." To these questions, Lady Eleanor says she responded with pleasure and also told the queen she would be happy "for a time."[91] Lady Eleanor was less charitable in her description of Charles's appearance during this exchange. The king, who had also apparently heard of Lady Eleanor, effectively interrupted her conversation with the queen with an accusation that she had broken her husband's heart by the way that she had predicted his death.[92] Thus, in Charles's eyes, Lady Eleanor had violated the rules of patriarchy.

Prophecy itself in either of its two senses, disclosing the will of God in history or foretelling specific events, injected a potentially explosive element into Lady Eleanor's relationships with the court. As a prophet, she assumed an authority that challenged that of the king. If she bowed to convention and devoted herself to seeking Charles's favor, she would be his servant rather than "the meek Virgin" to whom Daniel had revealed God's intentions. She claimed access to knowledge that others did not have, and, on the basis of that knowledge, she commented upon and even criticized the policies and practices of the monarch, his bishops, and his councillors. In predicting misfortune for members of the royal family, she risked being charged with treason, which by the statute of 1352 included compassing or imagining the death of the king, the queen, or the heir to the throne. Charles was sensitive to criticism and uneasy when parliaments or individuals offered him advice about public affairs. His declaration concerning his abrupt dissolution of parliament in March 1629 and the imprisonments and prosecutions that followed that dissolution served notice of the consequences that might be incurred by people who spoke out, and most tried to avoid confrontations with royal authority during the eleven years between 1629 and 1640, when Charles ruled without a parliament. Lady Eleanor, as we shall see, did not follow a similarly judicious course.

Courtiers who knew that Lady Eleanor had foretold her husband's death were interested in what she said. Each time her predictions proved accurate, she reinforced her authority, but, at the same time, she made those who listened to her more aware of the fragility of their lives. Since she frequently predicted death, her news was not welcome. When the queen gave birth to a son in March 1629, Lady Eleanor announced that the baby "should go to Christning and Burying in a day."[93] She also warned that the earl of Pembroke would live only to age 49.[94] Lady Berkshire, who had been one of those at court with whom Lady Eleanor had a good bit of contact and who was also a neighbor in St. James, personally experienced the vagaries of dealing with a prophetess. When Lady Eleanor turned down the lady's invitation to attend her son's christening, Lady Berkshire immediately began to worry about his fate. Lady Eleanor, pressed to explain, revealed that the son would die, and so he did.[95]

Probably the best known of Lady Eleanor's prophecies concerning the court was her word that the Duke of Buckingham "should not outlive August 1628."[96] Sir Edward Dering remembered it when he heard the news of Buckingham's death and thought he had known of the prediction since the previous August; the Rev. Joseph Mead mentioned it in his letter to Stuteville of 22 June 1628.[97] Lady Eleanor herself discussed it in retrospect in *Her Appeal* (1646), where she gave no precise date for her forecast. In an apparent departure from her pattern both before and afterward she did not personally apprise the duke of his fate but had informed some "persons of quality" who "told him from me."[98] She never explained why she took this course. Although she may have been trying to find a way of easing the obligations of her career, she more likely had such contempt for him that she disdained to approach him directly. In tracts written between her release from the tower in 1640 and her death in 1652 she minced few words in her criticism of him. Extending the popular imagery that by the 1620s had identified the Spanish Armada of 1588 with the dragon of antichrist and the dragon slain by St. George, she made Buckingham one of the Beast's "minions" in the *Restitution of Prophecy* and, in *The Revelation Interpreted*, he became the beast who received his power from the dragon (Revelation 13:4).[99] His title itself, Buckingham, came from the beast, and as "viscount vuilers" (Viscount Villiers) "these numerall letters" were, by her approximate calculations, "HIS: VIC LVVVI," 666, the number of the Beast (Revelation 13:18).[100] His public fault of association with the "Spanish Faction," demonstrated by his failure to lead an effective war against Spain, mirrored the wrongs he had done her by using his power as a patron to obstruct rather than assist either Sir John Davies or Sir Archibald Douglas.[101] Despite his name, George, Buckingham had become "So much bound to the *Dragon* his Patron, rather then to Saint *George.*"[102] What blasphemy they committed who looked on him with favor and after his death would canonize him "Saint *George* the second!"[103]

Lady Eleanor's prediction of Buckingham's assassination brought her into conflict with her husband. Douglas, like Davies, had little patience with a wife who would not accede to his authority. As she told the story almost two decades later (in 1646), the Douglas' made her prophecy concerning the duke the subject of a contest to determine who wore "the breeches" in their household. If she proved wrong, she promised that she would abandon prophecy.[104] Her accuracy allowed her to continue and to point to the occasion to confirm her power, but, as with her correctness about her husband's death, it fed the king's suspicion of her. He grieved over the loss of his favorite.[105] Charles, like both of Lady Eleanor's husbands, was a firm believer in patriarchy and disinclined to be sympathetic to rebellious women. In July 1631, one of Lord Scudamore's informants told the story of a "young woman burned in Smithfield for having poisoned her husband who was a most barbarous and cruwell man to her and . . . his own neerest of kindred . . . were suitors for her pardon" since he was so villainous "and the Queen laboured earnestlie for it, but howsoever the woeman was much pitied of all, yet the king thought it dangerous to spare hir, soe that he would not pardon her."[106]

Lady Eleanor dated Charles's rejection of her to "within a moneth" of the birth, on 29 May 1630, of the son who would become Charles II. The king, she claimed, sent a gentleman of his bedchamber to ask her not to keep the house she was taking near the court at St. James. Despite the absence of corroborating evidence for her allegation and despite the possibility that she may have meant it metaphorically rather than literally, Lady Eleanor's story is in accord with Charles's interest in decorum at court and his penchant for privacy. This may account for the otherwise unexplained warrant for her appearance before the Privy Council in December 1630.[107] The orders the king issued in January 1631 "for reformation of certain irregularities in the Court" included a command that nobles, both men and women, "use great distance and respect to the royal persons."[108] Her prophetic pretensions set her apart from other aristocrats around the court and gave Charles added reason to dislike her presence.

When the king's gentleman brought her the order and threatened her with other "courses" if she did not desist, Lady Eleanor answered that she would take her own measures against her husband, whom she believed had burned her papers in order to win Charles's favor.[109] Both Douglas and the Youngs, his kin, who had seemed to be encouraging him in his opposition to her prophesying, had subsequent misadventures that she deemed judgments. Particularly significant, Patrick Young, Douglas's uncle who had moved to the house at St. James that Lady Eleanor had left after the king's objection to her presence there, lost "no few of his Majesties choyce Books" when the house burned.[110] Douglas himself, as we shall see, eventually lost "both Reason and Speech," an appropriate fate for one who had destroyed prophecy.[111] Although the Scottish Youngs, who had been close to James I, would hardly have been important assets at Charles's court, their enmity helped to mark her publicly as a persona non grata.[112]

As it became evident that King Charles did not want Lady Eleanor around, even those courtiers such as the earl and countess of Carlisle, the earl of Holland, and Lord Goring, whom she mentions but who were not touched personally by her prophecies, may have wondered whether they really enjoyed her company. Unlike the religious communities who frequently provided support for members who wished to extend or deepen their spiritual lives, courtiers focused their attention upon obtaining material benefits for themselves from their monarch.[113] Their lives depended upon royal favor, and they were accustomed to a system by which they expected some return for interceding on behalf of a client. Lady Eleanor had little to offer except prophecy.[114]

For some courtiers, the trial and execution of Lady Eleanor's brother, Mervin, baron Audeley and earl of Castlehaven, in 1631 may have provided an additional reason to keep their distance. Castlehaven was condemned for sodomy and for being an accessory to a rape committed on his wife by a page. Although Prynne, in his 1633 denunciation of the evils perpetrated by stage plays, cited "a late example of a memorable act of justice on an English Peere," to prove that, by the statutes of England, sodomy was a "capitall" matter and although historians have drawn their own conclusions about what Lord Scudamore's correspondent termed the earl's "fowle and horrible offences," Cynthia

Herrup is persuasive in arguing that Castlehaven's greatest crime in the eyes of his contemporaries was threatening order by exploiting his patriarchal power by injuring his wife, Anne, daughter of Ferdinando Stanley, fifth earl of Derby, and his son for the benefit of his servants.[115] While no printed account of the proceedings appeared until 1642, newswriters followed them closely.[116] After being condemned by a jury of twenty-seven peers, with the lord keeper acting as lord high steward, the earl was executed on Tower Hill on 14 May 1631. The court's evidence came from servants and family, some of whom, as Lady Eleanor later pointed out, were papists.[117] She also raised questions about the special provisions that allowed Lady Castlehaven to give her testimony privately rather than in public as ordinary procedure required.[118] In contrast to Lady Eleanor herself, who had openly predicted her own husband's death and, as a result, had incurred sharp criticism by the king for her apparent treachery, Lady Castlehaven, who had covertly given evidence that led directly to her husband's conviction and execution, had received public sympathy. For Lady Eleanor, her brother's trial was yet another occasion when Charles I condoned hypocrisy and seemed to be assisting the work of antichrist. Castlehaven, who, just prior to his execution, had formally confessed his adherence to the Church of England, was judged guilty on the basis of statements by his wife, who was "a wicked woman" and a "whore"; by his brother Ferdinando, who stood to benefit materially from his words; and by the servants Broadway and Fitzpatrick O Donel, the latter of whom was a vagrant and a papist.[119]

If, like her husband or her sisters, Lady Eleanor spoke out in Mervin's behalf in 1631, her appeal has not survived. Amy, Elizabeth, and Christian addressed King Charles, asking him to stay the earl's execution and to examine those whose testimony had led to the judgment.[120] To justify such an examination, Sir Archibald Douglas submitted an information alleging that the witnesses against his brother-in-law had been bribed. For his trouble, Douglas found himself confined to the Fleet by order of the Privy Council the next day.[121] Several factors may explain Lady Eleanor's apparent distance from the proceedings. Among the scanty evidence concerning her personal life, there is none to indicate that, despite their proximity in age, she and Mervin were close. She may have openly opposed his marriage with the woman who testified against him and who, as the countess of Huntingdon's sister, was Lucy's aunt. Her brother's apostasy had created a barrier between them that his return to Protestantism had not entirely removed. Lady Eleanor may have feared too that, if she intervened, her sister-in-law would retaliate and would exacerbate the rift that had developed over Sir John Davies's estate. She later produced a letter that she claimed the countess had written to her in Mervin's name about a month after the two were married to warn her not to "rayse Scandall and lyes" upon his wife who had forgiven her after "in most lewde maner thou were founde with mee thy brother.... Neither were the rest of thy Lewd courses ever divulged by her."[122] While this letter may refer to incest, it could also be using lewd in a now obsolete sense of vulgar or lower class. Castlehaven's wife could seemingly have strengthened the case against him by testimony about incest.

After the earl's death, Lady Eleanor and Sir Archibald Douglas submitted the countess's letter with their undated petition to the king for recovery of £500 allegedly owed to Lady Eleanor by her brother.[123] Lady Eleanor also referred to the letter in *Woe to the House,* her broadside printed in 1633, where she employed prophetic phrases to proclaim the fate of that sister-in-law whom she accused of telling lies that led to Mervin's conviction. From Ana [*sic*] Stanley, Countess of Castlehaven, she made the anagram *A LYE SATAN,* and, to accompany it, she formed an anagram, *THAT JEZEBEL SLAIN,* for a second Stanley sister, Elizabeth, Countess of Huntingdon, Lucy's mother-in-law, who at the time of Davies's death had prompted two "men of Belial," Sir George Hastings and Thomas Gardiner, to bear false witness.[124] By maintaining that both women were like Jezebel, who had written letters in Ahab's name (1 Kings 21), Lady Eleanor deepened the rift between her and the Stanley family in a way that Alice, the Countess of Huntingdon's daughter, found unforgiveable.[125]

In tracts she published after 1640, especially *Word of God* (1644) and *Crying Charge* (1649), Lady Eleanor repeated her fierce protests against the proceedings by which her brother had been "unmercifully ... sentenced to death ... and cruelly executed att Tower-Hill accused falsely of two Crimes, what lewdnes could and malice produce."[126] In 1651, in *Restitution of Prophecy,* she referred to his widow as "Heretrix, of that extirpated House, Isle of Man," the House of Derby to whom she had earlier cried, "Woe." The arms of Derby, the red deer, could signify "that Scarlet Beast," the red dragon of Revelation 12.[127] The death of her second brother, Ferdinando, a year after Mervin at the very same hour seemed "the just hand of God displeased" with such an "unnaturall brother," one who was not only a "perverted Papist" but also, through his testimony, had helped to bring Mervin's execution.[128] Lady Eleanor interpreted her brothers' fates, like her own, as part of a larger prophetic story, but she omitted from her tale references to the imprisonment that her husband, Douglas, suffered as a consequence of his intervention on Mervin's behalf. Douglas's confinement may have been even shorter than the month indicated by the records of the Privy Council. One manuscript account of Castlehaven's trial and condemnation states that Sir Archibald's "imprisonment was deferred by reason of a sute he had depending before their Lordships," presumably some of the litigation concerning Davies's estate.[129] The date Lady Eleanor herself gives in a subsequent account of Douglas's seizure in St. Martin's church suggests that he did not remain in the Fleet for the entire time.

Lady Eleanor was in Berkshire on 1 June when, according to the account she published in 1646, Douglas, "was strooken bereft of his sences" while "in Martins Church at the Communion." No longer able to speak, he made instead "a noise like a Brute creature." She thought it "doubtlesse his heart changed into a Beasts too, for so [he] would put his head into a dish of Broth of Letice or Herbs and drink Oyl and Vinegar, and sometimes Beer all together, insatiable that way." He recognized nobody but her.[130] Her prediction that something along these lines would befall Douglas suggests that, even before the seizure, she had probably abandoned any hope that he would assist her in her mission and may have exaggerated his incapacity in order to emphasize the consequence of the wrongs she believed he had done her. She had signed a statement in March 1631 in the presence of several witnesses that if some "wonderful judgement from God" did not come to him within three months, she would walk to St. Paul's barefoot and in a sheet, the garb of a penitent.[131] Although we cannot definitely determine the date when it happened, Douglas did incur some serious mental or nervous disability that dashed Lady Eleanor's hopes that he might assist her in her mission.

The information about Douglas's condition is not very satisfactory. Lady Eleanor's most extensive comments about it come from *Her Appeal* of 1646. The presence of his name on subsequent documents and his apparent disposal of property raise questions about the credibility of both her description of him and the testimony, in 1642, of Dr. James Jackson, who had apparently treated Sir Archibald at the time. In answer to interrogatories administered in connection with Lucy's petition to the House of Lords concerning the manor of Pirton, Jackson claimed to have seen Douglas for about a fortnight twelve years previously but not since. The doctor reported that his patient sometimes said he was a prophet and would "utter extravigant buisnes as prophecies." At times, Douglas hid in his bed or tried to lock himself in his chamber. Once having obtained swords from a servant, he threatened to kill himself. Jackson withdrew from the case after he had diagnosed Douglas's condition as "mania" and concluded that the treatment had not had much effect. He believed that the "madnes proceeded of fiery biliose bloud" or from "vapours which oppressed his sences" and was "incurable." Jackson told Sir Peter Young, who had called him in, that he would not "loose any more tyme" on Douglas.[132] Even though Douglas's principal disability may have been his lack of cooperation with Lady Eleanor, that, in her eyes, placed him among the fools she later accused of confining the wise like herself in Bedlam.[133]

Sir Archibald's condition heightened the impact of the isolation Lady Eleanor experienced as a result of the deaths of her brothers and her quarrel with her daughter's in-laws. The frequency with which God seemed to be intervening in her life probably led her to think more seriously about her prophetic mission, and, in 1633, she took advantage of Douglas's indisposition in order to obtain permission to leave England on the pretext of going to the spa for his sake. Her real purpose was to travel to the Low Countries to have books—for which she had been unable to obtain a license in England—printed.[134] In deciding to make that journey, far more than in marrying Douglas, who claimed to be Charles's elder half-brother, Lady Eleanor admitted that she had failed to win support at court. With that step, she prepared the way for a confrontation with the king that resulted in her being called before the High Commission and marked a turning point in her prophetic career.

CHAPTER 3

"I will utter my grave matter upon the harp"

Next to her vision of 28 July 1625, the most significant experience for Lady Eleanor occurred in October 1633, when her books were seized and she herself was called before the Court of High Commission. These events and her journey to the Netherlands, which immediately preceded them, marked the beginning of a new phase of her life. By 1633, neither her marriage nor her heritage were bringing her the social legitimacy that her culture expected of women. Her husband's madness had made a travesty of the former, and her brother's execution had devalued the latter. With Lucy's in-laws continuing to impede the relationship between mother and daughter, Lady Eleanor was left to rely upon her own resources. Rather than accepting what would probably have been a life defined by her dependence upon Douglas and his inability to provide for her, she turned more seriously to prophecy. Her decision meant substituting one kind of imprisonment for another. She sacrificed participation in court life, but her straitened condition and tarnished connections would probably have forced her to abandon that in any case. She could take some consolation in knowing that she was not alone in her disillusionment with the monarchy of Charles I. Like some other dissidents, she went to the Low Countries and published works for which she could not procure the necessary permission in England. In Amsterdam, there were were several printers, including J. F. Stam, known for publishing books and *corantoes* or newsheets in English.[1]

The Registers of the Privy Council show that, on 26 June 1633, the Board granted a pass for "Sir Archibald Duglas and his Ladie with two men and two maydes" to go to the spa and to return within six months.[2] This, Lady Eleanor claimed in *Everlasting Gospel* (1649), was the pretext she had used to obtain a "license" to leave England "since none for printing to be had here."[3] Her date of departure is one of the many details about her trip and its aftermath that remains uncertain, although copies of three of her tracts from that autumn survive and her annotated manuscript copy of the official record of the High Commissioners' proceedings against her is preserved among the family papers in the Hastings MSS at the Huntington Library. Contemporary newsletters and her own comments in later tracts provide some additional information, although we have no printed "brief relation" comparable to that which appeared following the Star Chamber trial of Prynne, Burton, and Bastwick in June 1637. Much of the extant evidence about the entire sequence of events, and particularly Lady Eleanor's response to her hearing, comes from the 1640s, when she interpreted and reinterpreted what had happened in the light of her prophetic mission. Instead of succeeding in ending her career, the High Commissioners who sentenced her provided her with support for her prediction that the Day of Judgment was imminent and, thus, contributed to her development as a prophet.

The record from the High Commission mentions three schedules annexed to the articles against Lady Eleanor. These were probably *All the Kings of the Earth* and *Given to the Elector,* two of the three tracts she published that autumn, and her petition complaining to the king about Archbishop Laud. Her third tract, *Woe to the House,* a broadside, may have been included with *All the Kings of the Earth.* The two are bound together in the Domestic State Papers, although an independent copy of *Woe to the House* survives in the library of Worcester College, Oxford.[4]

Lady Eleanor most likely wrote *All the Kings of the Earth* before she left England. She dedicated the tract to King Charles's sister, Elizabeth, widow of Frederick, the Elector of the Palatine. Frederick's unsuccessful efforts to rule Bohemia had made him and his wife the symbols of the embattled Protestant cause on the continent and had led people to refer to Elizabeth as the Queen of Bohemia.[5] Since its establishment twelve years earlier, Elizabeth's court-in-exile at the Hague had attracted many well-born English travelers, including those who were critical of policies at home.[6] Lady Eleanor had specifically referred to the exiled queen in 1625 in the preface to *Warning to the Dragon,* which she concluded with a prayer for preservation of the Church, the King and Queen and "forren Princes, especially the Kings excellent Sister."[7] Prominent among that queen's friends had been Lucy, countess of Bedford, whose influence at the English court and patronage of literary figures prior to her death in 1627 could hardly have escaped Lady Eleanor's notice.[8] While frustration at her inability to attain a comparable position may have encouraged Lady Eleanor's prophesying, a lingering hope of success may have led her to seek Elizabeth's favor during her time in the Low Countries. To reinforce her plea and to explain her cause, Lady Eleanor most likely gave the queen a copy of *All the Kings of the Earth*. Throughout her career as a prophet, Lady Eleanor personally presented her writings to individuals for whom they were intended. The date printed on the tract is 13 September, nine days prior to the date of the letter Elizabeth wrote in Lady Eleanor's behalf to King Charles.[9]

Lady Eleanor took the title of her tract, *All the Kings of the Earth*, from Psalm 138. Identifying herself with Britain and Elizabeth with the divine power whose assistance could rescue her and the kingdom from the troubles they faced, she applied to the queen the words the psalmist addressed to God.[10] Had this statement not come from a prophet who was interpreting divine will and had it not been addressed to a member of the royal family in an era when monarchs claimed to be God's lieutenants, it could have been blasphemy, which she was quick to condemn on the part of others. She later printed the entire word in capital letters, BLASPHEMY, in *Revelation Interpreted* (1646), where she described its being on the head of the Beast, the Duke of Buckingham, and labeled the charges brought against her for her writings "Blasphemous."[11] To emphasize the significance of the queen's role in the desperate battle against the forces of the antichrist, the "Babylonian dragon," Lady Eleanor compared the defenders of true religion to the craftsmen of ancient Ephesus who had struggled (though in vain) "lest their Goddesse Diana, her temple should be despised."[12] With that reference to Diana, Lady Eleanor expressed contemporary hopes that James's daughter, Elizabeth, would follow in the footsteps of the late Queen Elizabeth in protecting Protestantism. On the title page of the tract she placed a star. In each of its six points was one word of the verse that announced its significance, "signe of the sonne of man," and in its center "Matthew 24," where Jesus talked about the fulfillment of Daniel's prophecies. Like her own vision in 1625 that had enabled her to understand the prophecies that had previously seemed so difficult and that she elsewhere described by the well-known image of the morning star, she hoped that her message would serve to guide the queen. At the bottom of the title page, beneath the six-pointed star, Lady Eleanor noted that the new star that had caused such a stir in 1572, eighteen years before her birth, was a portent of the "end of the world," which would come seventy-two years later, just as the destruction of Jerusalem had followed "seventy odd yeeres after the first Starre seen in the east."[13]

The text of *All the Kings of the Earth* consisted of the Geneva version of Daniel 7–12 with Lady Eleanor's gloss. She had discoursed at greater length upon the same material in 1625 in *Warning to the Dragon,* but, by 1633, she had become more critical of those who should have been protecting religion. If, as seems likely, she worked from the same original as she had in 1625, she revised and added to her marginal commentary as well as to her preface. Having presented her earlier tract to Archbishop Abbot, she dismissed the bishops with contempt this time. They had long ago, by the "largesse" of rulers, become "so haughtie" that they "stirred up kings to warre against Turks, to leave their Dominions under the bishops' Jurisdiction."[14] Instead of exhorting Charles to be Michael as she had previously, Lady Eleanor showed how the monarchs of recent history had made the same mistakes as rulers whose stories were told in the Bible. In Daniel 11:20, she saw Henry II of France who had raised taxes and died shortly after his reign began "neither in wrath, nor in battell" but while tilting; in the verses just preceding belonged Henry VIII of England who "for his owne behalfe rather then Religion causeth the shamefull marriage of his brothers wife to turn on the B[ishop] of Rome."[15] She was not breaking new ground with her criticism of the rulers. In his popular *History of the World,* which had seen several editions by 1633, Sir Walter Raleigh had also judged Henry VIII harshly and noted the consequences that fell upon Henry and other monarchs who had pursued worldly fame.[16] In contrast to these rulers, Lady Eleanor saluted the Queen of Bohemia, whom she described in her preface as "walking in the truth."

Lady Eleanor may have also presented a copy of *Woe to the House* to the Queen of Bohemia. This broadside told the ostensibly personal tale of wrongs that she and her late brother, Mervin, had suffered at the hands of two Jezebels of the House of Stanley,—Elizabeth, countess of Huntingdon, mother-in-law of Lady Eleanor's daughter, Lucy, and

Anna [*sic*], Mervin's wife, both daughters of the dowager countess of Derby. When seen through the mirror of prophecy, *Woe to the House* repeated the message of *All the Kings of the Earth* and a *Warning to the Dragon,* but, instead of disclosing the misdeeds of rulers, it focused upon women whose power for good or ill was a recurrent theme in Lady Eleanor's work and a motif particularly appropriate for a piece to be shown to a queen. It also was potentially dangerous in view of Protestant concerns about the influence wielded by Charles I's Catholic wife, Henrietta Maria, whom Lady Eleanor later made the target of tracts. The situation in 1633 offered an opportunity for another woman, the Queen of Bohemia, to intervene and, like Mary in giving birth to Jesus, help to heal the wounds that had been inflicted upon Lady Eleanor and, because she was God's prophet, upon Britain.

Elizabeth may have gotten the point. In writing to King Charles in Lady Eleanor's behalf, she explained that she could not refuse a woman of that quality, and, in what may be a direct reference to the grievances related in *Woe to the House,* confessed that, if the Lady Eleanor's story were true, she was to be "pitied." Elizabeth concluded her appeal by leaving the matter to her brother's judgment. She knew this was one of many pleas for favor that she sent him and may not have expected that it would affect his opinion.[17]

Lady Eleanor claimed that, while she was in the Low Countries, she published a third tract, *Given to the Elector,* who, in 1633, was Prince Charles of the Rhine, the Queen of Bohemia's son and King Charles's nephew. Although the title page of the extant copies reads, "Amsterdam: Printed by Frederick Stam. 1633," these copies come from reprintings of 1648 or 1651 that include marginal glosses pointing out how intervening events bore out the prophecy.[18] The text of the tract told, in verse, Daniel's story of the handwriting that appeared on the wall during Belshazzar's banquet and predicted his doom (Daniel 5). The tale was one of Lady Eleanor's favorites, and she cited it frequently in various contexts. In addition to the reprinting of 1648, she published two different versions of the tract under other titles, one in 1643 and another in 1649.[19]

Even more clearly than *All the Kings of the Earth* or *Woe to the House, Given to the Elector* shows signs that Lady Eleanor hoped that it might reach a larger audience than its dedicatee, the elector. She called it a song of "Babylon or Confusion" and noted that its verses could be sung to the tune of *Who list a Soldiers life,* a well-known ballad that she may also have known as *Lord Thomas and Fair Ellinor*.[20] In advising the elector of the dire consequences that might befall him if he did not heed God's signs, she was giving the same admonition to Charles Stuart, King of Great Britain.

> Against the Lord of Heaven thy King,
>   not humbling of thine heart,
> But stiffned hast with pride thy neck
>   unto thy future smart.
> Behold polluting holy things
>   with Sabbath so Divine,
> Idolatry and Revels in
>   that day and night made thine.
>
> But he in whose hands rests thy life,
>   even breath, and thy ways all,
> Thou hast not glorified him
>   sent this wrote on the Wall.
> God numbered thy Kingdom hath
>   ended; the Hand points here,
> In Ballance his weighed thee too,
>   the set hour drawing neer.[21]

Scholars have assumed that this last tract, because it might be conceived to have imagined the king's death, was most disturbing to authorities and, thus, the principal cause of Lady Eleanor's summons before the High Commission.[22] The warrant for her appearance commanded her to answer for "presuming to Imprint" books and for "preferring this detestable petition" to the king. Among the Domestic State Papers is a copy of a petition from "La. Elea. Tichet" complaining about the

B:BEAST ascended out of the bottomless pitt with seaven heads: Seaven year having made warre hath overcome, and killed them: Books [hers] sealed by the Prophets, by the Bishop of Lambeth [William Laud, newly translated from London to Canterbury on the death of former Archbishop George Abbot] horned like the Lambe, like a Wolfe harted, are condemned to be burned at Pauls-Crosse, where our Lord was also crucified.[23]

She herself acknowledged how much her petition may have annoyed Charles and Laud when she printed it in *As not Unknowne* (1645) and again in *Blasphemous Charge* (1649).

Laud, who, in his capacity as Bishop of London, may have denied Lady Eleanor permission to publish her tracts, formally began his primacy at Canterbury on 19 September, a week after the Queen of Bohemia wrote her letter to her brother, the king.[24] News of his appointment as archbishop began circulating almost immediately after George Abbot's death on 4 August and probably reached Lady Eleanor before 19 September, whether she was in the Low Countries or in England. As committed to his vision of the church as she was to hers, Laud quickly gave her reason for the view she expressed more than once, that 19 September 1633 had been a disastrous day.[25]

Upon her return to England, Lady Eleanor, as she later related, went to the archbishop "to give him a taste or warning of his judgment at hand, the hand writing (*Dan.* 5) served on him in his gallery."[26] Just as the handwriting on the wall in Daniel 5 had notified Belshazzar of what would happen if he did not turn from idolatry, hers informed Laud what his fate would be. What she gave him was probably the handwritten sheet, entitled by her "Handwriteing October 1633," and, like two of her printed tracts from 1633, preserved among the Domestic State Papers.[27] Rather than using anagrams, Lady Eleanor on this occasion employed another method then in vogue to find her text in her subject's name. By striking out the *a* and *d* of LAUD, she derived LV. This she interpreted to be the 55th psalm that promised that the Lord will sustain those who trust in him but destroy the others.

Laud responded by seizing her books and by protesting to the king. Lady Eleanor too turned immediately to Charles with the petition that resulted in her being called before the High Commission. Rather than heeding her plea to serve as the instrument for the resurrection of her books, Charles reacted against the description of his archbishop in which she had employed words similar to those of her "Handwriteing 1633." On 8 October, he ordered that Lady Eleanor be summoned before the High Commission. She emphasized the king's betrayal by placing that warrant immediately after her petition to him when she printed them in the 1640s.[28]

Quite apart from her own direct encounters with Laud either before or after he became archbishop, Lady Eleanor may have attracted the attention of the English authorities, who were keeping close watch on English books printed in Amsterdam.[29] The note she wrote to Lady Fairfax on a 1648 edition of *Given to the Elector* suggests that she had had some difficulty getting her books back to England and that the Lady's father, Lord Vere, who had relinquished his command of forces in the Netherlands after the siege of Maastricht in 1632, had helped her. Although this claim may be true, its value in demonstrating to Vere's daughter, who was married to the commander of the parliamentary forces, that she should grant similar support to prophecy may have justified a prophetic and figurative, rather than a literal, interpretation of facts.

If Lady Eleanor had escaped official notice prior to her return to England, she virtually ensured her prosecution when, returning home with her tracts, she took her "handwriting" to the archbishop and then appealed against him to the king. Laud struck the blow that hurt her most when, on 23 October before her own eyes, he burned her books.[30] Although she often mentioned her appearance before the High Commission in conjunction with that, 23 October, not the following day when she received the court's sentence, was the day she subsequently observed as a day of infamy. On one of her editions of the proceedings against her, she struck out the 4 of the 24th which would have been a Thursday and thus a regular day for the High Commission to sit and made the date the 23d.[31]

Lady Eleanor's emphasis upon her books was a conscious one, not a misremembering or an accidental observance of the wrong date. She remarked how, in 1641 on the anniversary of 23 October, "the Irish Massacre" occurred, and, in 1642, it was the Battle of Edgehill or Keinton.[32] To further illustrate what wrongs she had suffered, she might also have noted that the second Battle of Newbury (1644), which was not far from Englefield, occurred at that time in October and that troops moving in Berkshire and Oxfordshire had preceded the first Battle of Newbury too. When, in 1651, she gave her account of King Charles's reign, she told "How in the same moneth October, etc." of 1648 she had taken Fairfax a copy of "a Book, Entituled *Babylons Handwriting*, bearing date *Anno 1633*," apparently to convince him to bring Charles to justice.[33] The year 1633 also had significance because it began on a Monday which she thought was meant to be a "new sabbath" for the New Coming, just as Matthias

Regiſtro Curiæ Dominorum Regiorum
Commiſsionariorum ad Cauſas Ec-
cleſiaſticas. Extract.

Tertia Seſsio Termini Michaelis 1633.

Die Jovis *vicesimo quarto viz. die
menſis* Octobris *Anno Dom. mille-
simo ſexcentesimo iricesimotertio Coram
Reverendiſsimo in* Chriſto Patre *&*
Domino, Domino Gulielmo *providenc̄*
Divina Cantuar· Archiepiſcopo *to'ius*
Angliæ Primate *&* Metropolitano,
Richardo *eàdem providenc̄* Angliæ
Primate *&* Metropolitano Archiepiſ-
copo Eboracenſi, *Honorandis &* præno-
bilibus Comitibus Portland, Dorſet, *&*
Carliſle, *Epiſcopis* Elien', *&* Roffen'
& Oxon', *Dominis* Iohanne Lamb,
& Nathanaele Brent, *militibus legum
Doctoribus,* Matthæo VVren *de* Wind-
ſor,

Fig. 1.   The significance of 23 October.
Courtesy of the Folger Shakespeare Library.

had replaced Judas among the apostles. The regime's efforts during 1633 to suppress prophecy had violated Sunday, the old sabbath, which had seen the "first Resurrection or coming"; Monday, Moonday, would see the last.[34]

Lady Eleanor condemned both the king and his archbishop for their action. Laud she accused of rape and murder, an assertion that presages later attempts to portray Charles I as a "Man of Blood" and one that could justify execution.[35] The fact of the prelate's crime outweighed the specific number and identity of his victims, which she never disclosed but described variously to fit her immediate purpose. Laud had "ravished" her "childe."[36] Her books were her babes, and she could find no rationale for his crime against them. Her prophecies were legitimate; they must be received as truth. They were "no spurious offspring of Davids" whose attempt to inherit could justifiably be thwarted.[37] Unlike the deaths of her own sons and unlike the misfortunes of the House of Stuart, which she remarked upon in her tracts, the fate of her books was no blot upon her prophetic lineage, her authenticity.[38] They had been slain just as, in 1649 and 1650, were Dorislaus and Ascham, the Commonwealth's ambassadors, whose names she wrote in the margin of Thomason's copy of *Before the Lords Second Coming*.[39] Their "shrowded . . . embalmed bodies," were left at Doctors Commons in accord with the description in Revelation 11 of what would happen to the two witnesses.[40]

The loss of her books, her prophetic creations, compounded the injury Lady Eleanor had earlier suffered by the deaths of her sons. In denying her the role of prophet, the patriarchal regime destroyed a far greater maternal creation than that which she had borne in temporal motherhood. She was Mary: in writing, she was producing the children who would inaugurate the Second Coming. Their crucifixion, like Christ's, confirmed their mission.[41]

The heinous nature of Laud's crime provided the unstated backdrop for *Word of God*, the retrospective defense of her brother, Mervin, that Lady Eleanor published shortly after the archbishop's execution in January 1645. Whereas the earl of Castlehaven, she believed, had been falsely accused of rape, Laud was guilty of rape and murder in addition to the charges that the House of Commons had formally presented against him. Castlehaven, tried by his peers and unjustly condemned to die in 1631, would, like Zaccheus, the sinning publican (Luke 19) ultimately be rewarded, but the archbishop should expect no mercy.

Just as in the parable of the talents the calculations of the servant who feared his master's anger brought him loss instead of gain, Laud would pay dearly. He had aggravated his wrongdoing by claiming to act in the name of God. She denounced him in terms very similar to those that he and the other high commissioners had used against her.

Although Lady Eleanor complained about her judgment by the commission and regarded the destruction of her books as a crime, she welcomed, at least in retrospect, the opportunity that her hearing gave her to present to such an august group Daniel's message that the Day of Judgment would come in 1645. One sign indicating the truth of her words was the inability of Dr. Reeves, the king's advocate, to respond to what she had said. This she noted in her gloss to the version of the proceedings, which she published as *The Dragons Blasphemous Charge* in 1651.[42] Accustomed to defendants who, when faced with similar charges, sought to confound the court, Reeves may have found her apparent compliance unsettling.[43] She did not refuse to take the oath ex officio and thus decline to answer the articles of the charge, as did many nonconformists. Well informed about the law and litigation, she undoubtedly knew that the court imprisoned uncooperative defendants in order to convince them to answer and, if it obtained no answer, took the articles *pro confesso.* Principle as well as practicality led her to respond. Lady Eleanor needed to publish her prophecy. To follow Daniel's bidding and to preserve the meaning with which her vision had infused her life, she must speak to inform her contemporaries that the Day of Judgment was coming. She took the oath and confessed that she had, indeed, written the three books in question.

While her subsequent tracts and petitions might lead us to expect that Lady Eleanor would have used her answer to harangue her judges, there is no evidence that she attempted this. Her answer seems to have prompted none of the comment stirred by those that Prynne, Burton, and Bastwick presented in the Star Chamber in 1637. Neither she nor any of those who reported her appearance before the High Commission mention a long or contentious answer. Insofar as we can tell from the immediately contemporary sources, Lady Eleanor did not herself challenge the high commissioners' proceedings until she heard their sentence, although she probably authorized her attorney, John Wells (who had served her in the litigation following Davies's death), in an attempt to arrest the proctors concerned in her prosecution.[44]

The commissioners who debated how to deal with Lady Eleanor on

24 October 1633 most likely knew not only about her recent confrontation with Charles and Laud but also about some of her earlier prophecies. Her extract from the court's record indicates that most of her
judges agreed about what sentence might be appropriate for her. Having no need to mention her books, which had been disposed of the
previous day, they condemned her for interpreting the scriptures, for
being "a prophetess, falsely pretending to have receiv'd certain Revelations from God," for printing her books without license, for bringing
them into England, and for dispersing them.[45] Though they declared
her offenses against the king and court matters of "too high a nature"
for them to handle, they determined that she should be fined £3,000,
ordered to make a public submission, and committed as a close prisoner
to the Gatehouse during the king's pleasure.[46]

Perhaps the best-known anecdote about Lady Eleanor's hearing concerns an attempt by Sir John Lambe, Dean of the Arches, to discredit
her. According to Peter Heylyn, the unique source for the story, Lambe
responded to REVEALE O DANIEL (Eleanor Audelie), the anagram
with which she had signed All the Kings of the Earth, with an anagram
of his own, NEVER SOE MAD A LADIE (Dame Eleanor Davies). The
court, Heylyn claimed, erupted in laughter when Lambe not only read
his anagram aloud but also wrote it out and gave it to Lady Eleanor.
Although, given what we know about Lambe, Heylyn's tale is credible,
we cannot be certain that the incident occurred. The report appearing
in Cyprianus Anglicus, originally published in 1661, contains at least
two errors. Believing that she had used "Eleanor Davies" instead of
"Eleanor Audelie" for the anagram, Heylyn criticized her for having
an extra S and being short an L. He also asserted that Lambe's action
brought "the poor woman into such a confusion that afterwards she
either grew wiser or was less regarded," whereas we know that she did
not give up writing or making anagrams.[47] If Lambe did confront her
with a taste of her own medicine, she omitted him from any of her
catalogues of those who crossed her.[48] In contrast to Laud, the Dean
of the Arches was a relatively insignificant figure, and, in 1633, the
anagram was merely a taunt. Madness became a serious issue for her
later, after she had been confined to Bedlam.

Although Lady Eleanor's transcript of proceedings reported that the
Bishop of Rochester had suggested confinement to Bedlam, no one,
not even Lambe, who allegedly had cast the aspersion of madness upon
her, had seconded that proposal.[49] Lambe had declared his concurrence

with the most severe proposal and noted that she should be required "to acknowledge her Offence at *Pauls* Cross." Two of the commissioners, the earl of Carlisle and the earl of Portland, asked to be "spared" from judging her. We can only speculate about their reasons for doing so. Lady Eleanor mentioned Carlisle several times in references to her associations with court circles. Although she did not mention Portland, he too may have been an acquaintance. If either spoke in her defense, this does not appear in the record. Dorset, the third lay commissioner on this occasion, announced himself as for "the highest."[50] Lady Eleanor gives no hint about previous contacts with him, but they were both at court during the same period.

Because the Queen of Bohemia had appealed to the king on Lady Eleanor's behalf, the English resident at the Hague, Sir William Boswell, received a dispatch from Whitehall reporting the disposition of the case. That letter, dated 26 October, did not state the opinions of individual commissioners; instead it provided a summary of their assessment of Lady Eleanor. She was

a woman too well knowne and whose devellish practizes in her pretended prophecies have drawne upon her this weeke a severe censure in the high commission court: and might have cast her into further danger there being a mixture in them of treasonable conceptions, if the judges had not thought her possessed with a frantique spirit, to be conjured out of her by restrayning her libertie and disabling her to do hurt.[51]

Does this dispatch allow us to read between the lines of the official record or did the correspondent seek to explain the proceedings in a way that would absolve Charles from ignoring his sister's plea for Lady Eleanor and thus add his own gloss to the commissioners' statements in the register? The dispatch suggests that debate may have focused upon how to deal with Lady Eleanor rather than upon the more difficult question of whether or not she was mad. Did the judges expect that submission at Paul's Cross would free her of the "frantique spirit" that had taken control of her? If, instead, they intended to "conjure" it out of her by confining her to the Gatehouse, why, as her daughter, Lucy, asked in a subsequent petition, did they not see that she had access to spiritual counsel while there?[52]

For the commissioners, Lady Eleanor's case posed special problems. Like Frances, Viscountess Purbeck, who had come before the same

with Dr. *Worral*; and payment of Cofts.

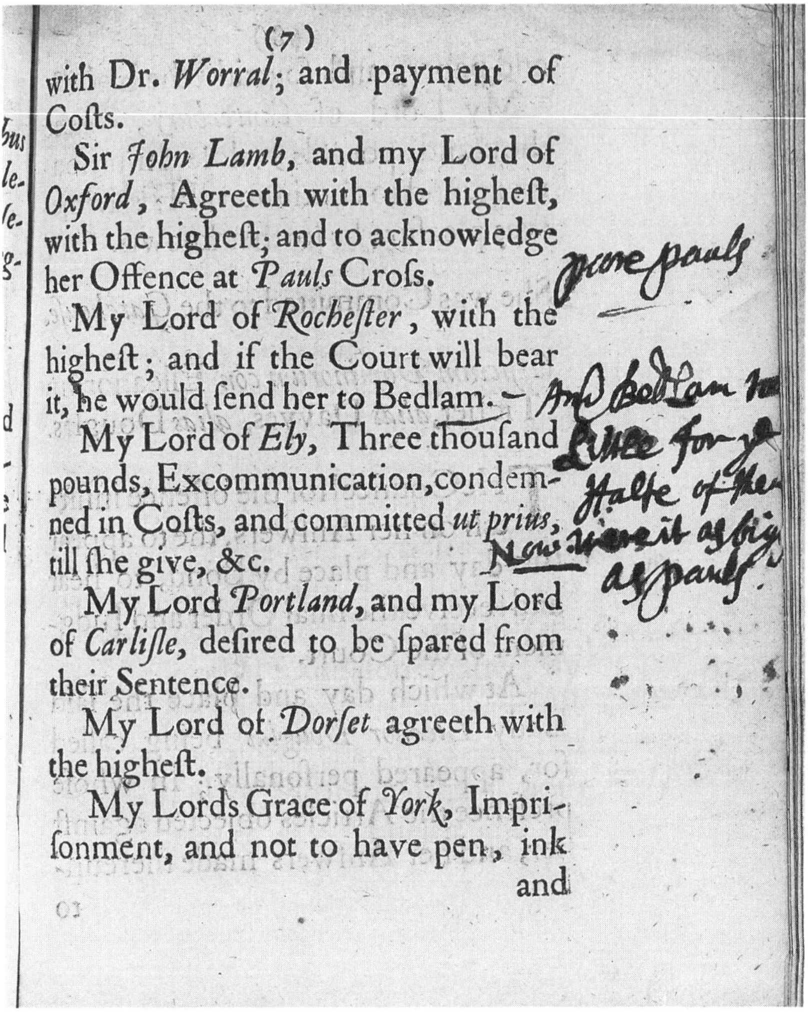

Sir *John Lamb*, and my Lord of *Oxford*, Agreeth with the higheft, with the higheft; and to acknowledge her Offence at *Pauls* Crofs.

My Lord of *Rochefter*, with the higheft; and if the Court will bear it, he would fend her to Bedlam.

My Lord of *Ely*, Three thoufand pounds, Excommunication, condemned in Cofts, and committed *ut prius*, till fhe give, &c.

My Lord *Portland*, and my Lord of *Carlifle*, defired to be fpared from their Sentence.

My Lord of *Dorfet* agreeth with the higheft.

My Lords Grace of *York*, Imprifonment, and not to have pen, ink and

Fig. 2.   The Commissioners' proposals for punishment.
Courtesy of the Folger Shakespeare Library.

court in 1627, Lady Eleanor expected to be treated as a woman of status, but, in contrast to Lady Purbeck and many of the women who appeared there, she did not appear in connection with either alleged adultery or a suit for alimony.[53] Nor had she been, like Sarah Jones and others, arrested on suspicion of having attended a conventicle.[54] Those appearing on charges of printing or distributing unlicensed books were men.[55] In some respects, Lady Eleanor's offense resembled those of the men accused of preaching false, scandalous, or offensive doctrine, and yet she had not preached. The court could not deal with her, as they frequently did with clergy, by ordering suspension or deprivation from a benefice, or with a physician, like Dr. John Bastwick, whom they suspended from his practice, in addition to demanding submission and acknowledgment of the offense.[56] The dilemma she presented them was not simply one of determining an appropriate sentence; they saw her as a violator of gender order. She had behaved in a way that "much unbeseemed her Sex."[57] She was, moreover, an aristocrat, albeit one whose family had fallen into disrepute. Would she follow the example of Viscountess Purbeck six years earlier and defy the court's sentence?

The procedures that allowed the High Commission considerable discretion in handling cases meant that they could make the punishment fit the crime and the offender. Although reports of the court's actions printed in the *Calendars of State Papers, Domestic,* begin four months after they had heard Lady Eleanor, a comparison of the penalties she incurred with those imposed during the year between February 1634 and February 1635 shows that she was treated severely. No one else received a fine of £3,000.[58] Only Amy Green, for "notorious adultery" was fined £2,000 and that was "subject to consideration."[59] Theophilus Brabourne, summoned because of his unauthorized publication of a book containing "erroneous, heretical and judaical opinions" incurred a fine of £1,000, the same day that Lady Eleanor was fined three times that amount.[60] In July 1634, Brabourne's sentence, which like hers also involved imprisonment in the Gatehouse, was suspended, his fine was respited, and he was ordered to go to the Bishop of Ely.[61] Bastwick's fine for bringing into the kingdom books he had had printed without a license "for corrupting his Majesty's subjects and raising schism in the church" was likewise £1,000. He was to be imprisoned in the Gatehouse until he gave bond for the performance of his sentence, but the sentence was respited for a month to see if he would submit himself.[62] Earlier, on the grounds that his wife was "great with child," he was able to avoid giving additional sureties for his appearance.[63]

While Brabourne and Bastwick were far from docile in their response to the commissioners' demands, they at times benefited from some of the opportunities that the court generally accorded to those who showed a willingness to cooperate and submit to its authority. The records suggest that imprisonment was, in itself, a means the commissioners used to encourage acquiesence. They imprisoned the Viscountess Purbeck after, not before, she refused to do the prescribed penance. In determining where they would send someone, they again relied upon discretion. This allowed them to separate such groups as the conventiclers and put two in each of several prisons.[64] The Gatehouse at Westminster, which was, according to Stow, in part the Bishop of London's prison for "clerks' convict" and in part "a gaol or prison for offenders thither committed," seems to have been the High Commission's choice for cases where the prisoner's status added to the signficance of his or her recalcitrance.[65] In the Gatehouse were individuals who refused to answer to the articles brought against them, declined to give sureties for their appearance, did not pay the fines or costs assessed upon them, or refused to acknowledge their errors.[66] Brabourne and Bastwick apparently negotiated, though the terms they proposed were hardly realistic.

Lady Eleanor did not play the game.[67] She frustrated the execution of her sentence without negotiating. Although the authorities imprisoned her in the Gatehouse at Westminster, they were no more successful in having her make a public submission than they were in forcing the Viscountess Purbeck to do penance. Her prophetic mission required that she resist the demand for a public submission that the commissioners commonly imposed upon political offenders. Complying would force her to deny the authenticity of her voice. This she could not do without declaring herself a fraud and, essentially, giving up her career as prophet.[68] How could she continue if she admitted that she should not have written the books in question?

Nor did Lady Eleanor pay her £3,000 fine. Surviving records of the High Commission show the fine still unpaid in February 1640, almost five years after she had been released from that confinement.[69] Lord Scudamore's correspondent told him that Lady Eleanor "was not moved at all with anything that was said or done to her." Responding to the sentence with "mad speeches" where "with a kind of despising the court, she told them they could do her no hurt and that she had the spirit of Elias and many such subtleties," she gave Laud a paper that she declared was his sentence.[70] When the Archbishop wrote to his friend, Wentworth, the Lord Deputy in Ireland, he mentioned that "the Lady Davis" had predicted that he "should very few days outlive the fifth of November."[71] This suggests that she had revised and specified the prognostication she made for him in her earlier "Handwriting."

Lady Eleanor summed up her view of the proceedings in words particularly appropriate for one sentenced to close imprisonment in the Gatehouse. Across the top of her manuscript copy of the transcript she wrote, "The gates of Hell shall not prevaile against her."[72] Her adaptation of Matthew 16:18 about the founding of the church allowed her to identify herself with the church and to assert that those who had committed her to prison were also defying the will of God. Thus, at the very moment that the High Commission was judging her, Lady Eleanor was judging them. She realized that, although they believed that they were curtailing her liberty, they were replacing the imprisonment of her spirit with that of her body. Previously, she had found herself confined by the authority of Davies, Douglas, the bishops, and the king. When she exchanged those bonds for the physical constraints of the Gatehouse in October 1633, she had moved from the hell that everyday life imposed upon a woman whose spirit longed for freedom to confinement in a place that, though deemed worse by her society, could not harm her more than the institutions and conventions of the world.

Lady Eleanor regarded her trial as a confirmation of the prophetic mantle that Daniel had laid upon her. Thanks to the High Commission, her prophecies had become a part of the public record of the kingdom.[73] She concluded her extract from the court's records with a note that expressed a thought that she repeated elsewhere, though never with words quite so fitting for the occasion. The title of the tract she had dedicated to the Queen of Bohemia said what she wanted to say, "All the Kings of the Earthe shall prayse thy name, Lord when they Heare the words of thy Mouth."[74] That court had heard the voice that her husbands had sought to silence. Although the king had earlier sent a gentleman of his bedchamber to ask her to give up her house at Whitehall, he had granted her an audience before his chief councillors and judges for ecclesiastical affairs in 1633.

With her repeated references to the destruction of her books, her hearing, and her sentence, Lady Eleanor displayed her anger. The court had condemned her and prophecy. She later published the court's official transcript of her case in *Blasphemous Charge,* a tract whose very title expresses her assessment of the proceedings. However great her notion of her own importance or her flair for drama may have been, she refrained from embroidering that record. The facts stated what she needed to say, and she reserved her views for glosses and for other tracts, where, in numerous references to the hearing and its aftermath, she vented her wrath upon both Archbishop Laud and Aquila Weeks, the Keeper of the Gatehouse.[75] As a preface to one edition of *Blasphemous Charge* published in 1649 at the time of the king's trial, she placed a letter to "King Charls Prisoner" in which she reminded him of his own offense at her trial in 1633.[76] In another 1649 edition of the same tract, she substituted an appeal to Charles on the "third day" to "speak the word" so that the "spirit of life" might enter the books that were murdered by Laud.[77] Two years later, in 1651, she printed the transcript of the High Commission's proceedings with the title *Dragons Blasphemous Charge,* one copy of which was endorsed, though not in Lady Eleanor's hand, for her daughter, "Lady Huntingdon."[78] In addition, she included excerpts from the record along with comments about it in *Her Appeal* (1646).[79]

In interpreting the events of 1633, Lady Eleanor pointed out the implications of the proceedings rather than challenging legal points, such as procedural irregularities or the severity of her sentence, as some others judged by the courts did. Although she never explicitly said that she felt that she had not received some of the privileges often given to those of status, her pride in her ancestry gave her added reason to regard the court's action as harsh. The treatment inflicted upon her indicated, confirmed, and reinforced the importance of her mission. What had happened made it easier for her to believe that God would judge Britain. While not suppressing her outrage, that understanding probably assisted her in enduring imprisonment.

The fame acquired by some who were imprisoned by the Caroline regime eluded Lady Eleanor. With whatever spiritual growth its testing brought came questions raised by her gender. The heroes among the political prisoners of the age were men, not women. Public acclaim went neither to those women who were suffering disapproval and persecution for their failure to abide by their societies' rules nor to those, such as Anne Hutchinson, who defied the authorities to write or preach publicly, but it went to those who were serving as patrons for the clergy or who were practicing godliness in their own lives.[80] The High Commission's sentence emphasized, for Lady Eleanor, the consequences of accepting life as a prophet. She might have been even more distressed if she had read the dispatch sent to Boswell in the Netherlands (cited previously). The court had rejected her and her message. They had questioned her legitimacy and ordered her to be imprisoned, and their judgment made it harder for her to dismiss the other obstacles she had encountered in the years following that "morning star" of July 1625. The trials she was experiencing and the strengthening of belief that accompanied them are comparable to those Petroff describes in what she calls the fourth stage of development for medieval visionaries, a stage that is sometimes accompanied by madness.[81]

The High Commission's proceedings left Lady Eleanor a close prisoner in the Gatehouse at Westminster. Apart from a letter to her sisters in which she announced her prediction that London would burn, none of her own writing survives from her confinement there.[82] Other sources provide only a partial picture of her condition. Her daughter Lucy, twenty-one years old, mother of several children, and freed from the awkward position created by the conflict between her mother and mother-in-law by the latter's death in January 1634, petitioned the king that Lady Eleanor might have air, a woman of her own to attend her, and a "grave divine" for her comfort and edification.[83] Seeing her mother in such circumstances probably shocked Lucy and prompted regrets that she had not been able to prevent the imprisonment. Although Lucy may have exaggerated her picture of Lady Eleanor's emotional suffering and that of the physical discomforts of prison in order to move Charles to action, the main points of the petition are probably valid. In her own 1647 petition to the Commons, Lady Eleanor recited, in terms similar to those Lucy had used at the time, the horrors of her confinement: not having a woman servant, not being allowed as much as a friend to visit her, and being "made subject to the base behavior of the Keeper and his officers (such an unchristianlike estate as is not fitt to be named by takeing advantage of that lowe estate of hers), shee being allowed neither pen nor inke, nor to have the Bible."[84]

Aquila Weeks, keeper of the Gatehouse, complained to the Council that Lady Eleanor had no means to support herself (and thus no means to pay Weeks) and probably had little inclination to make his prisoner

more comfortable.[85] Lady Eleanor later took revenge in her tracts,
where she made the most of his name, Aquila, the Latin word for eagle,
which was also a symbol of Rome.[86] Bastwick, who spent more than a
year and a half as a close prisoner in the Gatehouse shortly after Lady
Eleanor's confinement, mentioned the "ill usage" and many "domesti-
call affronts" he had received from the keeper in the course of *The
Letany* of grievances he published in 1637, when he assured Weeks
that, though he had cause to do so, he would not appeal against him.
Although identifying himself as a spiritual pilgrim rather than a
prophet, Bastwick, like Lady Eleanor, could serve his purpose by emphasizing how much he suffered in the hands of the forces of the
antichrist.[87] In contrast to their experience was that of the Viscountess
Purbeck, who, while imprisoned in the Gatehouse in 1635, resisted
the attempts of the keeper and his assistants to bring her before the
High Commission. The Viscountess apparently won some concessions
from her guards, and, with support from her friend, Sir Robert Howard, who bribed a turnkey, she escaped to France. Although depression
could account for the conditions Lady Eleanor was subjected to in the
Gatehouse, a more likely explanation is her interest in demonstrating
that she was, indeed, a prophet and that her warnings about evil were
justified. Daniel himself had endured being thrown in the lions' den,
and before she came to the throne, Elizabeth had survived imprisonment in the tower by her Catholic sister, Queen Mary. Lady Eleanor
may have been familiar with Christopher Lever's *Queene Elizabeths Teares*
(1607), which described Elizabeth's time in the tower as her "bearing
the Christian Crosse" and which suggested that the young woman had
found comfort in Daniel's example, which was depicted on hangings
there.

Tales of the strength of spirit with which martyrs had borne imprisonment and persecution, from the early Christian era to her own, set
a high standard for Lady Eleanor and other would-be imitators. William Waller's time in prison during the 1640s led him to ask, "What
is there in an imprisonment that should make that condition so formi-
dable?" Despite his belief that, in one sense, we are all prisoners during
life because our souls are imprisoned in our bodies, he felt as if he was
"a kind of living corps[e]."[88] Studies of prison life over the centuries
show that its mental impact is not inconsiderable, and Lady Eleanor
made many references to prisons in her tracts. Most of these convey an
image of darkness and evil, ultimate terror and anguish, hell without

redemption.[89] She associated "infernal furies" with the Gatehouse, yet she survived.[90]

In accord with the expectations that God would be with the prophets who suffered in his cause, Lady Eleanor had a visit from an "angel from heaven" during her time in the Gatehouse. Newswriter Rossingham told Lord Scudamore in February 1635 that she had written a letter informing the king that the angel had told her that London would be burned.[91] No such letter is extant, but one that she addressed that same month to her sisters, Amy, Elizabeth, and Christian, survives among the Domestic State Papers. Under the heading "Three Children of the Lord," Lady Eleanor interpreted Psalm 75, which had been the previous Sunday's scripture, for them. The wine in the cup in the hand of the Lord (verse 8) was "hott redd wine Burning . . . prepared for Babylon London." She continued with comments upon Psalm 79, the scripture for the next Sunday, the sevenfold reproach to be rendered to those who have reproached God (verses 11–12).[92] Rossingham noted that the judgment she predicted had come, but in the form of heavy snow instead of fire.[93] She remained silent about that.

For her sisters, Lady Eleanor described, as she did again later in a tract, her experience in the Gatehouse the preceding September (1634), during a full moon, the "prisoners fire and candle," when she was visited by an angel. The angel came and rested upon the bed for an hour before leaving with a farewell salute from his mouth and another farewell from the amber glove on his right hand that "left such an odoriferous scent when he was gone" because it had been "all oyled with Ambergreece."[94] That episode, like most of her references to her imprisonment, illustrated the power of prophecy rather than her experiences in the Gatehouse. She was resolved, as she said on her transcript of the hearing, that "The Gates of Hell shall not prevaile against her." In 1646, she concluded *Gatehouse Salutation* with triumphant lines. However much she may have suffered and struggled while in the Gatehouse, she had a purpose that, like others who suffered for their causes, enabled her to take advantage of what had happened.

Lady Eleanor's release from the Gatehouse came in June 1635, probably as a result of the efforts of Lucy, who, according to her mother's petition to the Commons in 1647, had paid £500 in that connection.[95] When Lucy's sister-in-law, Alice, heard the news, she feared that Lucy and Ferdinando would bring Lady Eleanor to Donnington, where they were living with the earl of Huntingdon. Alice reminded her father of the "dishonors and abuses shee [Lady Eleanor] most wickedly" laid upon "my late and most deare deceased mother and yourself," presumably in *Woe to the House,* where Lady Eleanor had attacked both the Countess of Huntingdon and the Countess's sister, wife to Lady Eleanor's brother, Mervin, earl of Castlehaven.[96] In a subsequent letter, Alice thanked her father for acting quickly to prevent her fears from being realized, but Lady Eleanor's own wishes may have been as important as those of the earl or of Ferdinando and Lucy in determining that she would not live with them.[97] Lady Eleanor went her own way.

CHAPTER 4

Prophet or "Mad Ladie"?

Less than two years after Lady Eleanor obtained her freedom from imprisonment in the Gatehouse, the Privy Council ordered her committed to Bedlam, the London hospital for the insane. That order, which put into effect the Bishop of Rochester's proposal to the High Commission in 1633, raises the oft-debated question of her mental condition. In the face of slim evidence about how she may have felt at the time of her release, we can do no more than speculate about this.

While in the Gatehouse, Lady Eleanor could concentrate upon thinking of herself as prophet, but, once free, she again encountered the tension between that role and society's expectations of her as an aristocratic woman. Had she written then, she might have reflected upon the paradox by which the bonds of marriage imprisoned her when she was no longer confined. Douglas's mental breakdown offered a metaphor for his lack of sympathy for her prophetic mission. His condition meant that her marital bondage seemed as senseless as the official reaction to her messages. She later excoriated him for having disposed of her property while she was in the Gatehouse, but, at this point, she made no effort to recoup her losses. It seems likely that she may have needed time to recover from her experiences of the preceding years, but, at the same time, she was probably searching for a way to continue prophecy in a world that did not want to hear her message.

If, in the summer of 1635, Lady Eleanor made an effort to contact Douglas or the uncle, Dean Young of Winchester, with whom he was apparently living, she does not say so. She did visit Lucy, Ferdinando, and their family briefly before departing for Bath in September 1635. Along the way she wrote Lucy that she expected to see them again in a week or two, but we do not know whether she actually did. In her postscript, she offered one of the images whose meanings, like many in her work, seem only partially evident to those not privy to her prophetic knowledge. By describing the church at "Alsstree" [Elstree] that she understood was, in fact, "Audeleys tree," so called for the trees which were thought to be 2,000 years old "standing in the possession of Munday," she invoked the family heritage with a pun. She may also have been referring to her designation of Monday as sabbath, which she elsewhere contrasted to the authorities' violations of it or to Anthony Mundaye, pursuivant of the High Commission, not the poet. She concluded, "My Monday will prevaile."[1]

While at Bath, Lady Eleanor may have written the tract that appears in manuscript among the Hastings Collection, "Bathe Daughter of Babylondon—Woeman Sitting on Seven Mountains Beholde."[2] Using Revelation 17:9 as the text, she equated Bath with Rome and Babylon and even started to name the "Mountains" of Bath: "Landsdowne, Clarknes Downe, Warlesdowne etc." She may have found special meaning in at least two of these: Lansdowne, the hill from which Fonthill was visible and on which William Beckford, the estate's later owner, built his tower; and Warlesdowne, probably Wirral hill, close to Glastonbury where Joseph of Arimathea was said to have landed.[3] The woman featured in the piece was the whore of Babylon, whose waters made Bath's identification with it natural. The possibilities offered by the imagery are probably not accidental. By going to Bath/Babylon seeking cures instead of going to London/righteousness (which was also the seat of government where decisions about policy were made), Lady Eleanor's contemporaries were going a-whoring rather than heeding the words of life that she brought. Although she tells us neither when she wrote this tract nor whether she presented it to anyone, it fits the frustrating situation she faced at this time, and its antipopish vehemence is consistent with her opposition to what she saw at Lichfield the following year.

By midsummer 1636, Lady Eleanor was staying at the Angel in Lichfield. The image of the angel was one of her favorites. It was an angel who came to her in September 1634, during her confinement in the Gatehouse, and it seems likely that she purposely decided to lodge at the inn of that name. Though Lichfield was not far from Donnington, where she could have paid frequent visits to the grandchildren she had written about so fondly the preceding autumn, she may have gone there because she saw an opportunity to deliver her message.[4] Tradition claimed that the name Lichfield meant field of corpses and that a thousand Christians had been martyred there in the time of the Roman emperor, Diocletian. The three spires of the cathedral, "the Ladies of the Vale," made it stand out. Robert Wright, Bishop of Coventry and Lichfield, was thought to be more interested in protecting his own financial interests than in caring for his diocese.[5] John Hayward, a prebendary there, wrote Cosin in 1634, that the church and diocese of Lichfield were "Augias stable." Rather than remain when the "principall governors . . . live upon the dung of this stable," Hayward chose to leave.[6] Although three travelers who had begun their journey 11 August 1634 claimed to have seen "a fayre Communion Cloth of Cloth of Gold for the High Altar" in the vestry at Lichfield, Laud's vicar-general, Sir Nathaniel Brent, who visited the cathedral in May 1636, reported that the east end of the church was "undecent."[7] Word of Laudian efforts to correct the situation may have led Lady Eleanor to the city. She was certainly present while remedial measures were being taken. By December, the cathedral was "very beautifully set out with hangings of arras behind the altar; the communion-table handsomely railed in; and the table itself set out in the best manner, and the bishop's seat fairly built."[8]

According to articles subsequently drawn by the High Commission, Lady Eleanor, about Michaelmas 1636, moved from the Angel into the cathedral close at Lichfield, to the home of Susan Walker whose husband, John, was a clerk.[9] That put her virtually on the scene of the changes that were occurring. With Susan Walker, Marie Noble, wife of the town clerk, Michael Noble, and other women, the articles alleged, Lady Eleanor spent a lot of time discussing religion. They went daily to the cathedral, where they employed a tactic that contemporaries used in quarrels and citizens often utilized in disputes with cathedral clergy. They defied the established seating arrangements that gave priority in the church to those of social rank and ecclesiastical office. First they occupied the places in the choir for gentlewomen and then those next to the bishop's throne reserved for wives of the bishop, dean, and canons. Neither Lady Eleanor nor her companions have left evidence about what specifically prompted their protest, but it seems likely that they, like laity elsewhere at the time, wanted to express their discontent with the clergy's innovations, such as the removal of the communion table from the nave of the church to the east end where, in accord with Catholic tradition, it became an altar, separated from the congregation by a rail. Lady Eleanor, who had objected to "Altars decked as a shop, shining with the light of so many Tapers and Candles" in *Warning to the Dragon* (1625), expressed her dislike for what she observed on her daily visits to the cathedral in "The Appeal to the Throne," a tract, now lost, that she sent to the bishop.[10] Apparently having received no answer, she sat upon his throne one morning, declared herself primate and metropolitan, and poured hot tar and wheat paste upon the new altar hangings that she later described as being coarse, woolen, and purple.[11]

Lady Eleanor's action that day in the cathedral dramatized her written challenge to authority. Not only did she claim access to information concerning divine will upon which she interpreted what she saw, she also had assumed the position of the bishop by occupying his throne. Her conduct in the cathedral, like that of the early Quakers' "going naked as a sign," conformed with the patterns set by the prophets of the Old Testament, who had performed various "signs and wonders."[12] By the time of her death, she had written extensively about both Daniel and Ezekiel and made numerous references to Elijah and others. In destroying the altar hanging, she, as prophet, was displaying God's anger and warning of future, more severe judgments upon those who defied divine will.

This is the only time in Lady Eleanor's life when she combined direct action with her written prophecies and the only time when she appears to have been part of a closely knit spiritual fellowship. Her earlier companions at the court seem to have been people, men as well as women, who saw each other occasionally rather than an intentional community and people whose concerns were primarily temporal. As a consequence of dissatisfaction with her inability to communicate her message in those circumstances, she may consciously have decided to take an approach more appropriate for her mission. Yet she says nothing about the women who seem to have played a critical role in supporting her at Lichfield. Her only references to her residence in the city come in *Restitution of Prophecy* (1651) and *Bethlehem* (1652), which she published shortly before her death, and she passes over her associates in silence even then. The distinctiveness that she claimed because she was a prophet and the noble birth of which she was so conscious separated her from the townswomen. In contrast to the medieval visionaries who identified themselves with communities, the Marian martyrs who found fellowship in prison, Anne Hutchinson whose associates were important to her, or the Quakers who valued their women's meetings, Lady Eleanor believed that she was an individual called by God to perform a specific duty. [13] She wrote to execute her responsibilities rather than to record her spiritual journey and consequently saw others as audience or instruments. The ladies with whom she had been at court earlier were part of the establishment to whom she was directing her message, although, as wives, they, like the women of Lichfield, were a subordinate part of it. For the authorities, on the other hand, mentioning Susan Walker and Marie Noble served a purpose. By presenting Lady Eleanor as a leader of a group of dissidents rather than a prophet, they could avoid the question of her authenticity, discount her rank, proceed to condemn her as a troublemaking woman and a coventicler, settle some local quarrels, and, at the same time, announce publicly to the community the consequences of challenging the ecclesiastical establishment. [14]

Both the commissioners' articles against Lady Eleanor's companions and the action that she took during her time with them suggest that Susan Walker and Marie Noble belong in the narrative. Their commitment was strong enough so that they continued to stand by Lady Eleanor when doing so brought them into conflict with officialdom. Like her, they threatened the domestic and public order of patriarchy. Susan Walker refused to force Lady Eleanor to leave her house, even when the Chancellor of the Diocese, the Canon Residentiary, and the Dean ordered her to do so. When challenged about her defense of Lady Eleanor by Sir Simon Weston's wife at a dinner party at the latter's home, Susan Walker responded by saying that Lady Eleanor had acted according to her conscience, which was more than Mr. Latham, the Dean's official, could do. [15]

In 1651, when she wrote *Restitution of Prophecy*, Lady Eleanor discussed the altar hanging at Lichfield within the context of the conflict between the Laudians, who wanted altars in the east ends of churches, and their opponents, who labeled altars popish and instead wanted communion tables set in the naves. She linked those tables with the "Lords Table" and the "Tables of the Law" (the Ten Commandments) and compared the "clerk-vicars" burial of the altar hanging in the "Dunghil" to preserve it during the Civil War with a parable she often cited, that about the servant who angered his lord by burying his talent and failing to use it. [16] Having the altar removed from the people was as ridiculous to her as having a centurion guarding the crucified Christ. [17]

Lady Eleanor's conduct prompted the Privy Council, on 17 December, to order that she be brought to London and committed to Bedlam, the hospital of St. Mary of Bethlehem that had been established in the thirteenth century and given as an asylum for the insane to the City of London by King Henry VIII.[18] Although thirty or more individuals crowded into Bedlam's twenty-one rooms during the 1620s, then, as today, most of those with mental disorders remained in society. Some were confined in houses of correction or elsewhere. The appointment of Dr. Crooke, physician to James I, as keeper of Bedlam in 1619 may have been an attempt to provide real medical attention to the "prisoners," as they were referred to in the records, but the Privy Council's inquiry into conditions there in 1632 revealed that Crooke had, for the most part, been providing custodial rather than rehabilitative care. He and other staff members had been lining their own pockets with money paid by the friends and parishes of the patients. Rarely did he accept, even with a warrant from the Lord Mayor or Aldermen, those who could not pay fees.[19] Although Crooke was not prosecuted as a result of those findings, he was removed from his position. When Lady Eleanor arrived early in 1637, there was little evidence that the inquiry had brought other significant changes in the administration of the hospital.[20]

In ordering her to be sent to Bedlam, the council declared Lady Eleanor's actions "being of soe fowle and strange a nature that we cannot conceive them to passe from any person but one wholey distracted of understanding." Her behavior on previous occasions, they asserted, supported this conclusion.[21] Our sources do not indicate whether the council had any debate prior to issuing this order or whether those present agreed about what they should do. The council's registers show that the order was signed by the Lord Treasurer (Bishop Juxon of London), the Duke of Lenox, the Marquis of Hamilton, the Lord Chamberlain (the earl of Pembroke), the earls of Northumberland and Dorset, Lord Cottington, Mr. Comptroller (Sir Henry Vane), and Mr. Secretry Coke. Of these, only Dorset had sat as a High Commissioner during Lady Eleanor's hearing three years earlier. At that time, he had advocated the "highest" penalty for her.

Concepts of madness discussed in contemporary sources included a variety of disorders attributable to causes ranging from the deaths of friends or family, disappointment in love, enthusiasm or fanatacism in religion, possession by evil spirits, or diseases in the body.[22] Robert

Burton distinguished between melancholy, his principal subject, and madness that sometimes was a consequence of extreme melancholy or despair.[23] From the notebooks that Richard Napier, a Buckinghamshire clergyman and astrological physician, kept about his patients, Michael MacDonald has identified four types of madness, two serious and violent, one exemplified by criminal behavior, the other by sickness, and two less serious, melancholy and lethargy.[24] The nature of the condition affected the kind of treatment that Napier recommended.

The popular stereotype of the mad person emphasized behavioral characteristics of the most seriously disturbed. The "madman," as he appeared on stage and in verse, was scarcely human.[25] Burton drew upon this stereotype for the madman he included among the ten figures pictured on the title page of the 1638 edition of his *Anatomy of Melancholy*. The accompanying rhyme listed the well-known attributes of the mad for the reader, "But see the Madman rage downe right With furious lookes, a ghastly sight. Naked in chaines bound doth he lye, And roares amaine he knowes not why?"[26] Although Roy Porter has suggested that this "quintessentially masculine" model dominated until a century after Lady Eleanor's day, we know that women too were confined to Bedlam in the early seventeenth century. Hysteria, religious ecstasy, and witchcraft were frequently among their alleged afflictions.[27]

The laws recognized the existence of madness under the terms *idiocy* or *lunacy*. Lunatics were individuals deemed temporarily insane, in contrast to idiots, the permanently insane. Differences between lunatics and idiots often disappeared in practice. For both, writs could institute proceedings to adjudge mental condition, and the Court of Wards had jurisdiction over the affairs of both.[28] Quarter-sessions records show that justices of the peace faced questions about lunatics and their living. The justices had much of the power that the medical profession exercises today. They decided when someone's mental condition made that person unable to work, when parish support was warranted, when confinement in a house of correction or elsewhere was necessary, and when criminal responsibility could be assigned.[29] Dalton advised justices of the peace that sureties of the peace should be granted neither to nor against a man of *non sane memorie* on his own request, yet, if there were cause, the justices should, on their authority, provide for the safety of such individuals.[30]

Both the laws' provisions and medical practices placed the

identification and treatment of madness in seventeenth-century Britain, as today, within the context of the beliefs and institutions of the society itself. Families, friends, and officials determined whether individuals were mad and how they should be treated, and persons who deviated from norms of conduct, particularly those who seemed to defy authority or become fanatics in religion, could be deemed mad. Even though they frequently appeared to be following a unique course, prophets fell into a special category, but only when they could convince their contemporaries that they were true prophets. Biblical evidence demonstrated the dire consequences that might result if false prophets were heeded. Ephraim Pagitt, preaching on Matthew 7:15, "Beware of false prophets, which come to you in sheep's clothing, but inwardly they are reavening wolves," in the church of St. Edmund the King in Lombard Street in the 1640s, told his congregation that they might hear "the madmen in Bedlam to prate as wisely" as false prophets. Are not those who run after false prophets as mad as those in Bedlam, he asked.[31] There were statutes against false prophecies. Dalton declared that justices of the peace could imprison for a year without bail any who "advisedly" published false prophecies "to the intent thereby to make any rebellion, insurrection, or other disturbances within the kings Dominions."[32]

Women prophets faced particular scrutiny. The very nature of women, which made them peculiarly receptive to God and thus accounted for the importance of their roles in the Bible and Christian tradition, also made them susceptible to being led astray by the devil.[33] Contemporary definitions of prophet included those preaching God's word. Like the individuals who wrote tracts describing how England's history corresponded to that outlined in the Bible, these preachers were, in their sermons, interpreting divine will within history. Earlier in the century, William Perkins had used "The Art or facultie of Prophecying" as the title for his well-known "treatise concerning the only true manner and method of preaching."[34] Whereas men did not need to prove themselves prophets in order to preach, women had to, since they were not ordinarily permitted to preach. Hierarchical structures placed them at a distinct disadvantage, and women who challenged conventions found themselves judged by superiors who were male.

Lady Eleanor confronted her contemporaries with questions about her conduct as a woman, her legitimacy as a prophet, and her defiance of the authorities of church and crown. She was not unique in using violence against altars newly placed in the east end of a church, but, in seating herself upon the bishop's throne, she publicly inverted patriarchy. The radicalness of that act set her apart from other apparent rebels and meant that declaring her mad defended authority in religion, monarchy, and the family.

A self-proclaimed prophet, Welshman Arise Evans, who, like Lady Eleanor was concerned about Henrietta Maria's popery and her influence on the king, went to Greenwich to deliver to Charles a message from God. Evans also predicted death for the king and besieged the court with his prophecies. Though he spent some time as a close prisoner in the Gatehouse and was released from there on the grounds of insanity, he, in contrast to Lady Eleanor, was never held in Bedlam. Evans claims that he obtained a certificate that he was distracted at the suggestion of Secretary Windebanke. The secretary said he needed that to protect himself, presumably from those who would accuse him of being lenient with the politically dangerous, if he freed Evans.[35] Madness in this instance could apparently excuse conduct that would otherwise be unacceptable. Once, during the 1640s, the Presbyterians whom Evans had antagonized petitioned the justices of the peace that he was distracted and tried to convince his wife to ask that he be sent to Bedlam, but they were not successful.[36] Whether because he was a man or because he seemed to pose a less serious threat to order, Evans escaped the fate that befell Lady Eleanor.

John Lilburne's case is another that illustrates how gender may have influenced the handling of dissent. Lilburne, did not mince words in attacking Laud and the bishops. Confined to the Fleet in 1638, he published *A Worke of the Beast or A Relation of a most unchristian censure, Executed upon John Lilburne* and *The Poore Mans Cry. Wherein is shewed the present miserable estate of mee John Lilburne, Close prisoner in the Fleete.* Did he land in the Fleet rather than Bedlam because he had not claimed to be a prophet? Or, since he was a man, could he publish and circulate unlicensed books without appearing to be mad?

In Beckington, Somerset, where "ryots" occurred about the setting up of an altar, the churchwardens were both excommunicated and imprisoned. A clothier named John Ashe, thought to be responsible for the trouble, was, according to one observer, "held to be both in opinion and faction a puritan."[37] His misdeed and those of his fellows could be understood as contesting policies, not threatening fundamental order itself. Even Enoch ap Evan, who, in 1633, murdered his mother and brother with whom he differed about religion, had not attempted to overturn patriarchy, and the authorities took pains to argue that he was not mad but a puritan.[38] Likewise Henry Burton, whose sermons preached on 5 November 1636 had made puritanism very much an issue at the time that Lady Eleanor was protesting at Lichfield, could be charged with seditious libel, not madness, and could be fined and imprisoned for his preaching. While Lady Eleanor's status may have given the authorities added cause for wanting to label her distracted and to confine her to Bedlam, gender gave her deeds a meaning distinct from that of most other dissidents during the 1630s.

Because the admissions registers for Bedlam are not extant for the early seventeenth century, we cannot determine how many aristocrats or gentry were confined there, how many individuals were sent by order of the Privy Council, which of the "prisoners" were women, or which were committed for political reasons. Other sources tell us about a few cases. In 1619, a fellow named Weekes had been sent to Bedlam for bringing King James "messages and admonitions from God."[39] Richard Farnham, described as a "false prophet" and "blasphemer," apparently spent some time in Bedlam in 1637, after the High Commission had imprisoned him in Newgate. Farnham's repeated petitions from Newgate to Laud, the Commission, and the Privy Council in February and March 1637 may explain his transfer. He told the archbishop that he stood by what he had written, since truth came from the spirit and noted that, if Laud were what a bishop should be, he would not keep the servants of God in prison.[40] About a year later, Farnham then being in Bedlam, the Privy Council ordered that he should have the liberty "usually afforded to others" in the hospital after he obtained a certificate from Bedlam's physician and apothecaries that he did not "appear either by worde or jesture to be madd or lunatic."[41] His alleged lunacy seems not to have been the only reason for his confinement, since the council did not release him upon receipt of the certificate, though in the following August when it appeared that he had persuaded a woman that her husband was dead and then married her, the court hearing her case proposed that he be transferred to Bridewell, since he was "not so distracted but that he is well able to work."[42]

In addition to rendering her acts more radical, Lady Eleanor's sex and status contributed to the authorities' problems in dealing with her. Although married, she could not be committed to the discipline of her husband; he himself was mad and being cared for by his family. She had one surviving child, Lucy, who had obtained Lady Eleanor's release from the Gatehouse in 1635. Records do not indicate whether Lucy attempted to intervene on Lady Eleanor's behalf following the incident at Lichfield. The antagonism toward Lady Eleanor that Lucy's sister-in-law, Alice, had expressed in 1635 may have meant that Lucy could not offer to have her mother in their household. Lucy may also have realized that, even if she had wanted to, she could not prevent Lady Eleanor from continuing her prophetic mission. A powerful spirit that would not submit to ordinary reason or practical considerations inspired Lady Eleanor's conduct. Whether one called it divine light, willfulness, or, as the authorities did, madness, it followed its own orders, not those of the world. What Lady Eleanor did at Lichfield so forcefully demonstrated her prophetic power to the Privy Council that they could hardly have had confidence in Lucy's ability to restrain her mother from further prophetic acts and would have been unlikely to heed any pleas for mitigation of their order concerning her.

By 1636, when she vandalized the cathedral at Lichfield, she had provided any who wanted it with considerable evidence of behavior that was extraordinary even for a prophet. The openness with which she conducted her mission made her violations of the norms of conduct seem all the more striking. Like modern dissenters who inform the authorities in advance about their acts of civil disobedience, Lady Eleanor, neither in her writing nor her actions, sought to conceal the unusual aspects of her life or her single-minded concentration on relating the message that Daniel gave to her. In defacing the altar hangings, she proved the truth of the defiant words with which she had summed up her attitude toward the High Commissioners and the sentence they imposed upon her, "The gates of Hell shall not prevaile against her." This behavior exhibits characteristics similar to those Petroff associated with a fifth, or participatory, stage of visionary experience.[43] Lady Eleanor openly confronted the rule of antichrist and offered herself for suffering; she participated in the cross. In her manuscript tract among the Domestic State Papers, dated "Litchfeild January 1636," she expressed continuing concern about the "howse of God['s] poluted smell." Citing Christ's casting out the devils (Matthew 8:28–34), she warned those in England to take heed of what they were doing.[44] She wrote that soon after her destruction of the altar hanging. At the time, she was still at liberty although probably aware of the stir her action had caused. Apparently the weather made it impossible for the council's messenger to travel and delayed his arrival in Lichfield until early February.[45]

Archbishop Laud, whom Lady Eleanor had dubbed the Beast from the Bottomless Pit at the time of his translation from London to Canterbury, was not among the councillors signing the order for her to be brought to Bedlam on 17 December. Although we cannot trace when he first heard about her exploits in Lichfield, his sensitivity to personal attacks and tendency to hold a grudge meant that he had added reasons for wishing to see her severely punished. In reporting to the king on 21 February 1637 on the state of his province during the preceding year, the archbishop commented that Bishop Wright had not given an adequate account of the "gross abuse" Lady Eleanor had committed in the church at Lichfield. "I most humbly beseech your Majesty," Laud continued, that she "may be so restrained, as she may have no more power to commit such horrible profanations."[46] Although Lady Eleanor was apparently in Bedlam by then, Laud seems to have believed that she might be there only temporarily.

The process by which the Privy Council committed Lady Eleanor to Bedlam was a summary one, like that by which it acted on a number of occasions, including its imprisonment of those who refused the forced loan. As she indicates, she received not so much as a hearing before her commitment.[47] Her companions, Susan Walker and Marie Noble, were questioned, though not until later. Edward Latham wrote to Sir John Lambe, 27 March 1637, to inquire what had happened to the instructions for articles he had sent up from Lichfield against those two women, and the copy of the articles against Marie Noble in the Domestic State Papers is dated January 1638.[48] In contrast, the council wasted no time in initiating action in Lady Eleanor's case. On 17 December 1636, they commanded a serjeant-at-arms to go to Lichfield for her, and, on the same day, they also wrote to the Governor of Bethlehem Hospital to receive her and keep her until he had further orders.[49] About ten days later they also directed a letter to the Lord Mayor of London asking his cooperation in arranging appropriate lodging for her at Bedlam.[50]

Evidence about Lady Eleanor's stay at Bedlam is scant: three entries in the Minutebooks of the Court of Governors of Bridewell and Bethlehem, a few references in the Registers of the Privy Council, a letter she wrote while there, and her later discussions of that period in her life. These sources indicate that provision for her care presented a problem. The council assured her family that she would be treated well at Bedlam and respected as a "person of honor."[51] When, at the beginning of her stay, she pointed out, as she did on many occasions, that she lacked the means to pay for her care, the council wrote both to her husband Douglas's uncle, Dean Young of Winchester, with whom Sir Archibald was living, to ask that £100 be sent, and to Lord Hastings for the £120 per annum payable from him to Lady Eleanor or Sir Archibald, presumably as a part of the settlement of the disputes about Sir John Davies's estate.[52] A subsequent order specified that, after the serjeant-at-arms had been reimbursed for bringing Lady Eleanor to London, Lord Hastings' money be distributed semiannually, £20 to Sir Archibald and £40 to the the clerk of the council for Lady Eleanor's maintenance.[53] The Court of Governors' order, 3 January 1638, that she should have no more than 20 shillings weekly, suggests that the money was being paid even though Richard Langley, the steward of the hospital whose conduct led to his suspension the next month, claimed at that time that he had received only 50 shillings for her and her servant for an entire year.[54]

At Bedlam, Lady Eleanor stayed in the steward's house in rooms that, according to the President of the Court of Governors, were "reserved for such persons as the Governors should place there."[55] On 16 August 1637, approximately six months after her arrival, Langley, the steward, asked the court that she be moved. He complained that "she used all the meanes she could to escape" though the minutes recorded, he "could make noe proofe of it." Lady Eleanor, for her part, protested that the steward had "used ill words" to her.[56] The following February, when another six months had elapsed, Langley appealed to the Privy Council "in regard there is of late a convenient roome built on purpose for her within the said hospitall that she might be removed thither." He also asked the council for "satisfaction" for the expenses he had incurred by having her in his "private house." The council agreed that she should be moved to the lodging Langley mentioned and ordered that he should have "reasonable satisfaction" but not all at once.[57] When the Court of Governors met just a week later, accusations that Langley and his wife were "very unquiet uncivell and ungoverned people, and that they doe very oftentimes come home both together very farre gone in drincke and that 11. and 12. of Clocke at night and then very much disturbe the Lady Davies" were among those that led to Langley's suspension from his office.[58]

We do not have to decide between Lady Eleanor's claims about Langley and his about her to acknowledge that having her as an uninvited and unwilling houseguest would hardly have been easy.[59] She probably insisted on the recognition of her rank as the daughter of a baron, demanded the treatment appropriate for a prophet, and would not have hesitated to exhort Langley and his wife to mend their ways if she thought they were behaving improperly. If, as seems likely, she suspected Langley of profiting from his position, she, who tenaciously guarded her own financial resources would have seized every opportunity to put obstacles in his path.

When she wrote to Lucy on 9 April 1637, when she had been in Bedlam for only about 6 weeks, Lady Eleanor described her situation in much more agreeable words than the quarrels with Langley or contemporary descriptions of the hospital would imply. She told Lucy "for this place, thoughe princes persecute etc I want not therein: a greater on my side accompanied with prayers of his people. Bedlems gatehouses birds and bulles which may imprisone put there; but honore and truthe cannot put out of countenance." The hope she expressed to Lucy that "my preferment is now on the winge," the desire to reassure her daughter about her well-being, and the spiritual strength that allowed her to place tribulation in this world in a greater perspective may explain the difference.[60]

Lady Eleanor's quarters at Bedlam removed her from the scenes described in the prose and verse of her day. Though she did not actually live among the screaming, naked, chained, and scarcely human beings called Bedlamites, she was close enough to see and to hear the horrors that contemporaries make resemble Hieronymous Bosch's vision of Hell in the *Garden of Earthly Delights*.[61] As she put it in her petition to the House of Commons on 22 September 1647, going from the Gatehouse to Bedlam was "the grave exchanged for Hell." She complained that she could not "goe forth to receive the Sacrament unlesse she would take itt there in the house of such restlesse cursing to bring the cup of blessing."[62] Both this complaint and her subsequent descriptions of the hospital as a "loathsome *Prison,* infected with those *foul Spirits* day and night Blaspheming" enabled her to emphasize the wrongs committed by those who placed her in Bedlam.[63] When she petitioned the Commons in 1647, she claimed that those responsible had presumed that, by doing so, "to make her ever incapable of anie complaint but ever held or taken to be person *non Compos mentis* to the perpetuall blott and infame of her familie and posteritie."[64] Their sins against her were the sins that were condemning Britain to Judgment. As a prophet, she could cloak her own desire to heal her wounded pride with denunciations of those who had punished God's messenger. They had proclaimed "the invincible truth . . . madness."[65] She emphasized this after her stay in Bedlam by putting her own prophecies into language that others would find difficult to understand. Thus, she demonstrated how those who thought her mad were themselves incapable of comprehending what she wrote. In 1649 she made the point with an anagram. The Archbishop's "House at *Lambeth* with its scituation not onely pointed to, but of its denomination borrow'd from the house of *Bethlam,* otherwise called *Bedlam.*"[66] Her anger and embarrassment about her commitment to Bedlam fed on her knowledge that Londoners found amusement in watching those in the hospital. In April 1636, less than a year before Lady Eleanor found herself in Bedlam, the king and queen had themselves gone to "to see the mad folks" there and had been "madly entertained."[67]

As is true of many who have been imprisoned for political reasons over the centuries, Lady Eleanor seems to have gained courage and fortitude during her stay in Bedlam. In April 1638, shortly after she had been dislodged from the steward's home to other accommodations at the hospital, she was transferred again, this time to the Tower of London, a place openly recognized as a prison for traitors.[68] We have no evidence about the council's reasons for moving her and thus cannot determine whether they abandoned efforts to claim that she was mad since they had neither subdued her nor eradicated the threat she posed. We do not know whether they considered the implications of of their decision. It may have come as a response to appeals from Lucy against her mother's remaining in Bedlam. The tower, though far from a comfortable spot, at least had been a place where, over the years, many nobles and even monarchs had been imprisoned. Although Lady Eleanor herself later referred to the tower in *Bride's Preparation* and noted that instead of providing for the city's safety as it was intended, it was turned into a prison, "a place of teares and death," she said little about her own stay there.[69] She failed to even mention the tower in 1647, when she summarized her sufferings in a petition to the House of Commons.[70] Although imprisonment in the tower manifested the obdurateness of the regime, it did not contribute as easily as Bedlam did to her arguments that associated wisdom with prophecy and madness with those who questioned it.

Records about the conditions under which Lady Eleanor was held in the Tower of London are as slight as her own comments about her confinement there. In deference to her rank, she was probably lodged in special quarters there too, though, in the tower, as in the Gatehouse, she could not freely send and receive communications. In October 1638, in explaining to Lucy why she had not written, she

pleaded the dull place; the danger to write here . . . as for newes safe that so shamfull better smothered then mouthed, never time, begetting such cittye monsters impudency she may blushe to speak them and other disasters such would affright very cruely. Bad to h[e]are of. So for information of this kinde leave those that have not heard to theire books and balads.[71]

Whether she corresponded with others than family members, we do not know. Her reference to cousins who ask to be remembered to Lucy suggests that she may have received a letter from one of her sisters.[72] Her contacts with Dr. James Sibbald, minister at Clerkenwell, may date from this period. Sibbald, who was associated with the Royalists during the 1640s, gained some notoriety in 1649 when he served as confessor to James Hamilton, earl of Cambridge, just prior to the latter's execution. Lady Eleanor does not tell us whether she or Sibbald himself took the initial steps in their relationship. She subsequently feared he would reveal what she had told him in confidence to those who might use the same information to prove her madness.[73]

From the tower, Lady Eleanor begged Lucy for news about the children and poured out her love and grief when she heard the news of the death of Lucy's son, John, in 1639.[74] She also continued her prophetic career and, in 1639, as she had done in 1635, predicted that London would burn. Stating this time that London would be destroyed by fire before Easter, she caused some alarm in the city, especially when fires broke out. Thomas Smith, who reported this in a letter to Pennington, believed she was still in Bedlam and thought it likely she would remain there for the rest of her life.[75]

Lady Eleanor's release from the tower came on 6 September 1640, when the crown was under a great deal of political pressure. The Scots had invaded England, and rather than rallying to their king's call for support, the English were refusing to pay shipmoney, resisting military service, entering churches and tearing down altars and rails, and protesting against the Convocation of the Clergy's continuing to meet after parliament had been dissolved in May. By their vote of subsidies and approval of new canons, the clergy had seemed to overthrow law and religion. In August, a dozen members of the nobility petitioned Charles to summon another parliament, and, early in September, he announced that he would instead call a Council of Peers.[76] Immediately after that decision, the Privy Council wrote to Lady Eleanor's son-in-law, Ferdinando, informing him that, in response to the appeals he and Lucy had made, the king had decided to free Lady Eleanor. They warned that the king's willingness to agree to this "doth proceed from a confidence . . . that you will prevent and keep her . . . from giving any further scandalls or cause for further restraint."[77] His mercy went virtually unnoticed by political observers, who were commenting on matters they deemed far more important than Lady Eleanor. Charles himself probably regarded his deed as a personal favor rather than a public act. He may have hoped, in return, to gain support from Ferdinando whom he summoned to the House of Lords for the first time in November, but he should not have counted on any gratitude from the earl of Huntingdon whose relationship with Lady Eleanor was decidedly cold.[78]

With that order from the council, Lady Eleanor concluded a period when the king, the archbishop, and the Privy Council used their authority to obstruct prophecy. They effectively restricted her ability to publish her warnings but, at the same time, convinced her of the truth of Daniel's message. As for John Lilburne and others, the punishments she suffered showed her how far Britain was from listening to God's word and its promise of redemption. The energy in her subsequent writing came from her acceptance of her role and her recognition of her identity with the women of power in the Bible. She was, after 1640, even more than previously, one of the women whom God over the years had designated to be a divine instrument.

CHAPTER 5

The *Bride's Preparation*

In September 1640, when Lady Eleanor obtained her freedom, four years and four months remained before the date Daniel had told her Judgment would occur. This chapter focuses upon that interval and her preparations for the long-awaited moment. She resumed writing, and her tracts demonstrated how Britain's political crisis, divisions, and war fulfilled the biblical texts. Casting herself as the Bride who would become the Lamb's wife (Revelation 21:9), she hailed Archbishop Laud's execution (in January 1645) as a climactic moment. Although it was not itself the Judgment, it marked the end of an era and intensified her anticipation of the apocalypse.

Despite some correlation between significant moments of Lady Eleanor's career and those of British politics in the first half of the 1640s, her prophetic activities do not neatly coincide with the best-known events. What happened, what she did at the time, and what she subsequently said about the occasion represent three separate though interwoven strands of her story. Her experience falls into three periods: about nine months of quiescence following her discharge from the Tower of London in the autumn of 1640; an interval (from 1641 to 1643) of approximately two-and-one-half years of observation, reflection, and criticism of Britain and her rulers; and then, in 1644, a time of prophetic activity more specifically concerned with the scenario of Judgment and Restitution. In her prophecies, she emphasized such occurrences as the the king's departure from Whitehall and Westminster, the Irish "Rebellion" of October 1641, the outbreak of fighting in 1642, and the meeting of the Westminster Assembly; in contrast, she paid little heed to such matters as the Grand Remonstrance or the Militia Ordinance, which traditionally receive attention in histories.

During the months immediately following Lady Eleanor's release from imprisonment, when both in Parliament and the country politicking was intense, we know little about her. Although she later declared that Michaelmas, the feast of St. Michael the Archangel, and the season of Virgo, the astrological sign of the virgin, was a time of prophetic consequence, neither in 1640 nor subsequently did she note that she herself had emerged from confinement then. She may have spent the autumn and winter of 1640 recovering from what, like her imprisonment in the Gatehouse, had probably been a traumatic experience. Before determining what to do next she may have wanted to assess the changing political situation.

For a time, Lady Eleanor may have believed that her work was over. Late in September 1640, King Charles met his Council of Peers at York and announced that he would issue writs for a parliament to assemble at Westminster on 3 November. The MPs could assume the responsibility of preparing the way for the Second Coming. To some, the summoning of what was to become the Long Parliament appeared as a providential act. Individuals and communities flooded Parliament from its outset with cries for redress of grievances in church and state, and people who had remained silent during the 1630s began to express their opinions. Parliament promptly impeached not only the Lord Lieutenant of Ireland, the earl of Strafford, but also Archbishop Laud, the man whom Lady Eleanor had designated as the Beast from the Bottomless Pit in 1633. In response to appeals from Prynne, Burton, Bastwick, Lilburne, Leighton, and Smart, outspoken critics of Laudianism who were still imprisoned in November 1640, the Houses initiated investigations of their cases, and, from January until May, the Commons issued a series of orders reversing proceedings against them.[1]

We have no evidence to indicate whether Lady Eleanor went and stayed with Lucy and Ferdinando in the fall of 1640 or whether she immediately found her own lodgings. By Whitsuntide 1641 (Whitsunday was 13 June that year) when she brought out *Her Appeale*, she was living in Kensington, at the "Angell signe."[2] There, not far from Westminster, she probably followed the proceedings by which Parliament, as she later put it in *Restitution of Prophecy*, had given the earl of Strafford "his *quietus est, Easter* Term (*Anno* 41)."[3] His execution on 12 May, the passage of the bill against the dissolution of the Parliament, and the Lords' consideration of the bill to exclude the bishops from parliament gave new meaning to the long, continuing wars in

Germany and to England's recent conflict with Scotland and troubles in Ireland. These events seemed to confirm the Day of Judgment's approach. In contrast to the ministers who, in their sermons to the Commons during the spring and early summer of 1641, addressed such immediate issues as the reforms Parliament had achieved or those that should follow, Lady Eleanor, in *Her Appeal* of 1641, wrote about more general questions of the course of history.[4] She concentrated upon the central task of prophecy and suggested parallels that made the reign of Charles I correspond to the end of time predicted by Daniel. Charles had consented to Strafford's execution just as Nebuchadnezzar (in Daniel 2:12–13) had ordered his wisemen destroyed.[5] Like Daniel, who had been thrown in the Lion's den, she had been imprisoned in the Gatehouse, confined to Bedlam, and then moved to the tower.[6] She had endured imprisonment and suffering because she believed she could not delay publishing her message until she could obtain authorization and had thus proceeded without a license. The passage of time since 1633 made her suit that they prepare the kingdom for Judgment all the more pressing.[7]

Lady Eleanor addressed her statement at Whitsun 1641 not to the archbishop, whose predecessor she had approached in 1625, or the king, to whom she had gone in 1633, but to "the High Court of Parliament" and she asked them not for personal relief but to give credence to her prophecy.[8] Although she would seek parliamentary assistance in recovering her property before 1647, until then she did not ask Parliament to compensate her for the imprisonment and other wrongs she had suffered at the hands of Charles and Laud.

Between May 1641 and the beginning of 1645 Lady Eleanor produced twelve tracts, almost twice as many as she had written during the preceding sixteen years. Seven of the twelve appeared in 1644. The situation offered her what must have appeared to be an exciting opportunity to fulfill her mission. She would be the Bride married to the Lamb at the Second Coming, and, with the abolition (in the summer of 1641) of the courts of Star Chamber and High Commission where writers and printers of "dangerous" books had been prosecuted, publication became less hazardous. She developed her previous interpretation of Britain's history and, with it, her sense of her own role in that history. Drawing upon the latest news from diurnals and elsewhere, she adapted her message to meet the circumstances of the moment. While she certainly could have obtained news in the country, her desire to influence the course of events, not just observe them, meant that she needed to be on the scene. Thus, during much of the remainder of her life, she seems to have resided in the London area: in Kensington in 1641, in Knightsbridge in 1643, in Whitehall in 1649, and "in London" when she died in 1652. Despite the energy with which she sought to recover Englefield and Pirton, the estates that she had claimed at the time of Davies's death and lost during her imprisonment in the 1630s, she seems to have made neither one a principal residence when she did obtain possession.

More than a year elapsed between Lady Eleanor's publication of *Her Appeal* and that of the next of her tracts. In the interim, Lucy initiated proceedings to enable her mother to regain the rectory of Pirton. While Lady Eleanor was in the Gatehouse and thus could not intervene, Sir Archibald Douglas, by failing to pay what was due on a mortgage to Francis Poulton, had, Lucy argued, lost the Hertfordshire rectory that Davies had designated as his wife's jointure. By 1642, Poulton, who had taken advantage of Douglas's default and his "weaknes and insanity," had contrived to get possession of Pirton for forty years, by using an extent upon an old statute, a device that Ferdinando had accused Lady Eleanor herself of employing during their earlier quarrels about the property. Through such means Poulton had already recovered more than he had loaned in the mortgage and thus, although the petition did not explicitly make the claim, might be considered a usurer.[9]

Upon her release from confinement, Lady Eleanor no longer had the Privy Council to extract financial support for her from the parties responsible. She still held the position of a married woman who had no access to income of her own and was thus supposedly provided for by her husband. Without property, Lucy claimed her mother was "utterly destitute of all meanes, ether to prosecute a suite at lawe or to subsist." Lucy said a second cause for her petition was Lord Hastings's inability to continue to support his mother-in-law. Although she may have been acting at his behest, it seems more likely that Lucy was attempting to improve the family's financial situation and to reduce the lingering tension between her husband and mother. Time and again the family correspondence shows her as the one who took practical steps to deal with realities while Ferdinando tended to disregard them. From the experiences of conflict that ensued upon her father's death, Lucy apparently learned how to steer a course in which she could satisfy Ferdinando's expectations of his wife and Lady

Eleanor's of her daughter without becoming becoming a party to their disputes. That earlier litigation had left the Hastings with some of Davies's estate that Lady Eleanor had claimed, and with Matthew Davies, they had, in a deed dated 22 January 1634 (while she was in the Gatehouse), conveyed the manor of Pirton, except the "joynture, dower, or estate" which she had in it, to Poulton.[10]

Addressing her petition to the House of Lords, among whom Ferdinando had been sitting, and probably hoping to gain some sympathy because of her noble connections, Lucy maintained that he, by virtue of his losses as a result of the "Rebellion" in Ireland, was, "much disabled . . . to make any provision" for his mother-in-law, whose dower the Irish "rebells" had also possessed. The claim allowed her to take advantage of the emotions stirred by the events of the preceding autumn. It had some basis in fact, but the Hastings's fiscal plight was longstanding. They had exacerbated it through debts incurred during the extensive litigation following Davies's death.[11] Lady Eleanor's financial situation is difficult to assess. Amid her prophetic priorities, aristocratic tastes, and lack of concern with paying bills, little solid evidence survives about the extent and value of the Irish lands she had inherited from her father or about any other sources of income she may have had. Her alleged poverty was at least partly allegorical. When she subsequently referred to Ireland in her tracts, she labeled the disturbance that Lucy called rebellion a "massacre," and noted how its occurrence on 23 October marked the anniversary of her hearing before the High Commission and the burning of her books in 1633. Although she had lost a source of income, she took comfort in the belief that those who failed to heed her message were themselves being judged.

Although Lady Eleanor did not seek relief in her own name until September 1644, after Douglas's death, letters between her and Lucy from May and June 1643 show that she was both well informed and very much interested in the process of Lucy's petition in her behalf. It seems likely that Lucy had consulted her mother before preparing the petition in January 1642. Two questions that recognize Lady Eleanor's role are appended to the petition among the Main Papers of the House of Lords. They ask whether a wife can recover what her husband alienated and "whether the wife shalbe admitted to plead *non compos mentis* in her husband?"[12]

The Lords responded to Lucy's petition that they call Francis Poulton before them and question him by referring the petition to the Lord

Keeper for relief in equity instead of calling witnesses to the House. They thereby attempted to make good their stated desire to give the cause for recovery of Pirton "all convenient expedition."[13] Three weeks later, pushing again for action, they ordered Lord Keeper Littleton to hear and determine the case without any formal suit being filed in Chancery or to make a recommendation to them so they could proceed.[14] On 25 March, almost two months after Lucy had submitted her petition, Littleton reported that his efforts to mediate the case had failed, and the Lords themselves then prepared to hear the dispute.[15] Interrogatories drawn up in April concerning Douglas's mental condition became the second act in what would be a long drama.[16]

In view of Lady Eleanor's stay in Bedlam, the argument, that by acting when he was "not of sound mind or memory" Douglas had contributed to their predicament, had potential repercussions, and yet it was an argument that manifested the madness in society.[17] Proving Douglas's insanity in order to invalidate his disposal of property required testimony in court, whereas the Privy Council had summarily declared the prophet who was warning of evil mad and had ordered her confined to Bedlam.

To support her contention about Douglas's condition, Lucy had "a doctor of physick," James Jackson, of the parish of St. Dunstans in the West, called as a witness. According to a copy of a deposition he gave on 20 April 1642, Jackson testified that Douglas had claimed to be a prophet and had attempted suicide.[18] Lady Eleanor, who herself never mentioned Jackson, made the contrast between her own condition and Douglas's clearer when, in the course of a tract written in 1646, she described him as having become a beast. To one preoccupied with the apocalyptic contest between the bestial and angelic forces, this identified him as an opponent of true prophecy.[19] Condemning to Bedlam a woman whose acts could be understood within the context of the disputes then raging about altars and episcopacy and shortly afterwards requiring legal proceedings to establish the mental condition of a man who had lost the faculties that distinguished humans from animals was evidence of the irrationality that prevailed at the time.

Although with their articles the Poultons established that Jackson had not had contact with Douglas since the occasion when he had treated him twelve years earlier, Lady Eleanor apparently feared that they would try to bolster their case by challenging her sanity.[20] She was sufficiently worried so that on 30 April 1642, she wrote Dr. James Sibbald, minister of Clerkenwell, who she had heard would be called to testify. Having consulted Sibbald and shown him some of her writings, she feared that he would violate her confidence. Although she does not say so, it seems likely that he had visited her while she was in the Tower of London, where, as a woman prisoner, she would have been expected to accept his instruction, not to speak as she wanted. Under the pressures of prison life she may have said something to him that she subsequently regretted. The changing political atmosphere provided added reason why she may have wanted to disavow views she had expressed previously. In her letter, Lady Eleanor reminded Sibbald that he had promised to "be secret" and appealed to his conscience to keep that promise. By the time she had finished, she was no longer feeling powerless and dependent upon his goodwill. She had determined a course of action by which she believed she could vindicate herself from any accusation he made.

Withall Consider, when this on mine othe I will justifie: what will a learned Assembly thinke of you; my Bosome Friend: unto whom now, this I doe write; and sayeth—I protest before God this my selfe hath dictat; and written; without the help or knowledge of any; which I thinke, that few to this purpose could have done it much better, (though I say it) And that a man of very small understanding could not have done it so well.[21]

How could anyone consider her insane when she, a woman and thus one not expected to be able to write, composed a letter that would be impressive if written by a man?

Whether Sibbald testified is not clear. Poulton's death, shortly thereafter, meant that his will had to be proved before the suit could proceed. Lucy petitioned again on 24 May to ask for speedy action and to request specifically that, until her mother was otherwise provided for, she should be given a portion of the annuity that Douglas had bought with money he had obtained from Poulton for Pirton. Lady Eleanor, she claimed, was "utterly destitute of all meanes of subsistance even to ye provision of bread."[22] Although the Lords may not have been convinced of the truth of Lucy's rhetoric, they referred her petition to a presumably sympathetic committee, the earls of Holland, Stamford, and Portland, and barons Mandeville and Robartes.[23] It was Holland whom Lucy wrote in March 1644 when she wanted to obtain protection for herself and her family, and Holland who Lady Eleanor reported later that year was asking for Lucy.[24]

After the probate of Poulton's will on 17 June, Lucy petitioned once more. This time she asked the Lords to examine Poulton's heir and executors. In their answers, the Poultons maintained that Douglas was sane, that he had paid off the mortgage and recovered the property, and that, in subsequent transactions, he had mortgaged Pirton to one George Benyon, redeemed it, and then leased it to Poulton for sixty years.[25] They also produced affidavits taken in March from Douglas and from James Kenrick who was one of the witnesses to the lease between Douglas and Poulton and who also testified to Douglas's disposal of the money he had received from Poulton.[26] In his statement, Douglas accused Lady Eleanor and Lucy, for their own private advantage and for "disparagement" of his person, of seeking to void the lease he had made. He had, he said, acted with good reason, because his wife was "committed to prison," because of "her age"—she would have been in her forties and probably not expected to live much longer—because of "the debte and danger she hade brought" him into, and because she had procured the mortgage of Pirton so that she could have the money, a claim that, in view of her chronic indebtedness, seems plausible.[27]

On 23 September, when the Lords heard counsel of both sides, Mr. Herne (who represented the Poultons) raised objections and demanded the judgment of the House on points similar to those appended to Lucy's initial petition nine months earlier: whether a married woman without the consent of her husband could bring a suit on behalf of another married woman and whether it was proper for the Lords to hear the question of Douglas's sanity. Lucy's counsel, Mr. Chute, protested that the objection was too late—the answer had been put in—but at that point the hearing was interrupted when the Lords received a message about a more pressing issue.[28] Lady Eleanor found her cause pushed aside while Parliament turned to the affairs of the kingdom. Although she expressed hopes the following May that "a smaler matter" would "finish" Pirton than would be necessary to reclaim Englefield, she was still seeking resolution in September 1644, two months after Douglas's death.[29] The Lords could not find a remedy as long as the Poultons and Douglas were prepared to resist with all the provisions of the law that incapacitated married women.

In August 1642, a month before the Lords' abortive hearing of Lucy's suit concerning Pirton, King Charles had raised his standard at

Nottingham to rally troops to fight with him against what he perceived as a rebellious parliament. Although for several months Lady Eleanor apparently watched the ensuing conflict in silence and, perhaps, horror that her predictions were seemingly being fulfilled, she noticed and later commented that in 1642, as in 1641, events demonstrated the significance of the day when her books had been burned in 1633. On 23 October, royalist forces defeated a parliamentary army at Edgehill.[30]

Toward the end of November, reports circulated concerning the Queen's efforts to solicit funds and troops from continental rulers to enable Charles to recapture authority. People who had long worried about a "popish plot" against English religion and liberty were convinced to pour more resources into resistance. In *Samsons Fall, Presented to the House 1642*, published January 1643, Lady Eleanor reflected upon the fate of Britain's monarch in the context of the biblical story of Samson and Delilah (Judges 16), a story to which her own experiences gave greater meaning. Charles I, like Samson, had been "overcome by *a Womans importunity*." He had "violated his *Vow* or solemn Obligation" and revealed "The Almighties Counsel . . . to his Adversary." Lady Eleanor's accusation was a serious one. Not only did it question whether the king, the very man who had earlier admonished her for predicting her husband's death, was himself upholding patriarchal authority, but it also asked whether he was abiding by his coronation oath to maintain the laws and customs. Even those who understood the coronation oath in its most absolute terms believed that if the king broke his oath, he had sinned and God might punish him.[31] The recent suits over property that Douglas had alienated may have reminded Lady Eleanor that she had violated her own vow in marrying him, but Charles had done worse. He had ignored her prophetic warnings and, instead, had fallen prey to "the inchanting notes" of Henrietta Maria; thus, he who had imprisoned God's prophet had been "brought into thralldom."[32] Blinded from seeing the truth by love for the woman in league with the Papist Philistines, Samson became blind in actuality when they put out his eyes, and with his act of vengeance Britain's Samson, whose blindness was figurative rather than real, achieved what the Gunpowder Plot of 1605 had set out to do. The house Charles brought down upon himself was the kingdom, "our *British* Union, fast knit and bound, soon dissolved after" or "*Great Britains* Lyon rent in pieces."[33] Although Lady Eleanor had personal reasons for her awareness of the connection of England and Wales with Scotland that came about with the death of Elizabeth and the accession of James, the creation of Britain had been a prominent theme in histories of the period.

The "moral" that Charles had missed was, Lady Eleanor said, "to vulgar apprehensions visible." Anyone who frequented alehouses, where one would not expect to find a woman of her class, was familiar with Samson and Delilah, for "the bare walls [were] not without it."[34] She herself probably knew that biblical commentators, such as Thomas Taylor, whose *Christ Revealed* had been published in 1635, made Samson a type of Christ. In offering themselves to death, both Samson and Christ "most overcame their enemies when they seemed most overcome by them."[35] However radical that parallel might seem when applied in 1642 or 1643 to Charles I, it took into account the apocalyptic expectations upon which Lady Eleanor based her work. The civil wars were part of the preparation for Judgment and the Second Coming. Only a year before she wrote, John Milton, in his *The Reason of Church Government*, had also compared the king to Samson, but rather than identifying Catholic Henrietta Maria with Delilah, as Lady Eleanor did, Milton accused Charles of "laying down his head among the strumpet flatteries of Prelates."[36] Closer to Lady Eleanor's image was that of the parliamentarians who, in later responses to royalist presentations of Charles as the Martyr, argued that a king who was "overpowered with the Inchantments of a woman" should be discounted.[37]

However well known her theme may have been, Lady Eleanor's real audience for *Samsons Fall* was Parliament. She concluded the tract with a petition "To the most Honorable, The High Court of Parliament assembled."[38] Time was so "precious" that "there is nothing but a supernatural course to be taken, touching the *Cure* of such unnatural conditioned *Times*." The only *"Balm* and *Soveraign* Remedy" was the "Almighty his *Word*."[39] Claiming "rare operation and vertue given" to her, she offered to assist Parliament by bringing to them the king who had fled from Whitehall the preceding January and thus been "absent so long." She also said she would obtain a pass for the "Cavaliers," the king's supporters, to go to the Low Countries and Germany.[40]

In contrast to the bands of women who petitioned Parliament on several occasions during the 1640s, Lady Eleanor made no effort to present herself as the voice of a group. She shared with those women concerns about religion and opposition to the bishops, but she interpreted the events that were occurring from a different perspective. She was an aristocrat, and she spoke as a prophet. Distinguished from the women petitioners by her expertise and her status, she took no notice of them in her own works though she must have been aware of their activities.[41]

Parliament failed to accept Lady Eleanor's offer of help, and events seemed more desperate by early spring. In April 1643, she published two tracts, *Samsons Legacie,* a revision and elaboration of *Samsons Fall,* and *Amend, Amend,* in which she offered a new version of the poem she had addressed to the elector ten years earlier. Both tracts show how closely she followed public events and adapted her message to them.[42]

In the twenty-four pages of *Samsons Legacie* that replaced the twelve pages of *Samsons Fall,* Lady Eleanor included some phrases directly from the earlier tract, but, in the later version, she dramatized the contrast between Samson before and after he lost his hair and was *"stript of that great strength of his."*[43] With anagrams, she derived SAMSON from JAMES SON and RACHEL (a Hebrew word for sheep) from CHARLES. These names, which she maintained the king had acquired when he was "baptized" in the "teares" of his godparents, illustrated how the British lion had become a sheep.[44]

In *Samsons Legacie,* Lady Eleanor also extended her critique of Charles I and her discussion of the impact of the war on Britain. The "plundering and *intolerable* Theifts" of *"our bleeding dayes"* and the fighting that had caused "more slaine in one yeare, then since the Conquest in the Reigne of so many Kings and Queenes" were the consequence of Charles's apostasy. *"Without President* or Example of Progenitors," he had separated himself from "his Head—Kingdoms Parliament" that was then assembled for "rooting . . . out *blind Herisie,* [that is popery,] *Her* Majesties *darling."*[45] Charles, whose council had ordered her confined in the madhouse, was himself manifesting "great Imbecillitie in subjecting himselfe to a Womans waywardnesse." Like the ancient Israelites who had rejected Samuel because they wanted to be like everyone else and have a king to reign over them, the English had rejected the Elizabethan Church for that of the "LIBERTINES and ROMES CHURCH."[46] They were renouncing their place as an elect nation. Among the signs of their turning away from God were the "FALSE-HAIRE" (long hair) of the Cavaliers, the profanation of the sabbath with playing of cards and dice, the "LORDS house haunted by *Spirits of Divels* . . . holding their Spiritual Courts there" which fill the prisons with those they called *"Puritans:* and now, *Rownd-Heads."* (The High Commission often sat at St. Paul's in London.) In Britain as in Israel when the "sons of God became Tyrants, and carnall," disastrous consequences would follow.[47] The word *fox,* whose letters she found in Oxford (where Charles had made his capital), allowed her to link him, through Samson who had set the Philistines' fields afire by means of the tails of 300 foxes (Judges 15:4–5), with the tyrant Herod, whom Christ had called a fox (Luke 13:32). *"Reynold {sic} the Fox,"* she added. In conclusion, she reminded readers of the season—Easter, the time of resurrection, approached. She, who signed the tract, "From the Blessed *LADIE,* her *Day* in *Lent, etc.* 1643," and thus identified herself with the Virgin Mary at the Feast of the Annunciation, offered to "conjure and charge the aforesaid *Evill Spirits, or Legions, no more here to enter into this Kingdome from henceforth."*[48]

In *Amend, Amend,* Lady Eleanor turned to poetry to deal with some of the same issues she had treated in *Samsons Legacie.* In 1643, as in 1633 when she had directed a version of the poem to the elector, she specified that her work should be sung to the tune "Who list a Souldiers life to lead," but she reshaped her content in light of the changed political situation. The Day of Judgment approached, and she addressed King Charles himself, BELCHAZER, BE-CHARLES. He had become "the Faithless Steward" instead of the "faithful and wise Steward whom his Lord shall make ruler over his household" (Luke 12:42) or instead of Michael, as she had hoped.[49] The pun, one that she used again later, allowed her an unstated comparison between Charles Stuart's mishandling of his opportunity to save Britain and Douglas's poor stewardship of her mortgaged property. She emphasized in *Amend, Amend* both Daniel's (her) role and the wickedness of Belshazzar (Charles).

> Of Mene Mene to Thee Sent
> Even twise fullfil'd to bee:
> The hand pointing at Twenty-five,
> Heavenly Palmistry,
> Which Yeare reveal Gods Dreadfull day,
> Whose *hand-mayd* for a Signe:
> Our Troubles fore-told as come to passe,
> how never such a Time. . . .
> SIR Amend, you know what . . .[50]

Soon after publishing these tracts, Lady Eleanor wrote Lucy that she had entered a suit in the House of Lords for Englefield, which was then in the hands of the Catholic Marquess of Winchester, whose estates the Commons did not order sequestered until October.[51] There is no evidence to corroborate Lady Eleanor's statements about these proceedings or to show on what grounds she based her claim. Although Lucy and Ferdinando with Matthew Davies had conveyed Englefield to the marquess by virtue of a deed of 14 May 1635, Lady Eleanor, at least in her tracts, did not charge them with poor stewardship.[52] Her loss of Englefield illustrated the evils Britain was suffering, and the apocalyptic events thereby announced undoubtedly turned her thoughts to the setting and moment when Daniel had spoken to her in 1625. Practical obstacles did not deter her. She told Lucy that Mr. Chute, who was serving as counsel in the case for Pirton, had refused to act in that stead again. Though he claimed he wanted to take no more cases, she thought he was uneasy about visibility during such unsettled times.[53]

Money, though probably less important, may also have been a consideration in Lady Eleanor's attempts to recover Englefield. Her chronic shortage of funds probably explains the relatively poor quality and varied printing of her tracts, which, in some cases, show extra lines crowded onto their final pages or have entire signatures missing (although her desire to keep adding to and revising her works can also account for some of the corrections on the extant copies and the sometimes haphazard appearance of the finished tracts).[54] In the same letter to Lucy where she announced her suit, Lady Eleanor mentioned her need to continue paying her servant whom, she assured Lucy, she had paid "some wages" and the printer to whom she had given "some money." These expenses added to those of her "lodging and diett" and lawyers' fees.[55] While quick to claim money that she believed was hers, she was inclined to think that her needs were more important than those of people to whom she was indebted. When she wrote Lucy three weeks later, on 3 June, Lady Eleanor added a postscript, "As for my debts let them have patience a little while. I have written to ye Ld Maior to borrowe some money of ye city."[56]

To Lucy, at least, Lady Eleanor seems to have been genuinely grateful for both financial and moral support. Her appreciation may have been all the greater following her fears in the aftermath of Davies's death, that there would be a breach between them. In her letters to her daughter, Lady Eleanor expressed her thanks in more than just perfunctory terms. On 3 June, drawing upon the words of Christ when he said, "For whosoever shall do the will of my Father which is in heaven, the same is my brother, and sister, and mother" (Matthew 12:46–50), she told Lucy, "I am no less than His figure whose mother was his daughter. Hee having made you both to mee." Although the anagram, LUCIE HAST: LIVE CHAST, with which she followed that praise might be interpreted to warn Lucy [Hastings] against following her husband in his move from opposing to supporting the royalist forces, it may have simply been an injunction to live in accord with God's will. Lady Eleanor followed it with Christ's message to his disciples, "singe and rejoyse, your name is written in heavens" (Luke 10:20).[57] In *Her Blessing,* published the following year, she reiterated her gratitude. You "have bene your mothers Copartner, even You her alone and sole support under the Almighty."[58] Lucy had, in fact, performed the responsibilities that Davies and Douglas, as husbands, had betrayed. Although scholars have argued that ties between mothers and daughters tended to be close in this period, the bond between Lady Eleanor and Lucy seems to be especially affectionate and the tract dedicated to Lucy an adaptation of the well-known genre of paternal addresses to sons.[59]

Lucy's understanding and patience helped Lady Eleanor avoid despair as her attempt to reclaim Englefield met delays. In September she learned that Parliament would receive no more suits until November. "I have held out a ten yeares seige before wch had not ye liberty of goeing to lawe," she noted and likened her sufferings to those of the Church of Smyrna, which was counselled by the angel in Revelation 2:10 to fear not the suffering that would come. "Be thou faithfull unto the death, and I will give thee the crowne of life."[60] The passage that had attracted some attention when the Bishop of Bangor used it as the text for the sermon at Charles I's coronation allowed Lady Eleanor to invoke again a comparison of her situation and Britain's with that of the king.

In September 1643, Parliament accepted the Solemn League and Covenant with the Scots in order to have much-needed assistance for their struggle against the king. Their doing so resolved, for the moment, the question of peace or war in favor of war and confronted the assembly of clergy (and a few laity) that was also meeting at Westminster with an agreement to "reformation of religion in the kingdoms of England and Ireland, in doctrine, worship, discipline, and government, accord-

ing to the word of God, and the example of the best reformed churches."
The treaty did not use the term *Presbyterianism,* but it had committed
the English Parliament to preserving the "reformed religion in the
church of Scotland, in doctrine, worship, discipline, and government."
When the Westminster Assembly refused Lady Eleanor permission to
publish a book she had written interpreting revelation, she appealed
to Parliament in a twenty-page tract that appeared in November.[61]

In *Star to the Wise* she wove together with her quest to be heard her
exhortation to recognize wisdom and act upon it. Rather than focusing
upon the king's errors, she directed her words to the needs of the
war-torn kingdom. The House of Commons, which she addressed as
"the high Court of Parliament," had an awesome responsibility in light
of the implications of the Solemn League and Covenant and the meeting of the Westminster Assembly. She called upon them to do their
duty.

Events, she argued, had demonstrated the relevance of her message,
"The Revelations shewing Things which shall shortly come to passe."
Like the angel sent to deliver Peter from Herod (Acts 12:11), she was
sent to proclaim what "He that hath Ears to hear" should hear (Matthew 11:15) and thus to heal the "kings-evil," the disease, on this
occasion its "Malignant humors, for the most part resorting about the
Ears," customarily cured by the royal touch.[62] To justify further why
she, a woman, should be bringing the news that she presented in the
unlicensed volume, she noted that, preceding John's revelation from
the Isle of Patmos (Revelation 1:9) was an epistle (John's second)
written to a Lady, "the elect Lady" whom he told, "Having many
things to write unto you, I would not write with paper and ink: but I
trust to come unto you and speak face to face" (2 John 12). Thus, Lady
Eleanor, in claiming to be the bearer of what John had promised, took
for herself the title of Elect Lady that society had withheld from her
but had bestowed upon women who expressed their devotion within
existing conventions.[63] Why, she asked, in view of the scriptural prece-
dent, should it not

be revealed to us [on *"Great Britains* Islands"], before others in such case:
assoon to his handmaids as his menservants . . . so now, as well as then, when
she [Mary and Mary Magdalene] had the first happy sight of him [Christ],
after his rising, which was sent to tell and inform them [the disciples] where
they should meet him first.[64]

The Assembly's meeting in the seventeenth century at Westminster, the site of Henry VII's chapel, invoked for her the seven churches to whom John directed the book of Revelation. By associating other places and occurrences in her own day with those of the birth of Christ, including Bedlam and Bethlehem, she proclaimed the Second Coming, a time when everyone would be rewarded "according to his service."

The healing and correcting role that Lady Eleanor claimed for herself was similar to that in which Parliament had cast the Scottish army. The MPs, in agreeing that "an army of another Religion should come to defend the true Religion," were doing as Christ had when "He by the Devil cast out Devils" (Luke 11:14–17). She may also have been thinking that the "massacre" in Ireland two years earlier might be interpreted in the same way. Mixed with her defense of the Solemn League and Covenant was a certain amount of anxiety. The same words that condemned the English of popery could also censure them for the terms they had made with the Scots. "The sons of God" had accepted "the Daughters of men" as wives and subjected themselves to "their Sorceries" while accusing her, whose prophecies contained wisdom, of madness.[65] She herself was among those who were moving away from earlier beliefs in predestination toward a position closer to Arminianism although they would not call it that.[66] Two years later, in one of the books whose title resembles one that she wanted licensed in 1643, she emphatically condemned Arminianism, which she associated with the Duke of Buckingham and the "Spanish faction" of the 1620s.[67]

The disruption of civil war reinforced Lady Eleanor's belief in the approach of that date, nineteen-and-a half years after July 1625, that Daniel had announced to her and that she had confirmed by numerical calculations from scripture. Reiterating her attacks upon Charles as Belshazzar and Herod, she also applied to him the description contemporaries gave to the mad and to false prophets. She called the king a man possessed. Like Great Britain, Charles was divided against himself. Born in 1600 at the beginning of the seventeenth century, he, forty-three years old when she was writing, had been cast out of his kingdom during the seventeenth year of his reign. His time, too, was running out.[68]

Lady Eleanor exhorted the Commons to act. "Let the Executioner be without his fees no longer . . . here repair to the Second House [the House of Lords] for this License for the Lambe and the Bride, She having made her self ready, like *Joseph* and *Mary*," to give birth to a

new era, the Second Coming.[69] Whether she meant to appeal for the
execution of Laud, with whose impeachment the House had taken steps
to proceed on October 19, to call for the trial of Charles, and/or urge
preparations for the Day of Judgment, Lady Eleanor wanted the Commons to heed her words. She cast herself in a major role, that of the
bride, the lamb's wife, a role that she would claim more forcefully in
subsequent tracts.

After publishing her *Star to the Wise* in November 1643, Lady
Eleanor seems to have observed the events around her in silence for a
time. The opening of Laud's trial in the spring may have convinced
her that her responsibilities had been fulfilled. She apparently made
no effort to participate in the proceedings against him, either through
the publication of a tract or testimony in court.[70] Although the MPs
handling his prosecution dredged up many individuals whose complaints against the archbishop were mild compared to hers, they did
not attempt to include Lady Eleanor among their witnesses. She herself
did not come forward. Rather than seeking allies, she repeatedly emphasized her uniqueness as an aristocrat and a prophet. However much
they shared her contempt for Laud, the MPs prosecuting him had
reason to be uneasy about any alliance with her. They could not be
confident that she would not wreak far more havoc than they intended
and challenge the basis of patriarchy upon which they, as well as he,
relied.

As the days of testimony stretched into weeks and she watched and
waited for Parliament to judge Laud, Lady Eleanor achieved one victory
by returning to Englefield. The sole piece of evidence that documents
her arrival on the estate that she regarded as her promised land is a
letter that she wrote to Lucy on 10 June 1644. Thanks to her prophetic
syntax, it is difficult to determine whether she was commenting upon
the way in which she achieved possession or the state of the country as
a whole when she said, "Thes are to informe you since my being arrived
at Englefeild takne by violence the Canaan of this climat fallne on such
a streite at ye present thereby That without your assistance I am at a
stand or stopp." Although she found Englefield "a paradise . . . inferior
to none in as good estate as we left it, [it] hath not tasted of the lest
appearance of the sadd times," she still required some financial support
for a month or so "till grass mowed or the like." Otherwise, she would
have to cut down some trees.[71]

Paralleling Lady Eleanor's success in returning to Englefield was the victory of parliamentary forces at Marston Moor early in July. Both offered confirmation that Judgment and the Second Coming were imminent. Although she did not abandon justification of herself and her prophecies in *Restitution of Reprobates,* dated by Thomason 23 July 1644, she discussed what her contemporaries might expect in more detail than previously. From law, everyday life, and biblical typology, she drew examples to demonstrate the almost inconceivable contrast between what was and what would be. Making her tract "A General Pardon for *Reprobate Rebels,* all of them; Their *Restitution* as authoriz'd and affirmed; Matt. 18 [*sic*] Elias [or Elijah] truly shall first come," she attempted to explain how the pardon that followed Judgment would exceed any that people knew in the current society. From typology she drew such examples as Noah and Christ, Eve and Mary, Cain and sinners, and the Ark and Baptism that should have been familiar to readers. The similarity of the passage in Matthew 18:11 to that of Matthew 17:11 may explain the incorrect identification of the citation on the first page of text. It is one of very few of that kind of error in her work. Its appearance is particularly striking in *Restitution of Reprobates,* which includes more Latin quotations and trappings of scholarship than do many of her tracts.

Lady Eleanor declared that she was Elias, who Christ had promised would announce the Second Coming.[72] The role was proper for a woman—a woman (Eve) had been "the occasion of the worlds woe and undoing" and Mary had given birth to Christ. In response to another possible objection to her claim to have a "PLAISTER or PARDON" for the world, Lady Eleanor argued that her having information that Daniel was told should be closed till the end of time did not contradict the Bible. The promise of redemption was so all-encompassing that it defied human comprehension. This was not a mere pardon from purgatory; it was different. *"Nothing then impossible with Him."* She may have been alluding to her own situation when she cited, as an example of what would be, "that dispossessed Woman" who was "delivered that was at once of so many spirits or DIVELS."[73] Perhaps to offer consolation to her late brother's daughter-in-law, she corrected a copy of *Restitution of Reprobates* for presentation to the "Countess of Castlehaven." Later that year Lady Eleanor devoted an entire tract to her brother Mervin's cause.

When she heard that Sir Archibald Douglas, the husband from whom she had been so long estranged, had died on 28 July 1644, Lady

Eleanor may have hoped that widowhood would enable her to obtain prompt restitution of Pirton and other losses that had previously eluded her. In this she was disappointed. Presumably because Douglas's associates had interests in his estate that they did not wish to share with her, she had no part in his funeral. She later complained that she had been kept from him after her release from prison in order that the "lewd devises of those that had her in custody" should not come to his ear. "Though not a mile from her husband at his death, [she was] not allowed to know where he was buried."[74] News of his death nevertheless reached her, and she, alleging that he had died intestate, applied for and, on 22 August 1644, received administration of his estate.[75] Shortly afterward, a will was found and James Kenrick was named executor.[76]

Before that happened, Lady Eleanor herself took up the suit against the Poultons that Lucy had previously conducted in her behalf. A copy of her petition of 24 October 1644 to the Commissioners of the Great Seal indicates that, in addition to appealing to the House of Lords, she went to the Court of Chancery and, in that latter suit (I have found no copy of her petition to the Lords), she added to her plea for Pirton one for return of a diamond chain that she alleged that Douglas had "pawned or mortgaged" to Francis Poulton for about £150 in November 1630. She claimed that Poulton had declared that the chain was "in the country" when she had attempted to get it back prior to going overseas to see the Queen of Bohemia, presumably in 1633. Although she may have intended to pawn it again in order to obtain funds, she may have wanted the jewels to wear when she waited upon the Queen.[77] The chain, although a mark of worldly status and material wealth, symbolized the light of truth and riches of prophecy that she bore. Without it she would be like the "son of Man" judged for his iniquity (Ezekiel 28:13–16). This same chain was probably the one listed among the jewels at issue between the Douglases and Hastings in the aftermath of Sir John Davies's death. According to Judge Croke's report, a jury in the court of King's Bench, Trinity term, 1632, gave a special verdict that, although the jewels had belonged to Davies, although Lady Eleanor had used them during his life, and although she "being the Daughter of a Nobleman" ought to be able to "use them frequently '*ut ornamenta corporis sui*'" [as an ornament of her person], neither she nor Douglas could have them. They belonged instead to her daughter, Ferdinando's wife, Lucy, who was Davies's heir.[78] Lady

Eleanor and Sir Archibald had responded by petitioning Lord Keeper Coventry that the decision had gone against them because Ferdinando had contrived to have the hearing postponed until Douglas's witnesses could not attend.[79]

As a widow, Lady Eleanor had success in neither her efforts to regain the chain nor those to recover Pirton. In response to her petition in September 1644, the House of Lords had ordered an examination of the witnesses and two days later sent her petition to Poulton's heirs for an answer. Although according to depositions of the messengers, the Poultons evaded them and thus did not receive the Lords' orders, a copy of answers from Henry and Francis Poulton to a petition of the "Lady Elinor Douglas late wife of Sir Archibald Douglas knight deceased" survives among the Main Papers of the Lords.[80] Both in the Lords and in Chancery the Poultons staunchly maintained that they were legitimate owners of the disputed property. In their answers on 10 March 1647, Susan and William Poulton accused Lady Eleanor of "multiplicity of suits" and asked the court to award them costs.[81] Other documents among the records of Chancery include testimony from tenants of the manor, bills and answers from Lady Eleanor's suit in 1650 and 1651 against John Pargiter, a London goldsmith, who she alleged had collected rents and profits from the rectory, and papers from her prolonged dispute with clergyman Nathaniel Ward.[82] By persisting in these suits, Lady Eleanor demonstrated an unwillingness to compromise that accorded with her prophetic absolutism about right and wrong, even if it was impractical from other standpoints. She eventually achieved possession, but how that happened is not clear.

During that same autumn of 1644, Lady Eleanor picked up her pen to predict Laud's judgment. Prefacing *Apocalypsis Jesu Christi* with a recital for the benefit of the Westminster Assembly of her credentials as a prophet, she developed images and themes that she had used in July in *Restitution of Reprobates* and the preceding fall in *Star to the Wise*. Once again, she was the "Elect Lady" whom John addressed in his second epistle. Her name, "Elia. Tichet" [Eleanor Tuchet], itself demonstrated her association with Elias [Elijah] the Tisbite, the prophet, for whom God provided (1 Kings 17:19).[83] She reminded the Assembly that they met in Westminster Abbey in the presence of the history of the kingdom. Twenty-four kings, a grand jury, had ruled England since the Norman Conquest. Charles was the twenty-fifth. In his reign would come "a greater then he or the conqueror," he "on the white horse," Michael, who would destroy the beast, and the armies of the kings of the earth (Revelation 19:11−21).[84] She suggested specifically that under the astrological sign of Virgo (the heavenly virgin) that was, about Michaelmas, the feast of Michael and the very season when Laud had cast her into the wilderness in 1633, he would "receive his sentence to be cast out of heaven."[85]

In *Her Blessing,* published about the same time as *Apocalypsis Jesu Christi* and dated 23 September by Thomason, Lady Eleanor also took note of the significance of Michaelmas as described in the twelfth chapters of Daniel and Revelation, but, as the tract's full title suggested, her principal theme was motherhood. To her own daughter Lucy, who "so punctually have discharged that duty of the first commandment [to love God] with promise, in so much and such dishonour endured, have bene your mothers Copartner, even You, her alone and sole support under the Almighty," would go "the *Ancient of Dayes his Kingdom*" as a "portion." Lady Eleanor was at once the mother providing for a marriage portion and the prophet interpreting God's will for Lucy. In contrast were those who "preferred this worlds vanity and folly."[86]

At the beginning of the tract, Lady Eleanor had promised a "new Interpretation" of the seventh chapter of Daniel. Rather than filling her work up with *"Froath"* or "with differing Opinions of others," she would, she said, offer "BRITISH garments or . . . COATE."[87] Through heraldry she made the first beast of Daniel's vision England's lion rampant, the second the "she-bear" with three ribs (the *fleur de lis* of France) in her mouth, the third the Scottish "coat" of arms, and the fourth the Irish harp.[88] Particularly important for her argument was the second beast, with whom she evoked Queen Henrietta Maria who was "the Mother not of the Living Child but of Divisions and Massacres" evident in the wars that were splitting Britain apart. The queen was the woman whose willingness to divide the child convinced Solomon that the child was not hers (1 Kings 3:25−27).[89] She was Jezebel, the Samarian Queen who, like Actaeon, the huntsman in classical mythology, was devoured by dogs as a result of wrongdoing (1 Kings 21:23).[90] "As her name [Henrietta Maria] is, so is she the MARRAH: *The GALL of bitterness"* (Acts 8:23).[91]

The history of Britain showed how the end was coming. Monarchs had endured repeated misfortunes. Because three of the children of Henry VIII, *"first Heire of the red rose and the white,"* had been "Crown'd

Princes childlesse" and deceased "without Heires of their body," the throne had passed to Scotland to one who was "as *Unfortunate* in His *Progenie* and *Successor; As in His Predisessors* or *Parents.*"[92] The Parliament then sitting was the last and the war the final conflict between the forces of good and evil. People who failed to recognize this were like the women who sometimes miscalculated and were thus surprised when they went into labor. The signs were clear. Although the "late hand writing" had not appeared on the walls of the Banquetting House at Whitehall, it was "not unknown to London" since it had been "published and printed, 1633."[93] Lady Eleanor knew what was happening and that both she and Britain were in danger. Parliamentary forces were in disarray and their leaders divided. Instead of being the prelude to a sound defeat of the royalists, their July victory at Marston Moor stood out against a succession of losses and disappointments. "Satan because he knows his reigne or time to be short: is ready to devoure the Woman even for the truth of the Resurrection time revealed," yet, she asserted, her own role was to announce what was to come, even if she had to sacrifice herself in so doing. After Eve came Mary. It was *"most proper"* for a *"Woman by whom death came to be the Messenger of Life."*[94]

The second battle of Newbury occurred near Englefield that October and marked the eleventh anniversary of the burning of her books and her appearance before the High Commission. It also reminded Lady Eleanor of the warfare and destruction preceding the New Jerusalem. Aware of Parliament's preparation of propositions for peace, she published her own *Prayer or Petition for Peace November 22, 1644.*[95] In a confessional form, she enumerated the facts and the consequences of the nation's rebellion against God. "These late married Isles or united Kingdoms [were] now in widows forlorn woful Estate," a condition that, she knew, could be fraught with disputes and poverty, or, she continued with what may have been an analogy to her position while estranged from Douglas, the island's fate was "worse, as divorced."[96] Since 1642, "our Estate [has been] turned upside down. . . . [Our] storehouses exhausted, like those Rivers dryed up, and like the dead Trees, burnt up our Nation and Habitation, torn between two She-bears, like those Forty two ungratious Infants" in the biblical story.[97] In conclusion, she prayed, "O forsake us not! thou of unspeakable Mercy, cause thy face to shine upon us, for the Lords sake, our alone Savior Jesus Christ." She described him, here as elsewhere, in words significantly different from those of the Prayerbook. He was "made of the womans seed according to the flesh: A woman making her first witness of the resurrection tidings to them. Let thy mighty voyce be heard."[98]

Lady Eleanor continued her stream of tracts through the winter of 1644 and into 1645 as she awaited the end of the nineteen-and-a-half-year period from July 1625. Among her publications were two versions of a tract that she originally put out in 1644 and directed to Parliament and then revised and reissued in 1649, *Discovery* and *Sign*.[99] A third tract, *Prophetia* published in Latin and dated Christmas 1644, she issued in translation as *Prophesie* in the following year.[100] On the title page, both editions cite two of her favorite verses, Matthew 17:11, "Elias truly shall first come and restore all things," and Revelation 1:8, "I am Alpha and Omega," but whereas the English presents her as "the Lady Eleanor, etc.," the Latin is more formal. She is the Lady Eleanor, legate of Lusitania, resident in England.[101] The structure of the thirty-page tract, like its Latin text, suggests that it was directed to scholars. It offers three arguments about the Second Coming in succession: whether the date and hour can be known, what is to happen to the Gentiles, and the notion of eternal punishment.

Did Lady Eleanor herself compose this Latin tract, and, if the answer is yes, why does only one of her surviving publications appear in Latin? She herself provides no answer. We can hypothesize that the Latin is hers. She included Latin passages in other tracts and wrote Latin words in their margins in her own hand.[102] The argument and tone of *Prophetia* does not differ significantly from her other works. Though writing in English, rather than Latin, in *Of Errors* printed in 1645 and addressed to Parliament, she systematically exposed the errors she found in other works of prophecy. We can speculate that the lateness of the hour moved her, in December 1644, to make yet another effort to persuade the learned of her era to heed her prophecy before the nineteen and a half years of which Daniel had told her expired. In so doing, she once more departed from the expectations contemporaries had for women. If women were to write, they might write letters or prayers, certainly not scholarly Latin treatises.

Archbishop Laud's execution on 10 January 1645 was a moment that Lady Eleanor had long awaited. During his extended imprisonment and trial, she had repeatedly urged Parliament to make their judgment.[103] She later commented about the changes that would occur with the Second Coming. Images would fall and the Eucharist would not be "in privat administred, but powred out in the Presence of the holy Angels, and in the Presence of the *Lamb*" and the sacrament would be commemorative, not the "reall PRESENCE," that the Laudians had insisted upon.[104] She attempted to mark the occasion of her enemy's punishment and the validation of another of her predictions with a tract. Thomason managed to get a only fragment of it for his collection; he dated it 17 January and noted that it had been "Taken a printing." For its title she used a phrase from the Book of Revelation that became one of her favorites, *I am the first, and the last, the beginning and the ending* (Revelation 1:11, 17). Believing that her time of preparation would soon end and that a new era would begin, she wrote with a heightened sense of anticipation during the following months.

CHAPTER 6

A and O, the Beginning
and the Ending

For Lady Eleanor, Laud's death was the outstanding event of the winter of 1644–45. It came at the time when Daniel had told her that Judgment would occur, and changes in the political scene seemed to confirm that history was reaching a critical point. Parliament passed the Self-Denying Ordinance, created a New Model Army, authorized a reformed church discipline, and took steps toward establishing the Presbyterianism to which they had committed themselves in 1643 through their Solemn League and Covenant with the Scots. But, as the months passed, clouds of uncertainty hung over the future. Fresh conflicts developed without bringing resolution to longstanding problems. Lady Eleanor encountered obstacles in her own life, and, in her tracts, she merged her personal experiences into Britain's history and that of the godly (Israel) even more than previously. A prolonged imprisonment evoked memories of earlier detention and, like her losses of property, served her as a metaphor for general suffering from heavy taxation and from sequestration during the kingdom's continued bondage by the Beast. Rather than maintaining the high level of productivity that she had achieved in the first part of 1645, Lady Eleanor decreased her rate of publication in 1646 and 1647. In 1648, as hope began to replace the anxiety that had been troubling her, she once again began to pour her energy into writing. By January 1649, after renewed war had led to King Charles himself being brought to justice, she could quote with more confidence than she had since 1645 the words that were her theme during those four years: "I am Alpha and Omega, the beginning and the ending" (Revelation 1:8).

When the memory of Laud's death was still fresh, Lady Eleanor compared it with the execution of another Lord, her late brother, Mervin Lord Audeley and earl of Castlehaven who had been beheaded 10 May 1631. She addressed her tract, *Word of God*, to the City of London, whose leaders had played an influential role in the politics of the time and whose financial support was essential to the parliamentary cause early in 1645. Like Laud, Castlehaven had sought, at the end, to justify his religious beliefs to a doubting public.[1] For Lady Eleanor, the two differed significantly. She identified Castlehaven with Zaccheus, the sinning publican whom Christ promised salvation.[2] Her use of that comparison suggests she was not entirely blind to her brother's weaknesses, though she certainly believed that he, in contrast to Laud, did not deserve the sentence imposed upon him. Her desire to present Castlehaven as Zaccheus probably explains why she took the version of the parable of the talents that she quotes in the tract from Luke (19:12–27) rather than from Matthew (25:14–30), as she did on several other occasions when she cited it. Luke's rendering of the story also allowed her to appeal to London to provide what the Lord needed just as Bethphage and Bethany had allowed a colt to be taken for Christ (Luke 19:29–35).[3]

Lady Eleanor greeted spring in 1645 with announcements of her expectation of the fulfillment of her prophecy in two tracts, *As not Unknowne* and *Brides Preparation,* both dated 21 March by Thomason. *As not Unknowne,* one of her two extant tracts in the form of a broadsheet, reminded its readers that Laud's execution had brought to fruition the warning she had issued in 1633. The day of his judgment was "Doubtlesse an *houre and a day,* Not dreamed of in his *Diarie* where [he] sets down the 19 of *September* 1633," the day he was translated to Canterbury. He, the "Arch *B.B.* of *Lambeth* (or *Bethlam*) . . . [was] rewarded as he had shut up and silenced others." This, she noted, ought to remind the king that "how presumptious so ever the imprinting seemd then [in 1633] of those Books" in which she had warned him "beware the *handwriting,"* the events of the present demonstrated the truth of what she had said. In further justification of herself, she printed copies of her 1633 petition to him against Laud and of the ensuing order for her appearance before the High Commission.[4]

In her second tract of March 1645, Lady Eleanor invoked the images of spring and renewal, the concurrence of Lady Day, the Feast of the Annunciation, 25 March, with the beginning of the new year and the

Second Coming of Christ. Using as her text Revelation 21, "I John saw the holy Citie comming downe from Heaven as a Bride prepared," she followed John in identifying the Bride with the Lamb's wife and thus used more emphatically an image she had invoked earlier in *Star to the Wise*.[5] Whereas the gates of the Holy City were never shut and that city had need neither of a temple nor of sun or moon because it had God and the Lamb, how ironic it was that London's tower that was supposed to provide for the *"Cities safety* . . . was turned into a prison," where she herself had been confined, *"a place of teares and death."*[6] The publication, by order of Parliament, just a week or so earlier of *A Directory for the Public Worship of God,* which was to replace the Book of Common Prayer, may have added to her sense of anticipation, although she does not comment directly about this.

It was probably about that same time (in the spring of 1645) that Lady Eleanor wrote Lucy that she would not "so longe . . . have refrayned from vissiting you had not this bin ye long expected time come of seeing ye end of such a troublesome world."[7] Lady Eleanor had no doubt about her priorities. Obedience to Daniel came first. She signed the letter "Eleanor Da^{v}e Do^u," that is Eleanor Davies and Douglas, a signature which she would come to use to link herself with alpha and omega, the first and last.[8] But however important were her duties as a prophet, they did not eradicate her maternal concerns. She took time in her letter to write of her worries about Lucy's illness, to tell her daughter that the earl of Holland had asked about her, and to express her appreciation of Lady Elizabeth Hatton, who had "feasted" her.[9]

The title page of *Great Brittains Visitation* also shows 1645, but its content suggests that Lady Eleanor completed it late in 1644. Beginning with "The Apocalyps Prologue," she explained how the current age in Britain resembled that of the birth of Christ "when as City and Countrey opprest so: By such an universall imposd taxx . . . the infernall pit opened, where those Legions of Wormes or Locusts swarming out. Our Pruining Hookes have turned into Swords, our union into division."[10] This similarity underscored the chronology that predicted the Second Coming. As she had in *Star to the Wise,* she identified the Isle of Patmos with Britain, herself as messenger with John, and the four seasons and four evangelists with the four beasts.[11] Laud, though executed, remained an important element in her argument. Bishops, like ships, she noted, were "able to choake all with their smoakes and the like." Laud was the "contriver of this third kingdoms cumbustion." As archbishop, he had in his "custodie the Keys of the AByss [Archbishop's] power given him to imprison, Levie Taxes, wage warre at his pleasure."[12]

Lady Eleanor was still expecting the prophecy to be realized when she hailed Whitsun as the "last" such "feast."[13] For that occasion she offered "her creed or confession," a statement of her belief. She referred to "GOD, *the sole* Creator of *all* things," rather than to God the Father, as did the creeds of the prayerbook, and cited *"His* promise *made also; Concerning the* Womans *SEED."*[14] While her variations in wording were in some respects minor, they departed from the patriarchal language that was usual at the time. Lady Eleanor demonstrated by the content as well as by the fact of her writing that she was challenging ecclesiastical authority and gender order even though she shared some of Thomas Edwards's anxieties about sectarianism and error.[15] Edwards may have recognized this and forgiven her for writing as a woman, but she probably owed her escape from explicit condemnation in his *Gangraena* more to her singular position and lack of followers.[16]

The bulk of Lady Eleanor's creed concerned her belief in the "second *Comming* of the *holy Ghost,* immediately before the *day of Judgement."*[17] This is her most explicit statement of her expectations. As elsewhere, she demonstrated how scriptural texts, from both Old and New Testaments, applied to the events in Britain, particularly to the "plagues and Warre appointed the day of Judgements forerunner."[18] Across the title page of the Worcester College copy she added a note about the fall of Leicester to the royalists, 31 May 1645, just six days after Whitsunday. "Lecesters Loss," as she put it, left many of the city's defenders dead. She remembered Revelation 11 [:14]: "The second woe is past. etc."

Lady Eleanor expected the "third woe" (Revelation 11:14) would come about Michaelmas. She announced this in *Second Coming* which she wrote not long after her tract for Whitsuntide.[19] The parliamentary victory at Naseby on 14 June and the capture there of some of the king's correspondence probably contributed to her prediction. Although she does not mention them specifically, she does refer to the necessity of Laud's death in view of the evils that had plagued the kingdom. Britain was a spiritual Sodom—prophecy silenced, sabbath and festival days violated with "play-houses visited and drinking houses."[20] All these aspects of the antichrist's kingdom would be *"Cut off for Ever"* with the Second Coming.[21]

By the time she wrote *Second Coming,* Lady Eleanor may have begun to sense that events would not occur in the way that she had anticipated. In her postscript to the tract, she mentioned several erroneous beliefs. These she systematically refuted in *Of Errors,* which she addressed to Parliament and also published in 1645. Her more measured tone in *Of Errors* contrasts with the proclamations of imminent Judgment that she had published a few months before. As she realized that she had more time than she had thought, Lady Eleanor slowed down the pace and intensity of her writing. She may have felt a need to reassess what was happening so that she could continue to prophesy with confidence. Neither illness nor disinterest seem likely explanations of her temporarily reduced rate of publication, since subsequent references demonstrate that she was well informed about occurrences during the period. In 1648, for example, she related how, in October 1645, Cromwell's forces had savagely stormed, sacked, and burned Basing House, the seat of the papist Marquess of Winchester (who also held Englefield). Basing served as "such an Example not the like, unlucky *Babel* Towers, toward the increase of widows and fatherless, made to kiss the ground."[22]

In November 1645, Lady Eleanor published another *Prayer or Petition for Peace.* Except for the year, its title page was just as it had been in 1644. Most of the revisions in the body of the tract were stylistic, but there is one that may make a significant reference to the intense conflicts over church government in 1645. After praying on behalf of "those sheep yet not guilty or accessary to this trespass or capital Crime," she inserted "of deposing thee" to explain what the crime was before she continued with a reference to opposing "thy return."[23] Charles, the Scots, Parliament, and the army held religion hostage as they negotiated with each other about the terms of a settlement.

The transition to spring in 1646 brought Lady Eleanor hope once again, even though disputes continued to impede both her own affairs and the attempts to reach religious and political accord. The season itself promised a renewal of life, and she welcomed it with a tract *For the Blessed Feast of Easter.* In 1646, Easter fell on 29 March, just two days after the anniversary of King Charles's accession to the throne, a day he had repeatedly sought to have celebrated. She anticipated the inauguration of the reign of one "GREATER" than Charles. Believing that the victories of the parliamentary armies, *"Babylons* judgement, [were] the day of judgements forerunner," she saw Easter, the feast of the Resurrection, as the occasion for the Second Coming, the feast of the Lamb's marriage.[24] To be summoned to the Lamb's marriage supper was a "greater priveledge" than to receive a writ to attend Parliament, which she could not have as a woman. She did not explicitly mention the comparison that contemporary debates would have made obvious to readers—admission to communion, the Lord's Supper. The Lamb's feast would be "a greater shew then *St Georges* his coming at hand, or any other."[25] It would be a "new Modell, a new *Heaven and a new Earth, new Jerusalem,*" built on the foundations laid by the New Model Army, *"Albion{'s} Army"* whose leader was the Lamb.[26] In 1644, the seals of Revelation, chapters 6–8, had been unsealed; in 1645, victories had come, and the Lamb's marriage would follow.

As she had the preceding year, in 1646, Lady Eleanor watched expectantly during the forty-day period between Easter and Whitsun.[27] In *The Day of Judgements Modell,* dated by Thomason 15 May, two days before Whitsunday, she saw nature itself preparing for "a *Tryall before a Thron of Judicature"* with white robes that were customary for the newly baptized at Whitsun. "Wi[t]ness the fresh Boughes in their hands, *(all in white Robes) Where the innocent Lambe,* as it were, araigned before *Them."*[28] King Charles himself had surrendered to the Scots in April and was thus, by Whitsun, a prisoner. His wearing of white for his own coronation years before had served as prelude for what followed, the coming of *"Him that satt on the white HORSE, with his* Albion-trayn."[29] The lay elders whose role in the church was causing so much dispute in Parliament and in the Westminster Assembly would be the jury at the Day of Judgment. "Those *Elders* [were] NO ordinary MEN." They declared the "Prisoner" presented by the Lamb "one of their owne degree" and "the *Lamb acquits HIM here, though* Condemn'd."[30] She concluded by addressing another point in contemporary discussions. Her "Model or patterne" of Judgment, she maintained, was in conformity with scripture. "What Discipline Agreeable with the APOSTLES, Rules Included: where The PEOPLES approbation and Consent: . . . That Multitudes Holding up their HANDS, with Those Sealed ELDERS Verdict or Judgement."[31]

During the spring and early summer of 1646, Lady Eleanor probably also published three other tracts, *Her Appeal* (1646), *Je le tien,* and *Revelation Interpreted.* Although she used for *Her Appeal* a title very similar to that she had given a tract at Whitsuntide 1641, she was not merely offering a new edition of the earlier piece in 1646. Describing herself as "the Prophet of the most High, his Messenger" and the "Handmaid of the Holy Spirit," she addressed this new appeal to "Mr. Mace," probably Thomas May who served as "secretary" for Parliament at the time.[32] She explained that, "having in the burthen of his precious Word been my self a partaker, made a publique Example, no mean one, concerning the way before the Lords coming to be prepared," she thought it appropriate to "publish the same." Thus, whereas the former tract had interpreted the history of the kingdom to prove the imminence of the Second Coming, *Her Appeal* of 1646 related the events of her own career from its beginnings in 1625, when she took George Carr into her household and studied the books of Daniel and Revelation. In substantiation of her prophetic role she cited occasions when her predictions proved true and noted the judgments incurred by her husbands and others who had opposed her. The events that marked 23 October, the day when her books had been burned in 1633, were particularly significant; so too were the deaths of Sir Archibald Douglas and Archbishop Laud, which both occurred in 1644 according to the old calendar. In contrast to Laud, whose death came on a Friday, "the day our Lord descended, etc.," Douglas died on a Sunday, the day of "the Lords Resurrection." From the perspective of 1646, she could say that Sir Archibald was "with *Job* that good man with evil things." His experience, like the Archbishop's, nevertheless should warn Parliament to awake from its sleep to see what God had revealed.[33]

In *Revelation Interpreted,* rather than discussing her own life, Lady Eleanor explained how, from the vantage point of 1646, public events fit the biblical text. Charles had entrusted the wrong people with power, and the kingdom had suffered the consequences. One example was George Villiers, Duke of Buckingham, whom she attacked again with some of the same words in 1647 in *Excommunication out of Paradice.* His murder at Portsmouth in August 1628, which she had predicted, healed *"that foule Soare the* Kings-*Evill."*[34] Charles's inability to cure the maladies of the kingdom as kings were wont to do was itself worthy of note and a point she made even more explicit later. Assassination was an appropriate reward for Buckingham, whose blasphemy was like that of the French king, Henry IV who had met a similar fate.[35] In the guise of patronage, Buckingham had given away the kingdom's liberty and religion. His wide distribution of gifts, offices, and honors left none of his kin wanting. "The Other" major contributor to the factions and wars was Laud, whose Judgment she had also predicted. Thanks to him, "the TREASURERS Office [was in the hands of Bishop Juxon of London] ingrossed by the CLERGY," a circumstance that Lady Eleanor found deplorable because it extended the power of the forces of the antichrist.[36]

Lady Eleanor also took issue with the clergy in *Je le tien*. By using her family's motto for the tract's title, she defended her own claim to prophesy against the erroneous and dangerous convictions of those who declared that "the gift of Prophesie is extinguished."[37] Instead of doing their job, the clergy had ordered that the book of Revelation, on the grounds that it was obscure, need not be read with the rest of the Scripture each year.[38] These men failed to understand that "nothing so covered or hidden which shal not be proclaimed or preached on house tops" and thus deprived all of "those precious leaves for the healing of the Nations."[39] In making this point and in arguing against those who said the time of the Second Coming could not be known or that from hell there was no redemption, Lady Eleanor was addressing those who were then debating the settlement of religion. She drew heavily upon legal imagery to elaborate upon arguments she had made earlier in *Of Errors* (1645), in *Prophetia* (1644), and in its English translation *Prophecie* (1645). Anyone familiar with English law, she asserted, would know that attainders could be reversed, so why should that sentence God imposed upon Adam's house be irreversible? The royal prerogative allowed monarchs to free individuals who had been condemned to imprisonment in perpetuity. The Second Coming would bring the world's general pardon.[40] Rather than resigning themselves and abandoning hope, Lady Eleanor urged her readers to believe. On the last page she translated her title and family's motto, *Je le tien,* as "I Hold it." The words also evoked for her the message of Revelation 2:25, "Hold fast till I come," a message that was more important as she came to be less certain of the exact moment when the anticipated events would occur.[41] Laud had been executed at the conclusion of the nineteen-and-a-half years, but much of the old order of the Beast remained.

Lady Eleanor was in good spirits when she wrote Lucy on 23 May 1646. She may have heard of the King's apparently conciliatory letters to Parliament and the City, but she does not give a specific reason for her feelings. "I bless him ye Lord who have had so large a portion with mee: in my sufferings. Whereof mine ennimis now drinke ye dreggs."[42] Events soon proved that she had written prematurely. By

July, she found herself once again imprisoned, this time in the Wood Street Compter, one of the prisons of the sheriff of London. A successor of the Lord Mayor to whom she had written three years earlier to obtain a loan had signed the order. Her debts had caught up with her, and the action angered her especially because she was named in the warrant as "Eleanor Lady Davers alias Douglas."[43] The authorities thus mutilated the name that through puns, anagrams, and other devices, she had made an important element in her message. Their error attacked her identity and proved the disorder of the world whose end she was announcing.

As she told the story five years later in *Hells Destruction,* one Thomas Paine, a printer, had brought the action for debt against her.[44] The two had quarreled earlier over the printing of one of her tracts, perhaps *Prophetia,* which listed Paine as the publisher on the title page. She, having been since "put to the charge for Imprinting the same all over," had apparently refused to pay the sixty pounds he thought his due.[45] Her outrage at him was the greater because he, claiming he had lost her text, had contrived to get her to come to his house where he had her arrested. She, who enjoyed using her wit to reveal the inadequacies of others, had been outwitted. Then, once imprisoned, she was subjected to indignities far greater than those she had experienced during her earlier confinements, when her status as the daughter of a baron had served to protect her. First locked into her chamber by the keeper, then "between two of them carried down . . . [she was] instantly shut and bolted . . . into the Dungeon-Hole, Hells Epitomy, . . . left [without a candle] on the wet floor to take up her lodging, beyond any draught, by so many poysonous Vermin harbored." What is more, when she offered her captors no bribe or tip, they searched her coat pockets.[46] Whether understood factually as her experience or metaphorically for her sufferings, for Britain's (Israel's) distress, or for that of any individual prior to redemption, her description captured a sense of extreme discomfort and one of the relief that graciously and without payment would follow. She confessed that her stay in the dungeon had lasted only about an hour. The terrible storm that hit the city that evening, the Lord Mayor's commitment to the tower a year later, and the printer's sudden death all seemed to demonstrate the significance of the occasion.[47] This was another instance when those who committed injustice against her, God's prophet, experienced God's judgments.

From the Compter, Lady Eleanor was apparently transferred to the

Gatehouse, where she reflected upon her earlier confinement there and upon the quarrels and poverty that were afflicting the kingdom in the wake of war. Although the Scots handed the captive king over to the English, the chances for resolution must have seemed as remote as her own prospects of relief and release in February 1647. The contents of *Gatehouse Salutation,* the tract she published then, rhymed, but, except for the final lines, it was set in type as prose. She took the pains of childbirth, the prelude to new life, for its theme. Identifying herself with Mary, Bedlam with Bethlehem, the hours of labor with the "tedious hours" of imprisonment, she found comfort in the promise of eternity. Her final expression of faith,

> So Gates and Prison Doors be no
> more shut,
> The King of Glory comes, your
> souls lift up,

she proposed should be sung to the "Tune of *Magnificat,*" Mary's statement of her own faith.[48]

A fragment of another tract, also dated February 1646 [1647] and perhaps an enlarged edition of *Gatehouse Salutation,* survives in the British Library.[49] Like *Gatehouse Salutation,* this fragment is printed as prose but rhymes. Reciting the two woes that had already arrived, Lady Eleanor again announced the third. This time she thought it was "quickly assured to come." With it, as happens in the Book of Revelation, "Heavens gate" will open and the tables will turn so that the Beast and its allies will pay the price of their misdeeds. For five months, through the appropriate astrological signs, the torments will last, till the time of Aquarius, when she was writing. Aquarius was the bearer of water, the source of baptism and life. "Our Navy lastly ships Sea-Horses also those, whose stretcht out serpents fiery tails, no lesse power in their Nose [perhaps a pun on Noahs]; its masterpiece those GUNS hatch'd under serpents wing."[50]

Lady Eleanor was probably still imprisoned and thus able to use her own situation as a parallel for Britain's when she published *Mystery of General Redemption* sometime in 1647. In that tract, she discussed at some length the evidence that supported her claim that the Second Coming would bring redemption, that "the womans seed . . . [would] vanquish the Serpents power."[51] To emphasize the great gulf between riches and honor in this world and in the next described in Luke 16 with the example of Lazarus, she noted in the margin herself, Archbishop Laud, and Judge Richardson who had antagonized Laud and the king with his prohibition of churchales in Somerset.[52] She also invoked the king's name, *"Chasma,* a compound of Cha: and Ma: what a distance [or chasm] between them."[53] For part of her argument she cited the translation of the Latin *Secula* into English as *for Ever* in the final passages of Hebrews and Jude.[54] Elsewhere she mentioned the differences between the Greek and Hebrew wording and the English.[55] The result of these errors, she maintained, was distortion as great as would occur by substituting classical for biblical figures, Hercules for Samson, Ovid for David, or Seneca for Paul.[56] Although Lady Eleanor may have been able to review the linguistic as well as the scriptural arguments without reference to sources, the scholarship in the tract makes it seem as if she may have had some books with her on this occasion, in contrast to having been deprived of them when she was confined in the Gatehouse more than a decade earlier.

Lady Eleanor's return to the site of her previous confinement apparently revived her memories of the vision she had had while in the Gatehouse in September 1634. She related that vision in *Ezekiel the Prophet,* dated 2 April 1647, the very day, when, as she tells us in *Appearance,* published in 1650, she had another vision. On 2 April, when she apparently had received a writ challenging her claims to the manor of Pirton, she tells us that "a bold star facing the Moon . . . passed through her Body, at which time served that Writ bearing date the second of April: *I send thee to a rebellious house, etc. Ezek. 2 and cap. 12."*[57] The next morning, Southwark endured a terrible thunder storm that she declared was, "To the upper House a warning piece their discharge."[58]

Lady Eleanor added that same date, 2 April 1647, in the margin beside the opening lines of a second and longer tract drawn from Ezekiel, *Ezekiel, cap. 2.*[59] Both tracts depended upon the same text and story, one that Lady Eleanor cited on many other occasions. She herself could identify with Ezekiel's experience of dealing with a "rebellious nation" that paid little heed to his prophecy. The image of the wheel (Ezekiel 1:15–21) evoked clocks and the passsage of time, which the bells of Westminster Abbey had marked for her during her stay in the Gatehouse.[60] Despite their common features, these are two different works. In *Ezekiel, cap. 2,* Lady Eleanor focused upon the prophet's encounter with a rebellious nation rather than with descriptions of prophetic visions.[61] "Lest that [Judgment of such a nation] come to pass," she warned in her postscript, Britain should be prepared and not be taken without their wedding garments or without the robes of parliament essential for members when the monarch attended.

Signs of rebellion were evident in Britain in the spring of 1647. Discontent was growing and, with it, sympathy for the Levellers. Late in May, the officers concurred with their men's resistance to the parliamentary order to disband. They seized the king from the commissioners who were guarding him on Parliament's behalf and, on 5 June, took an Engagement not to disband until their honor was assured. They called for a General Council of the Army, composed of both officers and representatives of the soldiers, to consider their grievances. Soon afterward, the army issued the first of their political manifestos. By early August when they entered London, they had another, the Heads of Proposals, that they hoped could be the basis of a settlement with the king. Lady Eleanor took cognizance of the importance of the army by dedicating *Excommunication out of Paradice,* published that August, to Oliver Cromwell, to whom she later addressed other work. Confessing that she had not had the honor of meeting him, she told Cromwell that she hoped that he would follow in the footsteps of his ancestor, Thomas Cromwell, who had played a part in making the Bible available in English. Her message to Oliver concerning the nature of mercy and the true meaning of baptism offered, in addition to its discussion of general issues concerning the new order, an unstated critique of the Heads of the Proposals, which had outlined a settlement that would not only eliminate the coercive power of bishops but also, by its removal of most other religious requirements, would fail to make necessary reforms. As her scriptural texts for the title page and her opening sentence, she used, respectively, Genesis 3 [:24] *"So he drove out the MAN"* [from the Garden of Eden] and 1 Peter 3. The latter chapter was one of the standard sources for those who wanted to argue that wives should obey their husbands. Rather than directly addressing the part of the text that ran counter to her own conduct, Lady Eleanor took a much broader approach and challenged practices that she regarded as contrary to scripture. Among these she included allowing "those knowing not good from evil, to be Baptized" and the claim that "Circumcision, appointed for males" gave them special status. Thus, she denounced "those Mother Midwives, *Joan Baptists* suffered to take that office upon them, because of *Ziporahs* circumcising her Son" (Exodus 4:25–26). On the other hand, she maintained that in accord with Acts 8:12, where both men and women who believed were baptized, baptism offered salavation just as Noah's ark had previously (1 Peter 3:20–21), and yet belief was more important.[62] The church was itself of age—the gospel, not the law, applied. The waters of baptism were those of life—not those of the sea from which the Beast rose. To illustrate her arguments, she mixed together a grab bag of marine figures and events, a number of which appear in others of her tracts. Like many contemporaries, she cited God's warning to England in the Spanish Armada, a story that, in her own fondness for tapestries, she remembered was depicted on hangings in the House of Lords.[63] The Duke of Buckingham, "Founder of the Spanish Faction" and Lord Admiral whom she had attacked the previous year in *Revelation Interpreted* was another example of the Beast that had risen from the sea.[64] So too was Walter Lord Devereux, the first earl of Essex, whose name sounded like water and who had been a treacherous military adventurer in Ireland.[65] What was needed, instead of beasts from the sea, was for "he that is athirst [to] take the water of life freely" (Revelation 21:6).[66]

Lady Eleanor followed her August appeal to Cromwell with a petition to the House of Commons in September. The efforts of Leveller leader John Lilburne, then imprisoned in the tower, to negotiate with Cromwell for his release may have prompted her to seek some relief. Reciting all that she had endured from 1633, when the High Commission had committed her to the Gatehouse, "And now in her widdowes estate [she] hath beene made subject to all arrest for debt, and is sometimes taken and carried to the Gatehouse, then to the Compter, then about to the Kings Bench without any respect of her" or consideration of the service that her father and her two husbands had given overseas as well as at home, she asked "to be relieved for such bondage and damages."[67] There is no evidence that her petition was even read in the House. The MPs had little reason to listen to her appeal. The status and connections that had won her attention earlier lacked sway in 1647. Her father was dead, she was widowed, and her son-in-law, the earl of Huntingdon, who had shown little enthusiasm for the parliamentary cause, was financially embarrassed. Like Jane Shore to whom she compared herself in that petition, she suffered when the powerful men with whom she had associated had passed from the scene.

Lady Eleanor was apparently still in custody in the King's Bench the following year when she published *Reader, The heavy hour at hand.*[68] Again citing passages from Ezekiel about the fate of a rebellious nation, she warned not, as she had before, of the danger from Rome but of the non-Christian "Turkish Armado's preparation." No one should be surprised by the day of Judgment. Among the many indications of its coming was the situation of the earl of Northumberland, *"sometime Admiral of the Seas,"* whom Parliament had put in the position of Noah by giving him custody of the king's two younger children in 1645 and of the Duke of York in the following year, after the fall of Oxford.[69] As admiral, Northumberland, like Buckingham before him, was someone whose association with water made him important—baptism was the source of life and naval strength was Britain's defense.[70] The house, Sion, where Northumberland exercised his guardianship of the royal children represented Zion, and he *"paralleld . . . that Northern scourge* The Assyrian Army." How wrong it was to make him the protector of "the houses of the Lord" and yet, like the Assyrian army, his power would not last.[71] His "Crest or Coat-Arms," which she described as the half moon, the crescent recognized as the symbol of the Islamic peoples—the enemies of Christianity—was a portent of the coming Judgment. Thus, she admonished, the "day [was] drawing near."[72] Although she may have written after the Duke of York escaped from Northumberland's custody on 21 April 1648, her failure to mention that explicitly makes a slightly earlier date for the tract more likely.

Lady Eleanor gave her prolonged suffering and that of Britain a prominent place in her writings in 1648. Her legal struggle to reclaim Pirton, of which the writ of 2 April 1647 had been a reminder, continued into the following year, when she gave it a more central role in a tract that appeared in two slightly different versions. In *And without Proving* and *Wherefore to Prove* she recited the injustices that she had suffered as a result of Laud's "taking prophesie for no other then madness" and having her imprisoned in 1633.[73] During that imprisonment, "pagling Projectors Plots" had resulted in her losing her "widows Estate," the land she claimed as jointure from her marriage with Sir John Davies. Not only had the plotters taken the opportunity to obtain Pirton, but, she added, the Marquess of Winchester, during the same period, had bought Englefield. The wrongfulness of his deed was evident because his Basing House had fallen.[74] What could she say when confronted by the forces of evil? Her dispute with the Poultons over Pirton reminded her of that "between the Archangel and the other (the Tempter)" over Moses' body. Unable to obtain relief from the law courts, she trusted in the Lord to rebuke those who deprived *"Zions* widow."[75]

Lady Eleanor's suit for restitution of her property also gave her the setting for another tract published later that year, *Writ of Restitution.* Venting her anger at those who tried to interfere with what she believed was legal process, she attacked the sheriff and undersheriff of Hertfordshire. They were, she maintained, men who had risen to positions for which they were not qualified.[76] In making this charge, she took an argument traditionally employed to defend the established order against women or others who challenged it. Thanks to the upheavals of war, it offered a ready means of discrediting authority. In contrast to the conduct of these upstart officials, Lady Eleanor placed that of her own "honest poor" solicitor, one Rand, who had served her for some years and who "would not be foold with pocket Errors."[77] Justice prevailed in this instance. Her cause triumphed in Trinity term when her right to the tithes of Pirton was recognized and the "unhealing hands" of the king removed. Thus she noted the contradiction between the reality of Charles's conduct and the traditions that ascribed healing powers to him as monarch. She may also have been aware of the argument, made in the fifteenth century, that an illegitimate monarch, as she judged Charles to be, could not heal.[78] Her victory undoubtedly made it easier for her to insist once more, as she had in her earlier tracts, that the Second Coming brought the promise of redemption. The strength of her faith that restitution would occur even allowed her to see, as she rarely admitted, some humor in the arguments she and her opponents had exchanged. Just as Adam had claimed to be "undone by the woman," Eve blamed the serpent, who in turn said "he came but to try her for his part, what would befal was above his reach."[79]

The growing tensions and the renewal of war in 1648 provided Lady Eleanor with additional evidence that the end approached. Her undated tract, *Apocalyps, Chap. 11,* probably comes from that year. Declaring Britain's story to be that told in Revelation 11, she wrote, she said in a handwritten dedication on one copy of the tract, "for dispelling thes Mists of dangerous consequence." The two slain witnesses of her biblical text she equated with Daniel and John, whose prophecies had been ignored and with her two books based on those texts, "Imprinted at *Holland, Anno* 1633 [and] immediately seized on, shrowded in a loose sheet of paper: their embalmd bodies about Doctors Commons, the good hour waiting for their resurrection wounded in that barbarous manner, assaulted by merciless, desperate men, unto a senceless, saltless age sent."[80] Her books of the "Prophets Testimony," "the invincible truth," had been "tearm'd madness"; their "dead bodies trodden underfoot daily, or swept out like weekly Occurrences," the host of newsbooks that had become a part of Civil War Britain.[81] She thus justified and vented the outrage she felt as author about the fate of her work at the same time that she reiterated her message about the coming of Judgment to the kingdom.

Anticipation of "the end of days" permeates *The Lady Eleanor Her Remonstrance to Great Britain,* which also appeared in 1648. Although she gives no indication in its surviving pages that she expected King Charles to be tried and executed, she reasserted her belief in the chronology that would place Judgment in the seventeenth century. She also talked about treason. People now knew "what place and Nation in the latter days to be visited, a people even charged with High Treason by the prophet, *Daniel* (cap. 9) from the King, princes and fathers, to our Judges that have judged us, having all rebelled, their ears (as it were) sealed up, or their understanding blocked." All had committed treason against God.[82]

Lady Eleanor directed another version of her message, *Of the general Great Days Approach* to "*His Excellency Sir* Thomas Fairfax *General*" during that same year, 1648. The content suggests that she may have written the tract in September, when Fairfax was involved in treating with the king at Newport, about the same time that Milton wrote his sonnet to Fairfax. Signing herself on the title page as "The Lady *Eleanor Da: & Do.,*" she headed the first page of text "A. & 0." [Alpha and Omega]. Her tone is that of authority: "*From him which is, and was, and is to come, the alone peace-maker,* his Majesty expressly these the Revelation by his Handmaid interpreted."[83] Here, using many of the same arguments and illustrations as elsewhere, she emphasized the shortness of time remaining and thus the necessity of heeding the prophecy of John and making preparations. While she did not say so explicitly, she may have been warning Fairfax against too ready acceptance of a church settlement that retained too much of the old order.[84]

That September Lady Eleanor also prepared a new edition of *Given to the Elector,* the poem she had originally written in 1633. She added two verses, headed "1648 *September,*" in which she reminded King

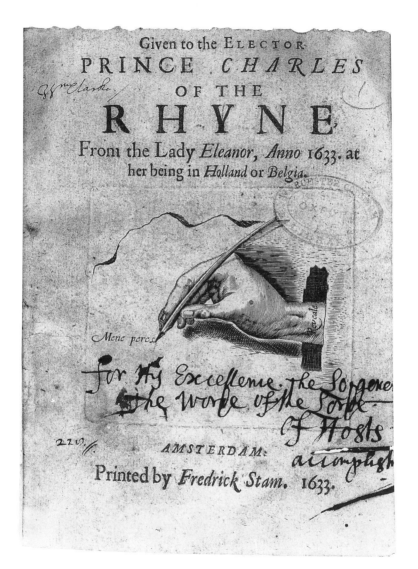

Fig. 3. Lady Eleanor's Message to Lord General Fairfax
1648, title page. Courtesy of the Provost and Fellows of
Worcester College, Oxford.

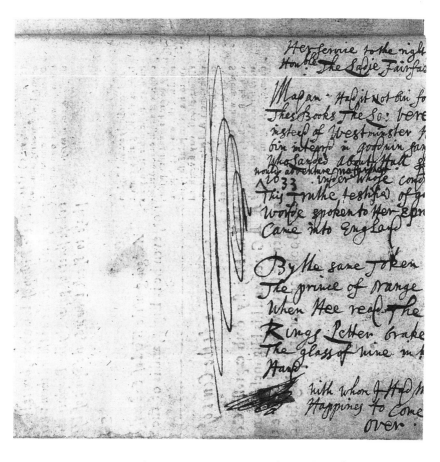

Fig. 4. Lady Eleanor's Message to Lady Fairfax, 1648,
verso of last page.
Courtesy of the Provost and Fellows of
Worcester College, Oxford.

Charles of the fate that had befallen his nephew, the elector, to whom she had first addressed the poem, and of his own imprisonment in 1645. She concluded with a warning,

> *From* Mene Mene, *doubled twice*
> *established even*
> *Parliaments Writs stoln too on thee;*
> *and so take leave, Amen.*[85]

One copy she inscribed "for His Excellence the Lo general the worde of the lorde of Hosts accomplishd."[86] This would seem to be a copy intended for Fairfax, but, in a postscript to a later edition of the tract, she claimed that on the version for the general she had "superscribed, THE ARMIES COMMISSION" and cited Jude 14: *"Behold he cometh with ten thousand of his saints to execute judgement on all"* and that, presumably as she gave him the tract, he had replied, *"But we are not all Saints."*[87] The last page of the copy so "superscribed" has her note to Lady Fairfax about the role that Lord Vere, Lady Fairfax's father, had played in 1633 by assisting Lady Eleanor in getting her books back to Westminster.[88] By February 1652, when she wrote *Restitution of Prophecy,* she seems to have interpreted her encounter with the Lord General in biblical metaphor. She says that when she gave him her tract, he "with Spectacles put on, read by him, That *watch word* superscribed, *Is a Candle to be put under a Bed, etc.* (useless and unsafe)."[89]

In the same edition of *Given to the Elector* that bore her printed postscript about her conversation with Fairfax in the autumn of 1648, Lady Eleanor declared that she then proceeded by "taking up at Whitehal her lodging where attending their coming to be a beholder of the Prophetical Tragedy."[90] Her retrospective claim may have some basis in fact. She addressed the Lord General again in January. In *Her Appeal from the Court to the Camp,* she asked him not to "Despise" prophecy. Relating "what she hath been a sufferer so many years for"—the message Daniel gave to her in 1625—she supported her argument by references to Matthew 24 and 25.[91] King Charles had not heeded those words of scripture. By marrying Henrietta Maria and by allowing her to influence his religious policies, he had made his marriage "a curse instead of a blessing." He, Charles Stuart, had been *"careless"* [the Latin form of Charles was Carolus] and thus "justly turned out of [his] Stewardship."[92]

To warn Fairfax of the consequences if he should be unfaithful in carrying out the mission to which she believed he had been appointed, Lady Eleanor cited one of her favorite examples, Lot's wife, who was turned to a pillar of salt when she violated God's command not to look back upon Sodom as she was leaving.[93] Lady Eleanor did not, however, expressly call for the king's trial and execution in *Appeal from Court to Camp,* and if she, like her contemporary prophet, Elizabeth Poole, actually came before the Council of the Army in late December or early January, she did not say so.[94] Her tract probably appeared before the trial opened and, thus, before the incident that occurred during the roll call of the court when a masked lady in the gallery (later identified as Lady Fairfax) cried out at Lord Fairfax's name, "he had more wit than to be there."[95]

Lady Eleanor took advantage of the opportunity afforded her by the king's trial to address both Charles himself and the court sitting in judgment of him. To the former she presented her own case and, to the latter, that of her late brother, Mervin, earl of Castlehaven. "For King *Charls* Prisoner, these," she wrote to remind him that he was now experiencing what he had ordered for her. *"Upon a reference from you* (1633.) *to these your Commissioners, I being Sentenced by them, as upon Record appears, because took upon me to be a Prophetess; first was Fined, and then to make publique Submission at* Pauls *so many times; that* Jericho *for ever cursed, and farther a close prisoner to continue at your pleasure. So,"* she continued in a new paragraph, *"be it known, you are hereby required to make a publique acknowledgement of such your capital Tresspass and high Offence; and first to:* Ask me forgiveness, *if so be you expect to finde Mercy in this world or the other."* She signed herself simply, "ELEANOR DOUGLAS." By entitling the tract, *The Blasphemous Charge against her,* Lady Eleanor underscored the seriousness of the king's offense. She may have had in mind Mark 3:28–29, "he that shall blaspheme against the Holy Ghost hath never forgiveness but is in danger of eternal damnation." After Charles's execution, most likely early in 1649, she printed her letter to him as a preface to a transcript of her trial before the High Commission in 1633 (to which she referred in that letter).[96] Later in 1649, she published another edition of the tract.[97] Instead of the letter to the king, Lady Eleanor prefaced this edition with a page reciting and explaining the significance of three dates: 28 July 1625, when she heard "the voice from heaven" speak to her; 10 January 1644 [1645], when Laud was executed; and January 1648 [1649], when

King Charles was beheaded.[98] Three final pages, following the transcript from 1633, discussed the chronology that meant that Charles's execution would herald the Day of Judgment.[99]

Lady Eleanor's appeal on her late brother's behalf to the court trying the king, *Crying Charge,* was, like *Blasphemous Charge,* printed in 1649 and likewise probably also intended for actual presentation, although we cannot prove this. In the margin of page 5 in the Folger's copy of the tract, Lady Eleanor wrote, as if to call his attention to what she was saying, the name of Bradshaw, who served as Lord President of the court that tried the king. She may have added this after August 1649, when parliament granted the judge some forfeited estates, including her brother's former home, Fonthill, that following his execution, had passed into the hands of Lord Cottington.[100] In *The Crying Charge,* she showed that court how, with Charles's consent, her brother, "Mervin E. *of* Castlehaven, *Lord* Audeley, *unmercifully was sentenced to death* Easter term 1631 *and in* May *cruelly executed at Tower-Hill, accused falsly of two Crimes, what lewdnes could and malice produce.*"[101] Arguing that the proceedings against Castlehaven had been, in several points, contrary to the law and that he had been in part a victim of scheming papists, "*his house utterly ruined chiefly, because* [he] *had declined Popery,*" she concluded by publishing a copy of his confession of faith to show that he had died a true believer in the Church of England.[102] Her implication was that King Charles should answer for Castlehaven's death at his trial.

Charles Stuart's being brought to Judgment seemed to confirm that Lady Eleanor would not have to wait much longer to see her prophecy fulfilled. If she was not present for the court's sessions in Westminster Hall, she may have been at the Banqueting House on 30 January, when the sentence on Charles was carried out. She was certainly familiar with some of the many contemporary accounts of the events. When she subsequently reissued *Given to the Elector,* she included details about the execution in her gloss and characteristically drew attention to the message of the words themselves. Whether taken in Latin or in English, her parenthetical identification of the ducks involved a pun: "As multitudes grazing at *S. James* of late; which forenoon the Ducks, *viz. Duces, etc.* mounted, or flew over the Scaffold."[103]

Charles's death, like that of Laud four years earlier, seemed to indicate that the Second Coming was at hand. In hopes that the moment for which she had waited so long was about to arrive, Lady Eleanor turned to prophecy with renewed vigor.

CHAPTER 7

The Lamb's Wife

Between the king's death in January 1649 and her own in July 1652 Lady Eleanor published prolifically. When 1649 failed to bring the long-awaited New Jerusalem, she looked to 1650, a "jubilee year." According to Leviticus 25:10–13, the fiftieth year was to be a year of liberation and restoration of possessions. For both her and Britain, a jubilee could inaugurate material as well as spiritual rewnewal. Like the era, she was herself aging. In 1650, she would enter her sixties. Even though her hopes and dreams clashed with reality, and those who came to power in the wake of monarchy seemed unable to replace the discredited regime with a new one, she continued to believe that the "Lamb's Marriage" would be soon.

Lady Eleanor was confident in the weeks and months that followed Charles's execution. That deed and the subsequent abolition of the monarchy removed a central symbol of the weaknesses of patriarchy and, by implication, suggested that the old order was no longer valid. Soon after the king's death, she wrote *The New Jerusalem* where she, *"The Prophetess of the most High, to all Nations and People, etc.,"* proclaimed "instead of a *Charls* the second, . . . a second *Saul*."[1] From Charles, she made the anagram *Rachel* and invoked again the reference to the story of Saul that she had used in the spring of 1643 in *Samsons Legacie*.[2] In looking to Charles, the English, who had been "blest . . . above all Kingdoms" in the reign of Elizabeth, "a virgin" Queen, had erred much as those Israelites who had demanded a king.[3] Charles had relied upon "evil Counsel infused by the Clergy" and had taken as a minister Buckingham, whose assassination made his mother "childless, she author of his unhappiness."[4] How much better it would have been if Archibald Douglas, "the supposed Son of King *James*," older brother of Charles by about a month, had not been deprived of his inheritance. Douglas, though he had burned "no few" of her manuscripts, had received the "first fruits of the Spirit." In the final pages of her tract, she printed letters that Douglas had sent to Dr. James Sibbald. These show that Sir Archibald saw himself as Elijah. He expressed his doubts about kneeling at the communion table and other traditions that seemed to violate the Word of God.[5]

Lady Eleanor demonstrated her sense that the events of the winter of 1648–49, like those of 1644–45, were signs that Judgment would soon follow by reprinting (with additions) several pieces that she had originally written on the earlier occasion. In June she wrote "A Prayer or Letter for the Peoples Conversion and Deliverance from their Distraction" and appended it to her *Prayer or Petition for Peace, November 22, 1644.*[6] Relating how, since her prayer, "Justice her Sword drawn . . . Kings, Princes, Head-Rulers, going to wrack, great Trees felled down, as well as those of lower growth amended," she asked "for a blessing on the Jubiles insuing year," 1650.[7] Five months later, in November, she published a different version of her letter as an appendix to a separate edition of the *Prayer* of 1644.[8] Although in June but not in November she specifically attacked such ills as the theater, she pointed out, with evidence about the appearance of new stars, about the occurrence of the St. Bartholomew's Day and Irish Massacres, and about other events, how chronology supported her prophecy in both instances.

The death of Lucy's eldest son, Henry, of smallpox on 24 June 1649 was another sign that the time of Judgment was approaching. When Henry died, Lady Eleanor felt a personal loss. In addition, she, like her contemporaries, saw the event as a symbol of the tragedy that was occurring in the world itself. Henry was heir to the earl of Huntingdon and about to be married to the daughter of the well-known physician, Sir Theodore Mayerne. "Divers persons of Nobility and Worth," including John Dryden and Andrew Marvel, contributed elegies for him to a volume that was published the following year, and many remarked about his extraordinary intellect and learning.[9] Lady Eleanor was not among the contributors to that tome; they were all male and saw Henry's death from a different perspective than she did. She had lost her own sons, though when they were at a much earlier age, and, just as she had when Henry's younger brother had died in 1639, she mourned for her grandson and for his mother. At that earlier bereavement, Lady Eleanor conveyed her thoughts in a letter to her daughter; this time she commemorated the sad event by publishing a tract. Two versions of her tract, printed in 1649, survive: *Sions Lamentation* and *Zach{arias}* 12. (The latter lacks the title and final pages of the former; otherwise the two are identical.) In writing, Lady Eleanor combined her roles of prophet and grandmother. She had interpreted Henry's "taking his leave of this life," like her own trials and tribulations, as a "warning piece" to England.[10] No one would escape the Day of Judgment. The boy's surname, *Hastings,* itself "declares much more what hastning required" to prepare for what was to come.[11] The text she used came from the second book of Esdras, which, she noted in a critical apposite, was "termed *Apocrypha,*" and thus part of the Bible that the authorities claimed was not to be regarded so highly as the rest (though the books were included in the Authorized Version of 1611). In Esdras, Lady Eleanor found a parallel story of a woman who "after so long time that had a son then nourished by her with so much travel [*sic*], grown up, came to take him a wife, when fell down and died."[12] Thus the Church, *"Sion,* the mother of all delivered into hands of hateful Jaylors a captive." Lucy's loss of her son meant that the "sackcloth and ashes were Hers." Even Ashby house, where the family lived, was in mourning; its towers had fallen in 1648 as a result of military action.[13] Yet Lucy's name, *Lucia,* pointed to the light, to the New Jerusalem that was to come.[14]

In August 1649, Lady Eleanor published yet another edition of the prophecy that had led to her imprisonment in 1633. This time, thanks to the king's execution and the end of the monarchy, her work had the official imprimatur and a new title.[15] Instead of reissuing the tract as *Given to the Elector,* as she had done in 1648, Lady Eleanor or her publisher called the version of 1649 *Strange and Wonderfull Prophesies.* Beginning with the title page itself, this edition advertised her record. It identified her as "The Lady Eleanor Audeley; who is yet alive, and lodgeth in White-Hall." The marginal glosses point out repeatedly how events, even in details such as Charles's not eating the night before his execution and his having a glass of wine the following morning, proved her predictions true. Although she had previously recited the judgments that she had foretold on many occasions, she probably did not write these notes. They were in the third person. Although she referred to herself in that way at times, their style is not hers. The gloss on her 1648 edition of the same text differed from these of 1649 in style as well as content. I have found no clues about who did the writing if she did not. Robert Ibbitson of Smithfield, the printer, handled much of the literature of the Commonwealth.[16]

A second of Lady Eleanor's tracts, which appeared in August but without the imprimatur, was directed to Sir Balthazar Gerbier, who had just announced his plans for an academy for sons of "Noble Families and lovers of Vertue."[17] Although his regulations for his scholars included daily prayer and observation of the sabbath, Gerbier had omitted the Bible, "the *Book of Life,*" from his curriculum.[18] The subjects he listed ranged from ancient and modern languages, writing, history, government, natural philosophy, mathematics, geography, cosmography, music, and drawing to fencing, dancing, and riding. She made no effort to challenge these; nor did she attack Gerbier himself, whose past as a courtier she would have known and found unconscionable for his ties with the Duke of Buckingham and for his sympathy for popery. She argued, instead, that Britain's recent experience and the conduct of people who, rather than heeding the prophecy of the Second Coming, "made their pastime as *Bedlam* for entertaining the *Holy Ghost*" necessitated attention to "the word of life."[19]

In October, Lady Eleanor decided to point out to the Council of State, which had assumed executive authority since the abolition of the monarchy, the work that they must do. Drawing texts from Amos and from several places in the New Testament, she reminded them that there were devils that must be cast out just as Princes Rupert and Maurice, the nephews of Charles I who had come to assist in the royalist cause, had been sent home, Archbishop Laud whose "House at *Lambeth* with its scituation not onely pointed to, but of its denomination borrow'd from the house of *Bethlam,* otherwise called *Bedlam*" had been executed, and the same had happened to *"Great Britains* last King, or *Englands* late Tyrant, into whom many Devils were entred from several parts."[20]

Lady Eleanor's many publications during 1649 testify to her own energy at the time, to her conviction that the moment for which she had been waiting was approaching, and to her persistence despite the Printing Act of that September, which imposed severe restrictions upon the press.[21] In November, when she issued additional revisions of her prayer for peace, she may also have reprinted *Discovery* and *Sign* with "some words of addition."[22] Because we have only the 1649 editions, we cannot identify what changes, apart from references to events between 1644 and 1649, she may have made in the earlier versions. For her text, she took the story of Hezekiah and Manasseh (2 Kings 20–21, 2 Chronicles 33, and Isaiah 39), with whom she identified James and Charles respectively. Charles's allowance of idolatry, in particular, was responsible for his own fate and the troubles of the kingdom.

Lady Eleanor turned her attention to her own role in bearing the prophecy of the Second Coming in *The Everlasting Gospel,* which, she claimed on the title page, was "Printed in the Year of our Redemption, *Decem.* 1649." She showed how the events of Charles's reign, beginning with her own experience on 28 July 1625, fit the gospel's words and how years could be added to the nineteen that she had originally predicted would precede Judgment.[23] Because of the plague that summer of 1625, "the Term [was] kept at *Reding,* County of *Berks,* other Courts at *Maidenhead* Town, the Parliament posting to *Oxford,* doing all homage to this *New born BABE,*" just as wise men from the East and others had flocked to see the Christ Child.[24] She continued the parallel through her hearing before the High Commission in 1633, the burning of her prophecy, her imprisonment, and the ensuing war. The trials and tribulations of Britain demonstrated the truth of her words. "Thou *Bedlam*-House, too little the Thousandeth part to contain of them distracted since her coming."[25]

Although Lady Eleanor focused most of her attention upon prophecy, she, because of her concern about preparation for the Second Coming, also paid heed to matters of doctrine and practice. In 1649, she published *The New Proclamation,* a letter that Lucy wrote her in answer to her question about the interpretation of Philippians 2:6, a passage about the relationship of God, Christ, and Holy Spirit. The proliferation of religious groups and the debates about how much toleration should be allowed had brought the issue of belief in the Trinity to the fore. Some advocates of liberty of conscience wanted to restrict freedom to Trinitarians and thus exclude the Socinians. Lucy, whose education extended beyond her mother's own very considerable learning, could examine the Greek text of Philippians 2:6 as well as its English translation and provide Lady Eleanor with the scholarly argument for "Trinity in Unity, and Unity in Trinity."[26] Lady Eleanor accepted and published her daughter's statement without comment of her own in yet another testimony to the trust between them. As we shall see, she had little enthusiasm for liberty of conscience.

The juxtaposition of the old and the new served as Lady Eleanor's theme for *Bill of Excommunication,* which she dated "From *White-Hall, fatal* 30 *of January, Jubile*" [1650], the first anniversary of Charles's execution. The tract's subtitle explained its purpose: *For abolishing henceforth the Sabbath Called Sunday or Firstday.* Relying upon the Book of Revelation for her text, she announced that the work contained three "Articles or Arguments": the renewal of prophecy, the replacement of the old sabbath (Sunday) with a new one, and the Second Coming.[27] In the forty pages of the tract, she wrote more fully about topics that she had previously discussed. Having some years earlier called for a new sabbath on Monday, she specified here that she had Monday in mind because it was Moon Day, a day associated with the "coelestial virgin Bride." She probably knew, although she did not mention it, that classical mythology's Artemis (Diana) was goddess of both virginity and the moon. The first day of the old week would become the last of the new week, just as "Jesus CHR:" was "a greater then *Cesar* slain then, or CH:R:[Charles R.] either of *Britains* three Isles, stiled Defenders or Saviors, etc. whose Coronations father and son both about *Easter, J*[ames], and *C*[harles] those first and last" of the Stuart kings.[28] Instead of "Maygames and Wakes . . . Heathen exercises" upon the sabbath, and instead of having Bibles with "presumptious prefaces annext" to allow bible reading once a week, except the Book of Revelation and other parts "such as may be best spared," the new order would nourish the spirit of prophecy and true religion.[29] To elaborate upon her argument, she discussed the messages to the angels of the seven churches (Revelation 2–3) and then proceeded, as she put it, to rephrase them "after the vulgar strain." Thus, Westminster Abbey, which she found lacking real commitment to its purpose, received her interpretation of the message to the angel of the church of Ephesus; those imprisoned in the Gatehouse, as she had been, "For the Holy Ghosts cause" that for the church of Smyrna to fear not; Westminster Hall, the seat of the courts of justice, that for Pergamos, a warning to use justice for the right cause; St. Peter's Cornhill, the "Cities Church," that for Thyatira to look to immorality around them; Whitehall Chapel, where Hugh Peters had preached to the court trying the king on 28 January 1649, that for Sardis to be watchful. Parliament itself received the message for Philadelphia, which contained a version of her family's motto, *"Je le tien"* and a statement, *"Eli-Amor vincet,"* in which she associated her name with that of Elias, God

(Eloi) and the City of God (Elia).[30] That message expressing confidence in Parliament's achievement and in the role it should continue to play in preparations for the Second Coming says much about Lady Eleanor's own political convictions. The final addressee she selected also expresses her views. St. Paul's, where the ecclesiastical courts often sat and where "Church-yard Drapers" conducting their business seemed to take priority over religion, received the message for Laodicea to buy *"white rayment* that the filthiness of their nakedness appear not."[31]

As the spring of the jubilee year, 1650, approached and Parliament debated whether they should continue their work of preparation for a new order or pass that responsibility on to a new body, Lady Eleanor once more outlined her views about Judgment. She began *Arraignment,* published at Lent 1650, "And who should be greatest or bear the sway; this Lesson appointed for the present, occasioned upon that dispute." Warning that the power of the army or its generals was nothing compared to that of God, "the Omnipotent General, Lord of Hosts," she paraphrased the words of Matthew 16:26 ("For what is a man profited, if he shall gain the whole world and lose his own soul?") to fit the contemporary example of Ferdinando Lord Fairfax, father of the Lord General, who had died 14 March 1648 as a result of a "festered Toe" from an injury to "a Corn [which] turned to a Gangren[e]." Rather "Then lose a foot, [he had] suffered his whole body to perish."[32]

Lady Eleanor reiterated her theme when she published *Appearance* sometime after July 1650. She admonished Parliament about their pretensions and contrasted their claims to authority with her own prophetic voice. "The Spirit after absent so long," was "greater then the Conqueror, Parliaments Prerogative not exempted." Unlike the Spirit, "those Heathen Potentates, [were] but like to Potters brittle Vessels broken in pieces, scattered, suddenly a Printers Press like."[33] On the other hand, she declared, with the same verse that she had used in proclaiming the futility of her own imprisonment in the Gatehouse in 1633, "hell gates shall not prevail against her" (Matthew 16:18). The pronouns with which she described the "prophetical everlasting Order" that the Spirit would introduce were feminine. She, herself, represented that Spirit who was the *"Queen of Peace,* or She-councellor." Thus, she wrote, *"She whose Throne heaven, earth her footstool from the uncreated,* saying, *I am A. and O. first and last, both beginning and ending, by whom all things were done: Not without her anything done or made."*[34] Her own statement was, "I am *A.* and *O. alias, Da:* and *Do:"* that is

Davies and Douglas, "by her first and last marriage."[35] Her family
offered other associations with the Book of Revelation through the
meaning of their titles. As the daughter of Baron Audeley or *"Oldfield,
in the Saxon* Tongue," she could claim to be part of the beginning of
Kings and House of Lords as well as part of their ending in her own
era. Touchet, her father's name, came from France; his title,
Castlehaven, from Ireland; Douglas, her second husband's name, from
Scotland; and her family's motto, *"Je le tien"* from the Book of Revelation itself.[36] Heaven became "her Joynture place," a place to which
her route was difficult just as was that for the lands she claimed as
jointure. This time equating Bethlehem with Berkshire rather than
Bedlam, she retold once more the story of her experience that early
morning in July 1625, her subsequent loss of both Englefield and
Pirton, the judgments that ensued, including one that had followed
her own visionary experience on the night of 2 April 1647.[37] The most
recent judgment had occurred when fire ravaged Holborn and "other
parts of the City" in July 1650, the very "same week she [was] cast
out of her lawful possession of *Englefield,* by that Counties Sheriff."[38]

In describing this loss of Englefield in *Appearance,* Lady Eleanor once
again showed how much that estate meant to her, even though she
apparently spent little time there. Elias Ashmole, who had some interest in prophecy and some contact with the Welsh prophet, Arise Evans,
made no reference to her in connection with his visits there during the
1640s.[39] Her reference to her dispossession from Englefield in the
summer of 1650 may also have served to represent the nation's loss of
the leadership of Fairfax, who, rather than agree to the invasion of
Scotland, resigned his position in June and was replaced by Cromwell.
Little evidence survives to corroborate her remarks in the tract, where
she said Berkshire's sheriff, who maintained he had power by the
"Committees Order," had come prepared to break down the doors.[40]
Records of the Committee for Compounding dated 2 July 1650 authorized the execution of a parliamentary order of the preceding September
to grant Englefield to Sir Thomas Jervois, who claimed that the Marquis of Winchester was indebted to him.[41] Lady Eleanor may have
contributed to her own dispossession by not paying her assessments
and/or otherwise antagonizing those in authority. She had apparently
not regained possession by the time she died two years later. Two days
after her death, the Committee for Compounding's proceedings show
an appeal by one Thomas Aldridge for two-thirds of a farm in

Englefield. Though the farm had been sequestered from Henry Englefield, Aldridge found his claims contested by those of Jervois, who said that it had been the Marquess of Winchester's.[42]

At the beginning of September, Lady Eleanor apparently was once again a prisoner. She dated *Before the Lords Second Coming* from the "Queens Bench," 2 September [1650]. Her belief in her role probably led her to give that name to the prison that had been known since Charles's execution as the Upper Bench. (It would have been the Queen's Bench in Elizabeth's reign, but would have been the King's Bench when Lady Eleanor was held there in 1648.) On the copy of the tract that Thomason acquired, she added a number of marginal notes. At the tract's conclusion, beside the date and place, she signed it with her own hand, "the Lambs wife," a designation used by other prophets and one that explicitly stated her own earlier assertions.[43] Thus she claimed for herself a marriage that, in contrast to the shortcomings in hers with Davis and later with Douglas, would create the healing power of the New Jerusalem. Evidence, much of which she had previously cited, demonstrated that the moment of the Second Coming would be soon. Her prophecies, she noted though "not by way of ostentation or self-ends," were "extant in several Courts since *an.* 1633."[44] In addition to the "festered wounds" imposed upon the nation by war, even the "wandring stars" announced the "inquity" of the "horrible Age."[45] The "Ignorance" of those who claimed to practice the "Trade called *Religion*" led them to abuse their "Tolleration or Liberty of conscience" to blaspheme against the Holy Ghost.[46] The witnesses (Revelation 11:3) who testified to the Second Coming had been "slain," so "Prophecies Lamp [was] extinguisht."[47] In the margin, she named those witnesses whom she sometimes identified as her own books and sometimes as Daniel and John, as the two English ambassadors, Dorislaus and Ascham, who had been killed abroad that summer. Cromwell's victory over the Scots at Dunbar on 3 September 1650, the day after she had dated *Before the Lords Second Coming,* provided the inspiration for yet another of her marginal notes.[48] In the same manner, she also recorded the burial, on 8 September, of the Lady Elizabeth, daughter of the late King Charles and said that she gave *Before the Lords Second Coming* to Parliament "two dayes afore ye Scotes Blowe" and that it was read 18 December, a claim that the *Commons Journal* does not confirm.

Many of the themes Lady Eleanor addressed in *Before the Lords Second*

Coming she took up again in *Elijah the Tishbite's Supplication,* which she dated October 1650.[49] Her own troubled widowhood gave the story of Elijah and the widow of Zarephath special meaning for her.[50] Just as Elijah had pleaded with God to show his presence, so she pleaded for action in the face of forces that were "arm'd to re-edifie *Babel.*" The danger from popery may have abated, but now a new enemy arose in the forces that had obtained permission to publish *"Cum privilegio"* the "Blasphemous" Koran.[51] Lady Eleanor's choice of Elijah for her model and the tone of her plea suggests that she was becoming discouraged as the months of the jubilee year passed without indication that the moment she had so long hoped for would arrive and without those in power making adequate preparations. Yet, on Thomason's copy of *Elijah the Tishbite,* she once again signed herself as the Lamb's wife.

Lady Eleanor turned to a more specific illustration of the justice that comes to those who do wrong in *The Lady Eleanor Douglas, dowager, her jubiles Plea or Appeal,* dated December 1650. Paralleling the case of the Stuart family and the ills that befell them was that of Sir John Stawell, a Somerset gentleman brought to trial for treason in July 1650.[52] Both families were reaping the punishments due those who had forsaken one wife for another. Although society penalized the women, its double standard wrongly allowed the men to escape the consequences of their misdeeds. Divine justice was rectifying what men overlooked. Charles Stuart's father, King James, had "two Wives, lived with both; the first, she Daughter of one Sir *Peter Yong:* His Son *Charls* about a Moneth yonger then Sir *Archibald Douglas* deceased."[53] The fates of James's children illustrated the judgment upon him, and that of Stawell the consequences of his grandfather's having married again after divorcing a wife found guilty of adultery, a case that attracted considerable attention in the Elizabethan era.[54] In addition to her personal tie with Douglas, her late husband, Lady Eleanor had a connection with Stawell, who was her sister Elizabeth's son and the holder of the Somerset manor of Aller that had formerly belonged to Sir John Davies.[55] She took advantage of the sequestration of Stawell's lands to prepare a petition to the House of Commons with a claim similar in tone to those she made for Englefield and Pirton. She maintained that she should have Aller since Stawell had not honored the promise he made to her, when he bought that estate, that he would give her "satisfaction" for her "right and title of dower in the . . . manor."[56] Here again, Lady Eleanor made an issue of the injustices that the law and patriarchal society imposed on women. She had been dependent upon Stawell's word and had to wait for her remedy until war gave her an opportunity to petition.

At about the same time that Lady Eleanor wrote the tract about the families of Stawell and Stuart, she was quarrelling with Gerrard Winstanley over what she believed was his attempt to take fiscal advantage of her. Like Lady Eleanor, Winstanley filled his prolific writings with metaphors and drew heavily from the Bible, but, instead of expecting the apocalyptic millenium as she did, he looked for the establishment of an ideal society. Rather than emphasizing his role as a prophet, he turned his attention to the poverty and suffering he saw around him. While she may have found some aspects of Winstanley's radical Christianity and concern about preparation for a new order appealing and may have sympathized with him in his conflicts with those in authority, Lady Eleanor may, at the same time, have had reservations about his beliefs and efforts to put them into practice. Contrasting with the desire for economic justice that he expressed in his tracts was Winstanley's reputation for "being dishonest and unprincipled" in financial dealings.[57] His attempt to establish a commune on St. George's Hill in Surrey in April 1649 probably troubled her aristocratic interests in property and his patriarchalism her spiritual feminism. Their differing agenda and personalities led to a bitter exchange.[58]

Winstanley became the target of Lady Eleanor's anger when he approached her in December 1650 about pay for those of his men who had helped with the harvest and had done other work for her at Pirton. When she received his detailed accounts of what was due, she left London for Pirton, where she confronted him in the barn and told him she was the prophetess Melchisedecke whom she had identified with the Queen of Peace in a marginal note in *Appearance*.[59] In response, Winstanley attacked her method of doing business. "What's the reason that divers men calle upon you for money, which you truly owe them, and you either putt them of[f] by long delays, or els makes them spend 10 tymes more to it in suites of law, whereas you have estate sufficient that you might pay all?" Her conduct, he thought, was contrary to that appropriate for the prophetess she claimed to be. Across his letter she wrote, "Hee is mistakne." She challenged his calculation of the work completed and then cited one of the biblical texts she frequently used, Matthew 25:19 and 26, "Affter Long time the Lord of thos servants commeth and reckoneth with Them" and "Lord know thou art a Hard Man and reapest Where Thou hast not sowne, and gatherest where thou hast not strawed."[60]

In listing all he had done for Lady Eleanor, Winstanley claimed to have gotten "the sequestracon taken" off her estate.[61] This was probably the judgment Nathaniel Ward had obtained against her as a result of his suit for repayment of £40, which she had originally borrowed from him in November 1645. In an answer dated 26 June 1651, Ward mentioned that some corn and goods of hers had been seized the preceding Michaelmas in that connection.[62] That seizure probably led Lady Eleanor, describing herself as being of Pirton, to file a complaint in Chancery against Ward on 2 November 1650, a month before Winstanley wrote his angry reproach to her. Among the issues in the dispute were the terms by which she had conferred upon Ward's brother-in-law, Nicholas East, the vicarage of Ickleford, which was among the rights of the manor and rectory of Pirton.[63] The commissioners who made the survey of church lands in 1650 had reported that "the Lady Ellenor Douglas of Purton parsonage receiveth all the tythes and proffittes ariseinge in the sayed parish" and that she had "time out of minde mainteyned a preachinge minister [there] . . . untill about six moneths last past but is at present destitute."[64] This evidence, which ignored the years during which the Poultons held the manor and rectory and contradicted the testimony presented about collection of the tythes in previous litigation, sounds very much as if it comes directly from Lady Eleanor herself.[65] She frequently claimed to be "destitute."

In 1651, the summer after her angry exchange with Winstanley, Lady Eleanor found herself pressed for payment of the half-tax for Pirton. According to the report her servant, Eleanor Hartley, sent to John Rand the following April, when the justices heard the matter, Lady Eleanor had refused on the grounds that parliament had more than she did. The authorities responded to this by seeking to interrupt her tithes. The reply her servants gave the justices was one Lady Eleanor might easily have made herself had she been present. They repeated their earlier defense that "whom soe ever should oppos my lady was free to take curse at the common law." Hartley added that she had pointed out that "my lady was other taxed."[66]

Even before Lady Eleanor faced proceedings stemming from her refusal to pay the half-tax for Pirton, she was tired of the continuing battles about money, property, and her prophetic claims. At Easter

1651, she vented some of her frustration in a tract, *Hells Destruction,* where she recited the events of her imprisonment in July 1646 by virtue of a warrant from the Lord Mayor that got her name wrong and thus left her "bereft both of her good Name and Liberty."[67] Presenting evidence from the Bible about the importance of names, she emphasized the difference between the writ of the Lord Mayor, which was "slime" or "Brick-bats" compared to the "Morter" or "Stone" of Holy Writ.[68] The latter's promise of redemption gave Lady Eleanor hope. She had seen the judgments that by Easter 1651, when she was writing, had fallen upon the Lord Mayor and others responsible for her "false Imprisonment."[69] She knew the message to the angel of the church of Smyrna (Revelation 2:10) and quoted it on her title page, *"Behold, the Devil shall cast some of you into Prison, that you may be tryed; and you shall have tribulation ten days* etc."[70] Springtime itself, with its annual and "infallible Messengers of Summers approach," made her especially aware of the meaning of Easter and intensified her anticipation of the Second Coming, but, in *Hells Destruction,* she expressed herself in a more serious tone than she had in her Easter writings of earlier years.[71]

Prophecy was Lady Eleanor's principal concern when she wrote *Of Times and Seasons Their Mystery,* which she dated 24 June, the day of St. John the Baptist, 1651.[72] Using Daniel 2:20–21 as her text, and, in accord with her argument in *Mystery of General Redemption,* changing the words from "for ever and ever" to "for Ages and Ages," she emphasized, as she had in *Hells Destruction,* how the power of God was of a different order than that of humans. It involved spirit as well as flesh. *"Miracles* and *Gifts of Tongues* [were] not Equivalent" to the divine *"breath of life."*[73] She argued, as she often did, by a multitude of images, many of which were associated with water, and by mixing together biblical, astrological, personal, and historical references. The time mentioned in the Book of Revelation for the Second Coming was at hand; the *"woman clothed or arrayed with the Sun, inthroned above the Moon, Crowned with twelve Stars"* (Revelation 12:1) would come. Like a prisoner, and, as Lady Eleanor herself had in 1633, the woman would "receive their judgement [and] thence even to be carried away by water." Michael, rather than Charles I (as Rubens had painted him), would take the role of St. George "this *Nations* Patron," and she, not the Henrietta Maria of Rubens' work, would represent England. By "rescuing a *Lady* from a *Monster,"* St. George would bring about change.[74]

"The Golden Zodiaks signs" (the twelve stars crowning the woman) themselves proclaimed this. Virgo, the sign of the virgin, came in September, just before Michaelmas, the time or season of "that skirmish in *Heaven*" when "the late *Luciferian Order*" would succumb like "those faln Stars; with Courts stiled, *Star-Chamber* and *High Commission*," the courts abolished in the early months of the Long Parliament.[75]

Before autumn, Lady Eleanor published another tract. *Serpents Excommunication,* in verse form, began with a subtitle, *"Coeli Jubilate* etc. *July, Anno* 1651. Their Sealed Pardon." Here again she contrasted divine Judgment with that the serpents had exercised on earth. The images appropriate to her theme—juries, bail, dispossession, leases, abuse of trust—also applied to her own legal battles over Pirton, which were probably much in her mind that July. At the conclusion of her poem, she printed a brief tribute to her written by M. Tuke, who described himself as a kinsman. Compared to her poetry, Tuke found that of the muses unappealing. *"Your Brass Doth far my* Caducaean Staff *surpass. As Arch-Types do Types: Whilest I look on Your* Streams, I *loath the Lake o* Helicon."[76] Lady Eleanor followed with some lines of praise for him and for his grandfather, Brian Tuke, who had served King Henry VIII and whose daughter was her own great grandmother.[77]

For Lady Eleanor, as for many of her contemporaries, Cromwell's victory over Charles II and the Scots at the Battle of Worcester on 3 September 1651 seemed to confirm that the forces of the antichrist would be conquered. At the end of October, she published a letter to Cromwell in which she offered *The Benediction From the A:lmighty O:mnipotent.* Although she did not here spell out, as she did on some occasions, the associations of *A* and *O* with her own heritage (Audeley and Oldfield) or with alpha and omega of the Book of Revelation, she referred to the letters as being of *"no mean Latitude"* and told Cromwell that by using *"The Flaming Sword* for expelling the Man" (Charles II), he *"Crowns with no Inferior Honor"* his name.[78] From that name O: Cromwell, she made, by replacing the C with an H, an anagram, "Howl Rome" (Jeremiah 25:34). His initials, O. C., which were also the first two letters of the Month of October, represented the eyes and the horns of the lamb (Revelation 5) and the sun and the moon that were, according to Acts 2, to be signs of the arrival of the age that Joel had predicted when sons and daughters would prophesy.

That victory over the royalists at Worcester may have encouraged Lady Eleanor to issue a new edition of her account of her appearance before the High Commission in 1633. The basic text was from her transcript of the proceedings, the same text she had published in 1649. Instead of continuing to call it *The Blasphemous Charge against Her,* she made it *The Dragons Blasphemous Charge against Her,* cited Isaiah 63 in addition to Matthew 10 on the title page, and added marginal glosses.[79] Some of the glosses were those she had made by hand on the Folger copy of her 1649 publication, but others referred to developments since that time.[80] On the prefatory page (2), where she listed important events, she noted beside the account of her experience on 28 July 1625 at Englefield, which she referred to as the field of the Angels on many occasions, "Since when English, The Angelical Language Its Prerogative Witness. All Writs, Reports, Judgements, etc. Enacted [November 1650] to be Printed in the English Tongue onely."[81]

By Christmas 1651 Lady Eleanor was once again in prison, this time in the Fleet where, between Christmas and Candlemas, she composed *Restitution of Prophecy.*[82] Into the tract's preface and fifty-two pages of text she packed even more images than usual and denounced the individuals and evils that she had long sought to expose and eradicate with special vehemence. Although she did not reveal the cause of this imprisonment, her confinement may account for the strength of feeling she conveyed in the tract. She also may too have sensed that she had only a few more months to live.

In *Restitution of Prophecy,* Lady Eleanor reexamined many of the issues and concerns she had treated in earlier works and tied together more comprehensively and more explicitly her own story with that of Britain. In a handwritten note at the beginning of the Folger copy of her tract she announced that she would be telling the history of Charles I's reign, which would conclude with his "arraignment." She contrasted the treatment accorded her and her "babes" with what they should have received. Unable to have her books *"licensed* or *fathered,"* she was sending them forth "in these plain *Swathe-bands."* Her experience paralleled that of the Virgin Mary at the birth of Christ; the Fleet Prison was her Stable. Its "darksom *grates close"* where "famished . . . no few" represented the suffering of "the true *Narrow way . . . that leads to life"* like the "Straits of the *Virgins-Womb."* She contrasted the narrow way with the *"Broad-way, Ebrieties* leading to destruction," a reference that also named Broadway, the servant of her late brother whose fate she mentioned later in the tract.[83]

In the body of *Restitution of Prophecy* Lady Eleanor wove together Charles I's life both with the biblical stories that led to the Second Coming and with her brother's trial and execution. Charles, in permitting the earl of Castlehaven's death, paved the way for his own subsequent judgment. Lady Eleanor also identified her sister-in-law, Anne Stanley, Lady Castlehaven, and Anne's mother, the Dowager Countess of Derby, with Henrietta Maria, and, as she had previously, called all three Jezebel, "more Mother *Jezebels* then one," and also the whore of Babylon.[84] By condemning these women as Jezebels, Lady Eleanor did not need to defend them as she did women whom she saw as victims of men. She was thus free to argue in her brother's behalf. Connecting her sister-in-law and the Dowager Countess of Derby even more closely with Jezebel, who was consumed by the dogs, and with the whore of Babylon, who was carried by the scarlet Beast, was the *"Red Deer* that Scarlet *Beast"* in the coat of arms of Derby and Strange. Even England itself had fallen to the Beast in exchanging its name *"Anglia* [the land of angels] for *Brute"* [Great Britain]. London, "of old called *TROY"* had become Babylon, and drinking, gaming, abuse of the sabbath, and other evils spread through the city.[85] Lady Eleanor illustrated her points with specific examples. One of these was the case of Sir Kenelm Digby, who, despite his popish religion, associations with the Queen, and alleged responsibility for his wife's sudden death in May 1633 by forcing her to drink "viper wine," had escaped the fate of Mervin, earl of Castlehaven.[86] The severe *"Thunder-claps . . .* and *Lightnings"* that occurred on 23 August 1651 impressed Lady Eleanor as they did Ralph Josselin, who noted in his diary on that occasion that he thought the Biblical texts of Joel 3:16 and Revelation 11 were being "fulfilled."[87]

For her principal text in *Restitution of Prophecy*, Lady Eleanor cited Matthew 25, whose number and text both fit her purposes. Charles's reign had begun in 1625 when he was twenty-five years old. That same year she heard Daniel's message; it was on the twenty-fifth day of the month that the Virgin Mary gave birth; and 1625 was also *"a Jubiles moiety,* Five times five."[88] She had used the parables of the wise and foolish virgins and the talents in Matthew 25 many times previously. Charles and his associates were like the foolish virgins or the servant who hid the master's talent in the earth. Even the earl of Strafford, "no *shallow Brain-piece,"* had paid for his misdeeds with his execution in 1641.[89] So too had Laud, whose wrongs she had enumerated time and time again. His title, *Canterbury*, which would have meant that he would be addressed as "Your Grace," gave her an opportunity to talk of *"Grace Buried"* and to note that the altar hanging at Lichfield that she and he had quarreled about had to be buried in the *"Dunghil"* when parliamentary forces invaded that city.[90]

In contrast to those who ignored or defied God's will, Lady Eleanor had taken pains to announce her message. She recounted her experiences in making presentations to Lord General Fairfax after she had despaired of help from King Charles.[91] She was *"the Lady Ele:,"* "the elect Lady" to whom John addressed his epistle, the last of the old prophets, Elias, A[lpha] and O[mega], and the Virgin whose Purification (Candlemas) preceded the new era.[92] Unlike Prynne, who, in *Histrio Mastix,* had condemned Candlemas for pagan Roman origins, Lady Eleanor, even in 1652, seemed not to challenge the traditional holidays of the Anglican calendar.[93]

By Good Friday 1652 when her next tract, *Tobit's Book,* appeared, Lady Eleanor had been released from the Fleet. Freedom allowed her to replace the multitude of individuals and conditions which she had denounced in *Restitution of Prophecy* with hope. The season itself and the promise of Easter that had often before inspired her writing probably also played a part in shaping *Tobits Book,* which she subtitled *A Lesson Appointed for Lent.* For her text she went to the tale from the Book of Tobit (in the Apocrypha), where the Angel chased away the Evil Spirit and, thanks to a fish, Tobit's sight was restored.[94] It was, like the tract she wrote during the same season in 1645, a tale of the "bride's preparation."

In the spring of 1652, Lady Eleanor, in her sixty-second year, may have been thinking about her personal preparations for death in addition to the nation's preparations for Judgment. *Bethlehem, Signifying The House of Bread: or War,* her final extant tract, appeared in June 1652, shortly before her death in early July. In that tract, she addressed herself to *"the healing of the present Evil"* and she talked more explicitly than anytime previously about what she had done at Lichfield in 1636, the *"Panick Terror"* of the authorities, and her subsequent confinement to Bedlam (Bethlehem Hospital).[95] Once again, she drew from the parable of the talents to talk about burial in many instances, including the burial of the truth, her burial in prison, and the subsequent burial of the altar hanging during the war.[96] In her concluding paragraphs, Lady Eleanor cited Acts 3 and offered what she may have realized would be a valedictory.

Prophets howsoever buried in the *Land of Oblivion:* which *Nations,* as much to say, avenge her shall of her Adversary thus supported: *My hand shall hold him fast, and my arm shall strengthen him, nor gates of Hell shall not prevail against her: O Hell or Fleet-Prison* (to wit, *where is thy Victory* now)?[97]

Thus, Lady Eleanor proceeded from the text of Acts to two other texts that had special meaning for her, Revelation 2:25, which she associated with her family's motto, *Je le tien,* hold fast till I come, and Matthew 16:18, Christ's message that the gates of Hell should not prevail against the Church.

Apart from these tracts, little remains to tell us about Lady Eleanor's final days. The book of "Disbursements from Loughborough Rents [1651–]1652," among the Hastings Manuscripts, shows that she and Lucy remained in touch. On 10 April Lucy sent her mother £10. In other entries, we learn of salmon or capon pies carried to London for "Lady Eleanor Douglas." The last entry that mentions Lady Eleanor is that of 3 June, when the carrier reported paying her "as my Lady order" £4.26.0 "to buye me lord Hastings," Lucy's son, Lady Eleanor's grandson, a coat.[98]

Lady Eleanor died on 5 July 1652 in London.[99] She was buried near Sir John Davies in St. Martin's-in-the-Fields with the epitaph Lucy prepared.

Who her illustrious birth And spirit equal to her race With Christian mildness tempered. Learned above her sex, Meek below her rank, Than most people greater Because more humble, In eminent beauty She possessed a lofty mind, In pleasing affability, singular modesty: In a woman's body a man's spirit, In most adverse circumstances a serene mind, In a wicked age unshaken piety and uprightness. Not for her did Luxury relax her strong soul, or Poverty narrow it: but each lot with equal countenance And mind, she not only took but ruled. Nay she was full of God to which fulness Neither a smiling world could have added, Nor from it a frowning world have taken away. Now for a long time sufficiently breathing of God and aspiring above, of her own And the Commonwealth's fate divining beforehand, And most sure of Eternal Salvation With a mighty and huge ardour into her Beloved Saviour's breast, she breathed forth her soul washed in His own blood. Taken away from things human she put on immortality on the fifth of July in the year of Salvation, 1652. Ps. 16. 9. My flesh also dwells securely because Thou wilt not leave my soul in the sepulchre.[100]

Exasperating to those who crossed her, Lady Eleanor nevertheless won the affection of those who knew her best. Her ill-paid servants, her daughter Lucy, and her grandchildren sensed an affection that made them willing to tolerate her demands and eccentricities. Lucy's attentiveness to her mother's needs went beyond the token measures that might be expected from a dutiful daughter. She attempted to preserve copies of the tracts and also devoted herself to ensuring that history would give Lady Eleanor proper recognition. Evidence among the Hastings manuscripts ties Lucy both indirectly and directly with the tribute to her mother in the fifth (1670) edition of Baker's *Chronicle of the Kings of England*. The third (1660) and fourth (1665) editions of the *Chronicle* had mentioned "the Lady Davies" briefly in the account of 1628. She "was reputed a great Prophetess" and had foretold the Duke of Buckingham's death. But in the fifth edition, she appeared in connection with her own death in 1652. The editor noted that, although she had predicted the Duke of Buckingham's murder and had been the "subject of critical discourse and censure among the wits of those times," DuMoulin's "elegant pen" showed how events proved that she had received a special gift of "divine knowledge."[101] Peter DuMoulin, a divine and tutor to the Boyles, earls of Cork, had written to Lucy in September 1654, to thank her for favorably receiving his verses and for sending him some of her own poetry.[102] For him, like Lucy, Lady Eleanor was a woman of learning and spirit rather than one whose beliefs and conduct were eccentric. But even this apparently did not satisfy Lucy, who vainly hoped that Roger L'Estrange would see that the text was revised in the next edition of the chronicle.[103] Over the centuries since, very few of those who have written about Lady Eleanor have been as kind as DuMoulin. Most have dismissed her prophetic claims as mad or fanatical, but, to Lucy, Lady Eleanor was a woman who was a prophet.

Conclusion

Lady Eleanor claimed power for herself and for her sex when she took up prophecy in 1625. She justified her rebellion against the established order in family and society on the very grounds that were the foundation for that order—religion. To prove the authenticity of her interpretation of both her own history and Britain's, she cited her visionary experience and the biblical tradition that was its source. Having been chosen to receive Daniel's command and the knowledge about the date for Judgment and the Second Coming, she was no longer subject to the constraints that applied to other women, whether they were noble or low-born, rich or poor. She was not bound in the position of the dependent wife struggling to satisfy her husband or the overburdened mother agonizing over a handicapped or dying child. Through her prolific writings she asserted a new identity that was free of the defects that her own had had. She made her father "first" instead of rather third-rate among the barons. As a prophet, she assumed the life-giving creative qualities of the Virgin and the Bride, the Lamb's Wife. Her books were a "plaister" that would heal the wounds inflicted upon the world by the Roman Whore of Babylon, just as the Virgin Mary's baby had brought salvation for those who suffered the consequences of Eve's wrongdoing. Unlike the male authors of most history, she emphasized women who made a difference, whether for good or ill.

By identifying herself with Britain and with the godly, Lady Eleanor combined the personal and political in her prophecies. She discussed her own experience but, at the same time, went beyond that to deliver a message that had general applicability. Contemporaries who were uneasy about a woman who published her writings found the content of Lady Eleanor's tracts disturbing. In asserting herself, she added to the threat that her message otherwise seemed to pose and laid herself open to the charge that she was mad.

Lady Eleanor reordered her world through her words. The universe that she constructed in her tracts offered her intellectual satisfaction and gave her power over situations that otherwise seemed impossible to affect. Employing a multitude of stylistic and literary devices from the dominant culture of the day to present the arguments that she took from well-known biblical texts and historical examples, she produced a devastating critique of the way Charles I and his ministers were using their authority. Their irrational, ungodly, and erroneous conduct was bringing divine wrath upon Britain, and the consequences would be catastrophic.

But Lady Eleanor was not merely a prophet of doom. With the promise of general redemption, she held forth the vision of a New Order. Those who had been deprived would win restitution of what they had lost; injustices would be rectified; the gospel would reign. She implied that life after the Second Coming would be very different from what had preceded it, and, indeed, her ideas pushed to their logical conclusions would significantly change the world she knew. Countering the potentially radical content of her prophecies was her apparent acceptance of existing institutions. She identified herself in terms of traditional signs of status, and, even after the execution of the "last king" in 1649, she continued to look for a leader who would "raise up the tabernacle of David" (Amos 9:11). Seeking the recognition and freedom that law, custom, and belief denied her, she incorporated her feminism within the lineage and property that were marks of aristocracy. However appealing it might be to attribute to her a concept of a differently structured society, she did not describe the New Jerusalem in detail. Doing so may have been beyond her imagination. It would certainly have taken her beyond her biblical mandate, and it would also have been impolitic. Although at times she seems to have thrown caution to the winds, her repeated justifications of her knowledge of the date for Judgment suggest that she was aware that her credibility was an issue.

The milieu that Lady Eleanor described is admittedly distinct from, but also related to, the early modern Britain where she lived. She reacted to what was happening and, at the same time, tried to influence future developments. Yet, apart from the seeming confirmation of her prediction of the death of Sir John Davies in 1626 and that of the

Duke of Buckingham in 1628 and apart from the drama of her hearing before the High Commission in 1633 and of the incident at Lichfield in 1636 which led to her commitment to Bedlam, she had relatively little impact upon her contemporaries. Her attitude toward them was ambivalent. While she seemed to long for acceptance at times, her aristocratic and prophetic stance set her apart. Caught up in the process of writing and delivering her message, she tended to conclude that those who did not hear were unworthy. They, in turn, denied her voice legitimacy and, consequently, had no need to respond to her. Despite her continuing appearance in history as a seventeenth-century fanatic, neither in the great house nor the village at Englefield have stories of her survived. She was one woman and her writings are among thousands of other pieces of evidence from that period. The discordancy of their feminist assumptions from the patriarchalism dominant throughout the spectrum of political and religious opinion stands as an important reminder of different points of view within the world in which she lived. Madness, like the anagrams popular in that era, was a construct of society. She believed the mad were those in power in Church and Kingdom. From her name, ELEANOR AUDELIE, she made REVEALE O DANIEL, whereas Sir John Lambe used DAME ELEANOR DAVIES to form NEVER SOE MAD A LADIE.

Appendix: Lady Eleanor's Tracts

C. J. Hindle's bibliography of Lady Eleanor's tracts, originally published in 1934 and revised in 1936, provided the first modern list of her works. Since that time we have seen the revision of Pollard and Redgrave's *Short-Title Catalogue,* both an original and a revised edition of Wing's *Short-Title Catalogue,* and the annotated bibliography of *Women and the Literature of the Seventeenth Century,* prepared by Hilda Smith and Susan Cardinale for the Greenwood Press (1990). Major collections of Lady Eleanor's tracts are in the Houghton Library at Harvard, the Folger Shakespeare Library, the British Library, the Bodleian Library, and the Library of Worcester College, Oxford. Other libraries hold copies of one or more of her tracts. The following chronological list of her writings is comprehensive, including both printed works and those in manuscript (the latter are indicated by quotation marks). Those titles in brackets are mentioned in other works but not themselves extant. I am currently editing thirty-eight of the tracts for the Women Writers Project in a volume to be published by Oxford University Press.

Chronological List of Lady Eleanor's Writings

1625

Warning to the Dragon

1633

All the Kings of the Earth
Woe to the House
Given to the Elector
"Handwriteing October 1633"

1636

"Bathe Daughter of Babylondon"
[Appeal to the Throne]
"Spirituall Antheme"

1641

Her Appeal (1641)

1642

Samsons Fall
To the High Court

1643

Samsons Legacie
Amend, Amend
[The Revelations Interpretation]
Star to the Wise

1644

Restitution of Reprobates
Apoc. J. C.
Her Blessing
Prayer (1644)
Discovery
Sign
Prophetia

1645

I am the First
Word of God
As not Unknowne
Brides Preparation
Great Brittains Visitation
For Whitsontyds
Second Coming
Of Errors
Prayer (1645)
Prophesie

1646

For the Blessed Feast
Day of Judgment
Her Appeal (1646)
Je le tien
Revelation Interpreted

1647

Gatehouse Salutation
Mystery of General Redemption
Ezekiel the Prophet
Ezekiel, cap. 2
Excommunication out of Paradice

1648

Reader
And without Proving [*Wherefore to Prove*]
Writ of Restitution
Apoc. chap. 11
Of the Great Days
Remonstrance
Given to the Elector

1649

Appeal from Court to Camp
Blasphemous Charge
Crying Charge
New Jerusalem
Prayer (1644) [*sic*]
Sions Lamentation [Zachariah 12]
Strange and Wonderful
For Gerbier
For the States
Sign
Discovery
Everlasting Gospel
New Proclamation

1650

Arraignment
Bill of Excommunication
Appearance
Before the Lords Second Coming
Elijah the Tishbite
Her Jubilee

1651

Hells Destruction
Of Times
Serpents Excommunication
Benediction
Dragons Blasphemous Charge
Given to the Elector

1652

Restitution of Prophecy
Tobits Book
Bethlehem

Notes

Introduction

1. See L. Woodbridge, *Women and the English Renaissance: Literature and the Nature of Womankind, 1540–1620* (Urbana: University of Illinois Press, 1984); K. Henderson and Barbara McManus, *Half Humankind: Contexts and Texts of the Controversy about Women in England, 1540–1640* (Urbana: University of Illinois Press, 1985); S. Hull, *Chaste, Silent and Obedient: English Books for Women, 1475–1640* (San Marino, Calif.: Huntington Library, 1982), 106–26; also M. P. Hannay, ed., *Silent But for the Word: Tudor Women as Patrons, Translators, and Writers of Religious Works* (Kent, Ohio: Kent State University Press, 1985), introduction; M. Ezell, *The Patriarch's Wife: Literary Evidence and the History of the Family* (Chapel Hill: University of North Carolina Press, 1987) makes some useful points about models of women's behavior and the reality of it.

2. See *The Diary of the Lady Anne Clifford,* with an introductory note by V. Sackville-West (London: William Heinemann, 1923).

3. See D. Grant, *Margaret the First* (London: Rupert Hart-Davis, 1957); S. Mendelson, *The Mental World of Stuart Women: Three Studies* (Amherst: University of Massachusetts Press, 1987).

4. H. Smith, *Reason's Disciples: Seventeenth-Century English Feminists* (Urbana: University of Illinois Press, 1982); see also M. Ferguson, ed., *First Feminists: British Women Writers, 1578–1799* (Bloomington: Indiana University Press, 1985).

5. See E. Graham, H. Hinds, E. Hobby, and H. Wilcox, eds., *Her Own Life; Autobiographical Writings by Seventeenth-Century Englishwomen* (London: Routledge, 1989).

6. See, for example, *Her Appeal* (1641), 16; *Prayer* (1644), 4.

7. E. Petroff, "Medieval Women Visionaries: Seven Stages to Power,"

Frontiers, 3, no. 1 (1978): 34–45; Petroff, *Medieval Women's Visionary Literature* (New York: Oxford University Press, 1986).

Chapter 1

1. See J. P. Rylands, "A Vellum Pedigree Roll of the Family of Touchet," *The Genealogist*, n.s., 36 (1920): 9–21.
2. *Appearance*, 8–9.
3. Two centuries earlier, Margery Kempe described herself as her father's daughter rather than her husband's wife.
4. *Star to the Wise*, 18; *Everlasting Gospel*, 3; *Her Appeal* (1641), 11.
5. HEH, Hastings MSS, Irish Papers, 15939; also see the questions her brother addressed to the commissioners for the office of earl marshal in 1612 (P.R.O., SP 14/71/39).
6. *Appearance*, 9; see T. Courtaux and la Marquis de Touchet, *Histoire Généalogique de la maison de Touchet* (Paris: Cabinet de l'Historiographe, 1911).
7. *Appearance*, 9.
8. *Restitution of Prophecy*, "To the Reader."
9. *Cal. St. P. Dom., 1547–80*, 439, 449; see also J. Foster, ed., *Alumni Oxonienses*. 4 vols. (Oxford, 1891–92).
10. One cannot be certain from the two of her letters among the Domestic State Papers (P.R.O., SP 12/172/116; SP 12/233/42) or those among the Thynne Papers (A. Wall, ed., *Two Elizabethan Women: Correspondence of Joan and Maria Thynne 1575–1611* (Wiltshire Record Society, vol. 38 [Devizes: Wiltshire Record Society, 1983], letters 38, 64).
11. *The Diary of the Lady Anne Clifford*, with an introductory note by V. Sackville-West (London: William Heinemann, 1923), xxvii.
12. Some of Maria's letters survive in the Thynne papers among the Manuscripts of the Marquis of Bath at Longleat; see Wall, *Two Elizabethan Women*, xxx, and letters 48, 49, 51, 52; also see A. Wall, "Elizabethan Precept and Feminine Practice: The Thynne Family of Longleat," *History*, 75, no. 243 (1990): 23–38.
13. E.g., *Her Blessing*, 30–31.
14. *Mystery of General Redemption*, 8–9; see also *Je le tien*, 22; *Of Times*, title page.
15. *Mystery of General Redemption*, 11–12. If she did know Greek, she surpassed her husband Davies (R. Krueger, ed., *The Poems of Sir John Davies* [Oxford: Clarendon Press, 1975], 421). She made a reference to the Hebrew in *Her Appeal* (1646), 8; annotations on the Harvard copy of *Hells Destruction* include what appear to be Greek words (6).
16. *Her Blessing*, 6–7, 36; *Restitution of Prophecy*, 34–35.

17. *All the Kings of the Earth,* Daniel 12, note E.

18. Transcripts appear among the Hastings MSS in the Huntington Library (HEH, Hastings MSS, Legal Papers, box 6, folder 1; box 5, folder 2).

19. Lady Eleanor's hand appears to be similar to that of her sister Maria (see Wall, *Two Elizabethan Women,* xxxii). See E. Hobby, *Virtue of Necessity: English Women's Writing 1649–88* (Ann Arbor: University of Michigan Press, 1989), 5; HEH, Hastings MSS, Correspondence, HA4849; see also D. Cressy, *Literacy and Social Order* (Cambridge: Cambridge University Press, 1980). I am grateful to Laetitia Yeandle of the Folger Shakespeare Library for her comments about Lady Eleanor's hand.

20. *Before the Lords Second Coming,* 11; *Remonstrance,* 8; *Restitution of Prophecy,* 19; see also L. Potter, *Secret Rites and Secret Writing: Royalist Literature, 1641–1660* (Cambridge: Cambridge University Press, 1989), 45.

21. *Warning to the Dragon,* general epistle and 1.

22. Marginal note to stanza 18, in *Given to the Elector,* 9; cf. stanzas 1 (3), 4 (4), and 15 (8).

23. I am grateful to Jean Klene for telling me of the entry in Lady Anne Southwell's commonplace book, a translation of Psalm 25, written by her "to the first earle of Castlehaven." Without more information, it is difficult to know how to interpret this.

24. See A. Wall, "Faction in Local Politics 1580–1620: Struggles for Supremacy in Wiltshire," *Wiltshire Archaeological Magazine* 62–63 (1980): 119–33.

25. See C. R. Mayes, "The Early Stuarts and the Irish Peerage," *English Historical Review* 73, no. 287 (1958): 227–51; M. A. E. Greene, ed., *Diary of John Rous,* Camden Society, vol. 66 (London: Camden Society, 1856), 60; *Word of God,* 12 and Castlehaven's confession.

26. See D. Dickson, "The Complexities of Biblical Typology in the Seventeenth Century," *Renaissance and Reformation,* n. s., 11, no. 3 (1987): 253–72.

27. R. Weigall, "An Elizabethan Gentlewoman," *Quarterly Review* 215 (1911): 125.

28. I have reached this conclusion by checking a number of her citations with both the Geneva Bible and the Authorized Version and her Latin passages with the Beza-Junius Bible. I am grateful to Amy Burnett for suggesting Beza-Junius as the Latin Bible she would most likely have used. Concerning Davies, see Krueger, *Poems,* 421.

29. See D. Willen, "Women and Religion in Early Modern England," in *Women in Reformation and Counter-Reformation Europe,* ed. Sherren Marshall (Bloomington: Indiana University Press, 1989), 140–65; P. Seaver, *Wallington's World: A Puritan Artisan in Seventeenth-Century London* (Stanford, Calif.: Stanford University Press, 1983). The only

preacher Lady Eleanor mentions is Reverend James Sibbald, who may have ministered to her while she was in the Tower of London.

30. See N. Smith, *Perfection Proclaimed: Language and Literature in English Radical Religion 1640–1660* (Oxford: Clarendon Press, 1989), esp. 32.

31. *Diary of Lady Anne Clifford*, 3–17. We also have nothing for Lady Eleanor comparable to the letter Lady Anne wrote to her father when she was eight. See G. Williamson, *Lady Anne Clifford: Countess of Dorset, Pembroke and Montgomery, 1590–1676: Her Life, Letters and Work*, 2d ed. (Wakefield: S. P. Publishers, 1967), xxi.

32. See Wall, *Two Elizabethan Women*, xxvi and letters 18, 19, 38, 42, 64; see also A. Wall, "The Feud and Shakespeare's *Romeo and Juliet:* a Reconsideration," *Sydney Studies in English*, 5 (1979–80): 84–95.

33. Lord and Lady Audeley were married before 8 July 1576; see *Calendar of Patent Rolls, 1572–82.*

34. Pawlisch describes the Touchets as a family "whose mental and emotional stability left much to be desired" (Hans Pawlisch, *Sir John Davies and the Conquest of Ireland* (Cambridge: Cambridge University Press, 1985), 27.

35. Audeley was captain of a company of foot at Ostend and then at Bergen in 1588 and 1589. Like other captains, he may, however, have been in England during some of that time. A list from the end of August 1588 notes him as having been absent since December (*Calendar of State Papers Foreign July-Dec. 1588*, 175, see also 262–63; 409–10; *Calendar of State Papers Foreign Jan.-July 1589*, 71, 175–76). Clifford's father, the earl of Cumberland, was at sea much of the time (*Diary of Lady Anne Clifford*, ix).

36. See Wall, *Two Elizabethan Women*, xxviii and letters 31, 38.

37. See R. Hoare, *The Modern History of South Wiltshire* (London: John Bowyer and Sons, 1829), 4:20; H. C. Johnson, ed., *Wiltshire County Records: Minutes of Proceedings in Sessions 1563 and 1574–1592* (Devizes: Wiltshire Archaeological and Natural History Society, Records Branch, 1949), passim. Lord Audeley occasionally performed local responsibilities; records show he was present at the Sessions as a justice of the peace during Easter 1585, Michaelmas 1589, and Epiphany 1591.

38. See W. Drake, *Fasticulus Mervinensis* (privately printed, 1873), 14–23 and appendix i. Mervin wrote to the earl of Salisbury on behalf of Lady Eleanor's sister Elizabeth in November 1607 (H.M.C., *Salisbury MSS* 19:319).

39. H. F. Chettle, "The Successive Houses at Fonthill," *Wiltshire Magazine* 49, no. 176 (1942): 505.

40. *A Pictorial and Descriptive Guide to Bath, Cheddar, Wells, Glastonbury, etc.*, 10th ed. rev. (London: Ward, Lock, and Co., 1938), 96, 101; J.

Britton, *Illustrations, Graphic and Literary of Fonthill Abbey Wiltshire* (London, 1823). Although one might suppose that Beckford would have enjoyed living where Lady Eleanor had, there is no evidence that he had any of her tracts among his library (*The Valuable Library of Books in Fonthill Abbey: A Catalogue . . . which will be sold by auction by Mr. Phillips* [9 September 1823]).

41. HEH, Hastings MSS, Religious Papers, box 1, folder 28, Bathe Daughter of Babylondon—Woeman sitting on seven mountains beholde—Revela. xvii.9. In addition to Landsdowne, she mentions Warlesdowne [Wirral] and Clarknes Downe.

42. *Before the Lords Second Coming*, 15. She also refers to Stonehenge in *Serpents Excommunication*, 5. She makes very few other geographical references.

43. *Cal. St. P. Ire., 1599–1600*, 32, 64. *Calendar of the Carew MSS* 4: no. 14.

44. *Cal. St. P. Ire. 1600–1601*, 310. H.M.C., *Salisbury MSS*, 16:52, 384; H.M.C., *Salisbury MSS*, 17:140; *Cal. St. P. Ire., 1603–1606*, 258.

45. *Cal. St. P. Ire. 1600*, 386; *Calendar of the Carew MSS* 3: no. 444.

46. Wall, *Two Elizabethan Women*, letter 54. Davies had apparently not seen Lady Audeley when she was in Ireland.

47. *Cal. St. P. Ire., 1608–1610*, 297; cf. the many social contacts of the Boyles (A. B. Grosart, ed., *The Lismore Papers* [London, 1886], vols. 1 and 2).

48. HEH, Hastings MSS, Irish Papers, HA 13964.

49. See L. Peck, *Northampton: Patronage and Policy at the Court of James I* (London: George Allen and Unwin, 1982), 9, 175–76.

50. H.M.C., *Salisbury MSS*, 20:112, also 16:52, 384.

51. Hindle, 5.

52. Bodl., MS. Carte 61, fol. 346.

53. *DNB*, s.v. "Davies, Sir John"; Davies left money for the poor of the parish of Tisbury in his will (P.R.O., PROB 11/150; HEH, Hastings MSS, Personal Papers, box 17, folder 20). See also Hoare, *South Wiltshire*, 4:134, 136, 153–54; Krueger, *Poems*, 233.

54. Wall, *Two Elizabethan Women*, letter 54. He mentions sister Anne, who married Edward Blount, and brother Mervin.

55. Pawlisch, *Davies*, 27. Pawlisch notes that John Hutchinson, *A Catalogue of Notable Middle Templars* ([London: Middle Temple, 1902], 244), includes Lord Audeley.

56. Wall, *Two Elizabethan Women*, letter 64.

57. HEH, Hastings MSS, Legal Papers, box 3, folder 2; also box 2, folder 12; cf. box 4, folder 4.

58. HEH, Hastings MSS, Deeds, HAD 3501 (20 March 1609); see also Bodl., MS Carte 61, fol. 580.

59. HEH, Hastings MSS, Legal Papers, box 3, folder 2; also box 2, folder 12; cf. box 4, folder 4. Ravenscroft was probably referring not to Lady Eleanor but to the manor of Pirton when he mentioned "your late purchase" in a letter to Davies on 10 June 1609 (Bodl., MS Carte 61, fol. 580).

60. *Cal. St. P. Ire, 1608–10*, 180, 297; HEH, Hastings MSS, Irish Papers, HA 13964. See also Pawlisch, *Davies,* 27–31.

61. N. E. McClure, ed., *The Letters of John Chamberlain* (Philadelphia: American Philosophical Society, 1939), 1: no. 113.

62. Davies was born in 1569, Lady Eleanor in 1590 (*DNB,* s.v. "Davies"). See *Samsons Fall,* 4.

63. Pawlisch, *Davies,* 18–21; cf. J. R. Brink, "Sir John Davies: His Life and Works" (Ph.D. diss., University of Wisconsin, 1972), 22–24.

64. Quoted in Pawlisch, *Davies,* 18; see R. P. Sorlien, ed., *The Diary of John Manningham of the Middle Temple 1602–1603* (Hanover, N.H.: University Press of New England, 1976), 235, 265.

65. The full title of the work Donne proposed for Davies was *The Justice of England: Vacation Exercises of John Davies on the Art of forming Anagrams approximately true and Posies to engrave on Rings* (see E. M. Simpson, ed., *The Courtiers Library,* with a trans. [London: Nonesuch Press, 1930]).

66. Especially *Day of Judgement;* see also *Arraignment; Writ of Restitution.*

67. *Ezekiel the Prophet,* 4–5; see also *Ezekiel, cap.* 2, 15–16, 21. On the opening page of both the Harvard and the Folger copies of *Ezekiel, cap.* 2, Lady Eleanor wrote, "His writ served of Rebellion Lamentation Mourning & Woe." I am grateful to Hugh Whitt for discussion of others who used the image of the roll.

68. I have not seen the original. The portrait was apparently sold from the collections of the Viscount Bearsted at Upton House. I am grateful to Jennifer Ramkalawon at the National Portrait Gallery for telling me about it. A reproduction appears in G. Reynolds, *Nicholas Hilliard and Isaac Oliver* (London: HMSO, 1971), no. 173; see also J. Finsten, *Isaac Oliver: Art at the Courts of Elizabeth I and James I,* 2 vols. (Garland: New York, 1981), cat. 61, "called" Lady Eleanor Davies. Finsten thus is less definite about the identification than Reynolds was. I am grateful to the Viscount Bearsted, the staff in the Photographic Division of the National Trust in the Severn Division of the National Trust's Historic Monuments and Buildings, Sir Roy Strong, and to Jim Murrell of the Department of Conservation at the Victoria and Albert Museum for their efforts in helping me in my unsuccessful search for the miniature.

69. The portrait of Maria, among the paintings at Longleat, is reproduced

as a frontispiece in Wall, *Two Elizabethan Women,* see also xxxii and note. Lucy's portrait, painted at the time of her marriage in 1623, by Marcus Ghaeraedts is reproduced in Roy Strong, *The English Icon* (London: Routledge and Kegan Paul, 1969), 273.

70. HLRO, Main Papers, 22 September 1647.

71. Sir T. More, *The History of King Richard III,* ed. R. Sylvester (New Haven: Yale University Press, 1976), 56. See also N. Rowe, *The Tragedy of Jane Shore,* ed. H. W. Pedicord (Lincoln: University of Nebraska Press, 1974), xv. I am grateful to Howard Norland for pointing out that Lady Eleanor's reference to "Jane" rather than "Mistress Shore" indicates that she knew the story not from More's history but from a later source. The story appears in L. Campbell, ed., *Mirror for Magistrates* (Cambridge: Cambridge University Press, 1938); also in M. Drayton, *Englands heroicall Epistles,* newly enlarged (London, 1599).

72. *Warning to the Dragon,* 94–95.

73. *Star to the Wise,* 3–6, 17.

74. *Samsons Legacie,* 9; cf. *Samsons Fall,* 7.

75. *Before the Lords Second Coming,* 20; see also *Word of God,* 12.

76. Pawlisch, *Davies,* 15–26; Krueger, *Poems,* xxxi–xlv.

77. F. Byrne, "Sir John Davies: an English Intellectual in Ireland, 1603–1619" (M.A. thesis, National University of Ireland, University College, Galway, 1985), 92. See also *Cal. St. P. Ire., 1608–10,* 451; *Cal. St. P. Ire., 1611–14,* 91; HEH, Hastings MSS, Irish Papers, HA 15076.

78. See T. W. Moody, "The Irish Parliament under Elizabeth and James I: A General Survey," *Proceedings of the Royal Irish Academy* 45, sec. C, no. 6 (1939): 41–81.

79. D. M. Waterman, "Sir John Davies and His Ulster Buildings, Castlederg and Castle Curlews, Co. Tyrone," *Ulster Journal of Archaeology* 23 (1960): 89–96.

80. HEH, Hastings MSS, Irish Papers, HA 15938.

81. HEH, Hastings MSS, Irish Papers, HA 15061.

82. HEH, Hastings MSS, Irish Papers, HA 15404; Correspondence, HM 1924. An inquiry to the National Archives in Dublin revealed that the grant of administration for Lord Audeley's estate was destroyed by fire in 1922.

83. HEH, Hastings MSS, Legal Papers, box 3, folder 1; Accounts and Financial Papers, box 8, folder 2. Sir Edward Blount, husband of sister Anne, was involved in Ulster, as were Lady Eleanor's brothers Mervin and Ferdinando. Two of Lady Eleanor's sisters, Mary, who married Sir Thomas Thynne, and Christian, wife of Henry Mervin, lived in Wiltshire and seem not to have participated in the Ulster plantation

(G. W. Marshall, ed., *The Visitation of Wiltshire, 1623* [London: Geo. Bell and Sons, 1882], 60; VCH, *Wiltshire* 13:160). Concerning Audeley's widow, see HEH, Hastings MSS, Legal Papers, box 3, folder 1.

84. HEH, Hastings MSS, Legal Papers, box 4, folder 6.

85. *Excommunication out of Paradice*, 12. She also describes paintings on alehouse walls (*Samsons Legacie*, 11; *Samsons Fall*, 7).

86. HEH, Hastings MSS, Genealogy, box 1, folder 12.

87. Anthony á Wood (*Athenae Oxonienses*), for example, mentions only one son, but see Bodl. MS. Carte 62, fols. 590—91. The dates of birth and death of neither are known.

88. HEH, Hastings MSS, Irish Papers, HA 15061.

89. Ed Taylor suggested this possible diagnosis. For descriptions of autistic children see B. Furneaux and B. Roberts, eds., *Autistic children*, (London: Routledge and Kegan Paul, 1977); B. Levinson and L. Osterweil, *Autism: Myth or Reality?* (Springfield, Ill.: Charles C. Thomas, 1984).

90. See *DNB*, s.v. "Davies."

91. HEH, Hastings MSS, Correspondence, HA 2337. She also recalled that Sir John Davies had died about the same time of year.

92. Krueger, *Poems*, 299. Wood also quotes the anagram and refers to an epitaph for the son of four verses "beginning Hic in visceribus terra" (432). Wood does not quote the epitaph in its entirety.

93. Krueger, *Poems*, xliv—xlix.

94. See L. Stone, *The Family, Sex, and Marriage in England 1500—1800* (New York: Harper and Row, 1977), 105; also R. J. Knapp, *Beyond Endurance: When a Child Dies* (New York: Schocken Books, 1986), 12—14; cf. L. Pollock, *Forgotten Children: Parent-Child relations from 1500—1900* (Cambridge: Cambridge University Press, 1983). I am grateful to Alan Booth for recommending current sociological research.

95. M. MacDonald, *Mystical Bedlam: Madness, Anxiety, and Healing in Seventeenth-Century England* (Cambridge: Cambridge University Press, 1981), 77—85 and 78, table 3.3.

96. HEH, Ellesmere MSS, EL 8376; cf. Ann Fashawe's comments in her diary when her daughter Ann died (*The Memoirs of Anne, Lady Halkett and Ann, Lady Fanshawe* [Oxford: Clarendon Press, 1979], 136, also see 137, 139).

97. HEH, Hastings MSS, Deeds, HAD 2414, 20 April 1609. The manor had been among the monastic estates acquired by Sir Anthony Denny in 1537—38 (*Letters and Papers of Henry VIII* 13: pt. 1, 384:47). Davies made some inquiries about Pirton before concluding his purchase (PRO, SP 46/69/34; SP 46/69/36). In 1612, Davies bought the Somerset manor of Aller, though not the manor house or demesne lands, from the earl of Huntingdon (VCH, *Somerset* 3:61—71).

98. For example, *Revelation Interpreted*, 4; *Restitution of Prophecy*, 12; *New Jerusalem*, 6ff. She later predicted the duke's death.

99. McClure, *Letters* 2: no. 410. Lady Jacob may have been the wife of Sir Robert Jacob, who was Solicitor in Ireland while Davies was Attorney.

100. P.R.O., SP 14/130/135. I have not been able to identify Kit Brooke or determine whether he was connected to Sir Richard Brooke a cousin of Lady Eleanor's. See HEH, Hastings MSS, Legal Papers, box 4, folder 1; box 3, folder 2; Irish Papers HA 14091.

101. P. Higgins, "The Reactions of Women with Special Reference to Women Petitioners," in *Politics, Religion and the English Civil War*, ed. B. Manning (London: Edward Arnold, 1973), 180.

102. M. Dalton, *The Countrey Justice* (London, 1635), cap. 107.

103. See L. Norsworthy, *The Lady of Bleeding Heart Yard: Lady Elizabeth Hatton* (1935; London: John Murray, 1938); see also Pawlisch, *Davies*, esp. 165ff. City women had a reputation for aggressiveness; see L. Woodbridge, *Women and the English Renaissance: Literature and the Nature of Womankind 1540–1620* (Urbana: University of Illinois Press, 1984), 171ff.

104. The indenture, dated 15 August, 20 Jac. [1622], was enrolled 27 August, 21 Jac. [1633] (P.R.O., C 54/2533). See also Bodl. MS Carte 289, fol. 24, letter from Sir John Davies to the earl of Huntingdon from Englefield, July 1623; also VCH, *Berkshire* 3:407. This predates the 13 December, 20 Jac., indenture of Vanlore's purchase from the earl of Kellie (HEH, Hastings MSS, Deeds, HAD 2066).

105. HEH, Hastings MSS, Legal Papers, box 4, folder 1. The project was in progress at the time of Davies's death.

106. HEH, Hastings MSS, Accounts and Financial Papers, box 8, folder 18; Personal Papers, box 17, folders 1–5, 8. Lucy's son, Theophilus claims the amount was £7,000 (Genealogy, box 1, folder 12).

107. See Bodl. MS Carte 289, fol. 64; also VCH, *Somerset* 3:61ff.

108. Lady Anne's daughter subsequently married her new husband's son.

109. E.g., A. Fraser, *The Weaker Vessel* (London: Weidenfeld and Nicolson, 1984), 155–56.

110. HEH, Hastings MSS, Correspondence, HA 1926, Sir John Davies to Henry, earl of Huntingdon, 22 March, 1624; HA 5737, Lucy to Ferdinando, 8 July 1624.

111. HEH, Hastings MSS, Legal Papers, box 4; also see HEH, Hastings MSS, Correspondence, Elizabeth, countess of Huntingdon's letters to Timothy Leving, e.g., HA 4824 (18 June [1618]); HA 4825 (18 May 1620).

112. See, for example, HEH, Hastings MSS, Correspondence, HA2. Concerning the marriage of children, see M. Ingram, *Church Courts, Sex,*

and Marriage in England, 1570–1640 (Cambridge: Cambridge University Press, 1987).

113. HEH, Hastings MSS, Personal Papers, box 17, folder 5; see also Genealogy, box 1, folder 12.

114. See, for example, HEH, Hastings MSS, Correspondence, HA 4823, 4825, 4827.

115. E.g., HEH, Hastings MSS, Correspondence, HA 4828, 4830–31, 4833–44.

116. HEH, Hastings MSS, Correspondence, HA 1926, 1928, 1930. Davies also discussed public affairs with the earl who himself wrote to Davies (HA 5482, 5483).

117. The binding, although from the seventeenth century, probably dates from after Lucy's death, since some of the annotation was lost when the tracts were clipped.

118. See Lucy's books, HEH, Hastings MSS, Personal Papers, box 18, folder 1; Religious Papers, box 2, folders 1–2.

119. HEH, Hastings MSS, Correspondence, HA 4858, Ferdinando to Lucy, 1 December 1624; also HA 4831, Elizabeth, countess of Huntingdon to Sir John Davies, [Nov.-Dec. 1624].

120. See HEH, Hastings Correspondence, HA 4830, Elizabeth, Countess of Huntingdon, to Sir John Davies [May 1625]; HA 4834, Elizabeth, Countess of Huntingdon, to Sir John Davies, 28 April 1625; HA 1931, Sir John Davies to Henry, earl of Huntingdon, 21 July 1625.

121. HEH, Hastings MSS, Correspondence, HA 1931.

122. E. Petroff, "Medieval Women Visionaries: Seven Stages to Power," *Frontiers,* 3, no.1 (1978): 35–36. The Countess of Warwick responded to the serious illness of her son in 1647 by turning to religion. See S. Mendelson, *The Mental World of Stuart Women: Three Studies* (Amherst: University of Massachusetts Press, 1987), 81–82. In Knapp's modern study, 70 percent of parents turned to religion in the wake of their child's death; 30 percent of these had what he calls a "genuine religious revitalization or conversion experience" (Knapp, *Beyond Endurance,* 34–35).

123. See her account in *Her Appeal* (1646), 4ff. Although extraordinary children were sometimes a topic of pamphlets, I am aware of none about Carr. See Wm. E. A. Axon, ed., "The Wonderful Child," *Chetham Miscellanies,* n.s., 1 (1901).

124. *Her Appeal* (1646), 4–7. See *The Historie of Frier Rush* (1620), which described itself as a story of "pleasant mirth and delight" directed to "young people."; see also L. de Bruyn, *Woman and the Devil in Sixteenth-Century Literature* (Tisbury: Compton Press, 1979), 91–94; C. John

Sommerville, "Puritan Humor or Entertainment for Children," *Albion* 21, no. 2 (1989): 227–40.

125. The judges committed the boy to the care of the Bishop of Coventry and Lichfield, who discovered he was "a counterfeit." See Richard Baddeley, *The Boy of Bilson* (London, 1622).

126. See Petroff, "Stages," 36–37; *All the Kings of the Earth.*

127. *All the Kings of the Earth,* Daniel 8:13–14, n. D and E.

128. *Her Appeal* (1646), 8–9; cf. *All the Kings of the Earth.*

129. *All the Kings of the Earth,* n. D for Daniel 8.

130. HEH, Hastings MSS, Correspondence, HA 1930; see also HA 1931.

131. Krueger, *Poems,* 421.

132. Petroff, "Stages," 37–38.

Chapter 2

1. *Her Appeal* (1641), 15; cf. *Her Appeal* (1646), 10; *Warning to the Dragon,* 100; *All the Kings of the Earth,* "To the renowned Princess." See also *Star to the Wise,* 18; *Samsons Legacie,* 18; *Her Blessing,* 7.

2. See *Warning to the Dragon,* General Epistle. Thomas Brightman describes his *A Revelation of the Revelation that is* (1615) as a "newe interpretation" of the Book of Revelation.

3. E. Petroff, "Medieval Women Visionaries: Seven Stages to Power," *Frontiers* 3, no. 1 (1978): 38–39.

4. See M. Reeves, *The Influence of Prophecy in the Later Middle Ages* (Oxford: Clarendon Press, 1969).

5. I am using patriarchy, here, in the broad sense so that it includes male dominance throughout the institutions of society, not just the legal and economic power of the male head over his household (see G. Lerner, *The Creation of Patriarchy* [Oxford: Oxford University Press, 1986), 238–39; also see G. Schochet, *Patriarchalism in Political Thought: The Authoritarian Family and Political Speculation and Attitudes Especially in Seventeenth-Century England* [Oxford: Basil Blackwell, 1975]; S. Amussen, *An Ordered Society: Gender and Class in Early Modern England* [Oxford: Basil Blackwell, 1988]).

6. *Star to the Wise,* 18ff.; *Dragons Blasphemous Charge,* 2; see also *Samsons Legacie,* 19; *Everlasting Gospel,* 3.

7. See W. Camden, *Britannia,* newly translated into English with large additions and improvements and published by Edmund Gibson (London, 1695), 142.

8. *Appearance,* 12. The road is no longer so close. The A4 runs from London through Reading and Theale (a mile or two from Englefield)

to Newbury, Bath, and Bristol. The old Roman road between London and Bristol was known in Berkshire as the Devil's Highway (J. Bond and L. Over, *Oxfordshire and Berkshire* [London: Ordnance Survey Historical Guides, 1988], 31). The first edition of the Ordnance Survey map of that area shows "Dead man Lane" between Englefield and Theale ([reprint; Newton Abbot: David and Charles, 1970], sheet 70). See also VCH, *Berkshire* 3:405.

9. *Star to the Wise,* 18ff.; see also I. Bennet, *Good and True Intelligence from Reading* (London, 1643).

10. *Everlasting Gospel,* 13. See A. Baker, *A Battlefield Atlas of the English Civil War* (London: I. A. N. Allan, 1986), 73–75.

11. *Appearance,* 12.

12. I am grateful to the Hon. William R. Benyon, present owner of Englefield, for sending me a copy of the brochure about the house.

13. HEH, Hastings MSS, Legal Papers, box 3, folder 2. See also HEH, Hastings MSS, Legal Papers, box 4, folder 1.

14. HEH, Hastings MSS, Legal Papers, box 3, folder 2 and box 4, folder 4.

15. HEH, Hastings MSS, Accounts and Financial Papers, box 9, folder 7.

16. *Her Appeal* (1641), 15; cf. the 1646 version of the tract, where she omits any reference to the warning about pride. Also see her description of the "musicall voyce" and warning in *All the Kings of the Earth.*

17. *Everlasting Gospel,* 4. She signed herself "The Morning Starre" in a letter to Dr. Sibbald that she printed in *New Jerusalem,* 20. See also *All the Kings of the Earth; Her Blessing,* 7; *Her Appeal* (1646), 11; *Great Brittains Visitation,* preface; Job 38:7; N. Smith, *Perfection Proclaimed: Language and Literature in English Radical Religion 1640–1660* (Oxford: Clarendon Press, 1989), 251; see Revelation 2:28, 22:16.

18. *Given to the Elector,* 5.

19. Theophilus Toxander, *Vox Coeli to England, or, Englands Fore-Warning from Heaving. Being a relation of true, strange, and wonderfull visions, and propheticall revelations, concerning these tragical sinfull times; and with what care and diligence reconciliation ought to be laboured for, between the king and parliament, having never been heretofore published* (London, 1646). St. Teresa also gives much fuller descriptions of her mystical experiences (F. de Ribera, *The Lyf of Mother Teresa of Jesus. Written by herself,* trans. W. M. [Antwerp, 1611]).

20. *All the Kings of the Earth.*

21. *Her Appeal* (1646), 8.

22. See A. Trapnel, *Strange and Wonderful Newes from White Hall* (London, 1654); see also N. Smith, *Perfection Proclaimed,* 45–52. Wight's experiences, like Gracy Cary's, were told by a man, Henry Jessey. Jessey, a

preacher in Wight's parish who counselled her, related her story as an example of divine grace (H. Jessey, *The exceeding Riches of Grace Advanced by the Spirit of Grace, in an Empty Nothing Creature, viz. Mrs. Sarah Wight* [London, 1647]; see also E. Hobby, *Virtue of Necessity: English Women's Writing 1649–88* (Ann Arbor: University of Michigan Press, 1989), 31–36; 67–69.

23. See N. Smith, *Perfection Proclaimed*, chap. 1; also G. Nuttall, "Puritan and Quaker Mysticism," *Theology* 78 (1975): 518–31; P. Mack, "The Prophet and Her Audience: Gender and Knowledge in The World Turned Upside Down," in *Reviving the Revolution*, ed. G. Eley and W. Hunt (London: Verso Books, 1988), 139–52.

24. See H. Dobin, *Merlin's Disciples: Prophecy, Poetry, and Power in Renaissance England* (Stanford, Calif.: Stanford University Press, 1990).

25. See K. V. Thomas, *Religion and the Decline of Magic* (Harmondsworth: Penguin, 1971), esp. 525–27; Dalton lists characteristics of witches to assist justices of the peace in identifying them (M. Dalton, *The Countrey Justice* [London, 1635], chap. 107).

26. See J. Kelly, "The Doubled Vision of Feminist Theory," *Feminist Studies*, 5, no. 1 (1979): 216–27. Also useful are M. Howell, *Women, Production, and Patriarchy in Late Medieval Cities* (Chicago: University of Chicago Press, 1986); I. Maclean, *The Renaissance Notion of Woman* (Cambridge: Cambridge University Press, 1980); L. Jardine, *Still Harping on Daughters: Women and Drama in the Age of Shakespeare* (Brighton: Harvester Press, 1983).

27. *Warning to the Dragon.*

28. *Her Blessing,* 7; *Given to the Elector* (Worcester College copy). See Hobby, *Virtue of Necessity,* 30.

29. de Ribera, *Lyf of Teresa,* 187. St. Teresa says that, for almost two years she, out of fear of deceit by the devil, resisted hearing, but she found resistance impossible. Cf. Julian of Norwich, who distinguishes "spiritual" from "bodily showings" or "showings" that were "words formed" in her "understanding" (*Showings,* trans. and introd. by J. Walsh [London: S.P.C.K., 1978], chap. 7, shorter text).

30. *Her Appeal* (1641), 11, 15–16; *All the Kings of the Earth.*

31. *Everlasting Gospel,* 3–8.

32. See A. Stafford, *The Femall Glory: The Life and Death of our Blessed Lady, the holy Virgin Mary,* facs. reprint with introd. by M. Sabine (1635; Delmar, N.Y.: Scholars' Facsimiles and Reprints, 1988); see also C. Levin, "Power, Politics, and Sexuality: Images of Elizabeth I," in *The Politics of Gender in Early Modern Europe,* ed. J. R. Brink, A. P. Coudert, and M. C. Horowitz, Sixteenth-Century Essays and Studies 12

(Kirksville, Mo.: Sixteenth Century Journal, 1989), 95–110; J. N. King, "The Godly Woman in Elizabethan Iconography," *Renaissance Quarterly*, 38, no. 1 (1985): 41–84.

33. I am grateful to Peter Blayney for identifying the printer who ultimately handled *Warning to the Dragon* as Bernard Alsop. Concerning Alsop, see H. Plomer, *A Dictionary of the Booksellers and Printers who were at work in England, Scotland and Ireland from 1641 to 1667* (London: Bibliographical Society, 1907), 3–4. She comments about her 1625 writing in *Star to the Wise*, where she says that the printed tract was burned in 1633.

34. For example, T. Brightman, *A Revelation of the Revelation that is* (London, 1615); *The Revelation of St. John Illustrated* (London, 1616). Brightman's work on Daniel, *A Most Comfortable Exposition of the last and most difficult part of the prophecie of Daniel*, was not published until 1635.

35. *All the Kings of the Earth.*

36. *Warning to the Dragon*, 8. See K. Firth, *The Apocalyptic Tradition in Reformation Britain, 1530–1645* (Oxford: Oxford University Press, 1979). Later, Lady Eleanor gave the beasts other meanings.

37. *Warning to the Dragon*, 9, 11, 14.

38. *Warning to the Dragon*, 85, 87, 92; in her preface, she refers to him "unto whom there is no accesse but by Faith" but makes no mention of predestination per se. Her tracts of the 1640s show her views had changed.

39. *Warning to the Dragon*, 84, 99.

40. *Warning to the Dragon*, 85, also 94–96; cf. G. S., *Sacrae Heptades or Seaven Problems concerning Antichrist* (London, 1625) which was apparently written just after the parliament and addressed to all kings, especially King Charles and to the King and Queen of Bohemia. In a much more scholarly discussion of Daniel and Revelations than Lady Eleanor's, the author warns of the progress of the antichrist.

41. See K. Fincham, "Prelacy and Politics: Archbishop Abbot's Defence of Protestant Orthodoxy," *Bulletin of the Institute of Historical Research* 61, no. 144 (1988): 36–64.

42. *Her Appeal* (1646), 11–12.

43. *Her Appeal* (1646), 12.

44. HEH, Hastings MSS, Correspondence, HA 1931.

45. Cf. P. Lake, "Feminine Piety and Personal Potency: The 'Emancipation' of Mrs. Jane Ratcliffe," *Seventeenth Century* 2 (1987): 143–65.

46. See J. T. Cliffe, *The Puritan Gentry* (London: Routledge and Kegan Paul, 1984).

47. *Her Appeal* (1646), 15.

48. Margery Kempe ultimately got her husband to agree to allow her to be chaste; see *The Book of Margery Kempe,* trans. B. A. Windeatt (Harmondsworth: Penguin, 1985).

49. *Her Appeal,* 15.

50. B. J. Todd, "The remarrying widow: a stereotype reconsidered," in *Women in English Society, 1500–1800,* ed. M. Prior (London: Methuen, 1985), 54–92.

51. See G. Fullerton, *The Life of Elisabeth Lady Falkland* (London: Burns and Oates, 1883).

52. HEH, Hastings MSS, Legal Papers, box 4, folder 1, testimony of Roshe.

53. HEH, Hastings MSS, Genealogical, box 1, folder 12. Davies was not the only spouse to impose such a condition. Henry, earl of Pembroke, had earlier done the same for his wife, Mary Sidney; see M. Hannay, *Philip's Phoenix: Mary Sidney, Coutness of Pembroke* (Oxford: Oxford University Press, 1990), 172.

54. Birch, *Charles I* 1:173–75.

55. *Her Appeal* (1646), 15; see also Anthony à Wood, *Athenae Oxonienses* (London, 1691), 1:432; Luke 6:21, 7:37–50. Tears were an important part of the spiritual experiences of Margery Kempe.

56. Birch, *Charles* 1:181–83.

57. *Her Appeal* (1646), 22.

58. HEH, Hastings MSS, Correspondence, HA 10543.

59. HEH, Hastings MSS, Correspondence, HA 5513; Hastings's testimony admits letters of administration were granted before the funeral (HEH, Hastings MSS, Legal Papers, box 4, folder 4). A copy of the letters of administration among the Hastings MSS shows a date of 10 December (HEH, Hastings MSS, Legal Papers, box 2, folder 12); the probate records are dated 16 December (P.R.O., PROB 11/150); the burial occurred 9 December (*The Register of St. Martin-in-the-Fields, London,* transc. and ed. J. V. Kitto, London: Harleian Society, vol. 46 [1936], 226).

60. HEH, Hastings MSS, Legal Papers, box 4, folder 1, testimony of Roshe, servant of Davies; Hastings's testimony corroborates this (folder 4). The church of Davies's day was pulled down in 1721. His monument probably went with the church. See J. McMaster, *A Short History of the Royal Parish of St. Martin-in-the-Fields* (London: Rugby Press, 1916), 26ff., 53–56. Some of the old grave stones (but apparently not his) are on the floor of the coffeehouse in the basement of the present church.

61. E.g., HEH, Hastings MSS, Correspondence, HA 2337, HA 2572.

62. HEH, Hastings MSS, Correspondence, HA 4840. See also L. Stone, *Crisis of the Aristocracy 1558–1641* (Oxford: Clarendon Press, 1965), 785.

63. Bodl., MS. Carte 62, fols. 590–91; see G. R. Potter and E. M. Simpson, eds., *The Sermons of John Donne* (Berkeley: University of California Press, 1953).

64. HEH, Hastings MSS, Legal Papers, box 4, folders 1 and 6; see also Accounts and Financial Papers, box 9, folder 7, a book of accounts from the end of November 1629 until 7 September 1630, which are for Englefield and include some of the Hastings's expenses for litigation in that connection.

65. See HEH, Hastings MSS, Legal papers, box 4, folders 1, 4, 5, 6, 7. There was some question about charges or extents laid on Pirton; see HEH, Hastings MSS, Correspondence, HA9738; Legal Papers, box 4, folder 4 and box 2, folder 12. The crown seized the manor in 1628 for payment of debts incurred by Arthur Denny, the previous holder (VCH, *Hertfordshire* 3:50).

66. See HEH, Hastings MSS, Legal Papers, box 4, folder 1, testimony of Bridget Crosse and Roshe.

67. See T. E., *The Lawes Resolutions of Womens Rights,* published in 1632, though claiming to be the work of an author then dead.

68. HEH, Hastings MSS, Correspondence, HA 4840.

69. HEH, Hastings MSS, Correspondence, HA 4840.

70. HEH, Hastings MSS, Correspondence, HA 2333.

71. HEH, Hastings MSS, Deeds, HAD 2416, dated 26 April 1627, leasing part of the manor of Pirton is in the names of Lady Eleanor and Sir Archibald as husband and wife. She says she married in three months in *Her Appeal* (1646), 15. HEH, Hastings MSS, Legal Papers, box 4, folder 7, says five months, but that would put the marriage in the beginning of May, after the date of the deed.

72. J. Nichols, *The Progresses, Processions, and Magnificent Festivities of King James* (London: Society of Antiquaries, 1828), 4:1010.

73. P.R.O., SP 16/117/25; see also F. R. Gordon, ed., *The Diary of John Young* (London: S.P.C.K., 1928), 4–5 and genealogical table; see also H. Young, *Sir Peter Young, Knt of Seaton* (Edinburgh: Neill and Co., 1896). I have found no evidence to substantiate Douglas's claim that James I was his father. I am grateful to Jenny Wormald and Maurice Lee for their response to my queries about this.

74. *Her Jubilee,* 3; see also *New Jerusalem,* 11.

75. *New Jerusalem,* 13–17; see also *Her Appeal* (1646), 36–37; also P.R.O., SP 16/395/14.

76. HEH, Hastings MSS, Legal Papers, box 2, folder 12, deposition of

William Smith; cf. the claim that someone impersonated Douglas, box 2, folder 12. I am grateful to Malcolm Smuts for information that Douglas, listed as paying 26s. for the poor in the accounts of the overseers for 1629, appears at an address near St. James's palace.

77. *Her Appeal* (1646), 15. Also see HEH, Hastings MSS, Legal Papers, box 4, folder 1, deposition of Bridget Crosse; box 4, folder 4, responses of Lord Hastings; box 3, folder 3, Gardiner's answers.

78. HEH, Hastings MSS, Genealogy, box 1, folder 12. Also see *Her Appeal* (1646), 15.

79. Sir Edward Coke died intestate (L. Norsworthy, *The Lady of Bleeding Heart Yard: Lady Elizabeth Hatton 1578–1646* [1935; London: John Murray, 1938], 215–16).

80. P.R.O., C 142/437; C 2, Chas I, H69/19.

81. HEH, Hastings MSS, Legal Papers, box 4, folder 4, Ferdinando's responses.

82. P.R.O., PROB 11/150; a copy is in HEH, Hastings MSS, Personal Papers, box 17, folder 20.

83. HEH, Hastings MSS, Correspondence, HA 5513.

84. HEH, Hastings MSS, Legal Papers, box 4, folder 1, depositions of Sir William Beecher, Dr. Thomas Reeves; box 3, folders 2, 5.

85. HEH, Hastings MSS, Legal Papers, box 2, folder 12. In April, Douglas had asked to be relieved of accompanying his troops (*Cal. St. P. Dom.*, *1627–8*, 146; see also *Acts of the Privy Council, Jan.-Aug. 1627*, 145, 150, 180, passim).

86. P.R.O., SP 16/117/25. See also W. A. Shaw, ed. *Letters of Denization and Acts of Naturalization*, Publications of the Huguenot Society of London, vol. 18 (London: Huguenot Society, 1911), 43.

87. HEH, Hastings MSS, Legal Papers, box 2, folder 12.

88. *Her Appeal* (1646), 28; H.M.C., *Fifth Report*, app. 25.

89. Croke, *The Third Part of the Reports*, 3d ed. (London, 1683), 343–47 (King's Bench, Hillary Term, 9 Car., Hastings v. Douglas, Trover and Conversion). I owe this citation to Paul Hardacre.

90. *Warning to the Dragon*, 85.

91. *Her Appeal* (1646), 17–18; cf. Sir John Davies's description of Henrietta Maria (HEH, Hastings MSS, Correspondence, HA 1931).

92. *Her Appeal* (1646), 18–19.

93. *Her Appeal* (1646), 19. Lady Eleanor says "conceived of," not gave birth to, but she would not have known that the child was a son until the birth (the baby was premature). In the margin, Lady Eleanor wrote "coming before Her time." See also Q. Bone, *Henrietta Maria: Queen of the Cavaliers* (Urbana: University of Illinois Press, 1972), 70.

94. Birch, *Charles I* 1:368; Kent Archives Office, Dering MSS,

U350/C2/19 (printed in L. Larking, ed., *Proceedings Principally in the County of Kent,* Camden Society, vol. 80 [London, 1862], xiin); see also *Her Appeal* (1646), 29.

95. *Her Appeal* (1646), 30–31.

96. Kent Archives Office, U350/C2.

97. Kent Archives Office, U350/C2; see also Birch, *Charles I* 1:368.

98. *Her Appeal* (1646), 19.

99. *Restitution of Prophecy,* 12; *Revelation Interpreted,* 4. See D. Cressy, *Bonfires and Bells: National Memory and the Protestant Calendar in Elizabethan and Stuart England* (Los Angeles: University of California Press, 1989), 126–27.

100. *Revelation Interpreted,* 7–8.

101. *Her Jubilee,* 3; *Revelation Interpreted,* 5; *New Jerusalem,* 6–11.

102. *Revelation Interpreted,* 5.

103. *Revelation Interpreted,* 14.

104. *Her Appeal* (1646), 19–20; also see *Appearance,* 14–15.

105. See R. Lockyer, *Buckingham* (1981; London: Longman, 1984), 454, 461, 466; see also P. Gregg, *King Charles I* (London: J. M. Dent and Sons, 1981), 176ff.

106. P.R.O., C 115/M30/8082.

107. *Acts of the Privy Council, 1630–31,* no. 415 (14 December 1630). It is possible that her summons had to do with her brother who was being held as a close prisoner in the Tower of London that December, but her failure to mention the summons in her discussions of his case makes it seem unlikely that this was the explanation. See P.R.O., C 115/M30/8074.

108. *Cal. St. P. Dom., 1629–31,* 478; see J. Richards, "'His Nowe Majestie' and the English Monarchy: The Kingship of Charles I before 1640," *Past and Present,* no. 113 (1986): 70–96; see also M. Smuts, "The Court and its Neighborhood: Royal Policy and Urban Growth in the Early Stuart West End," paper presented at conference "One Imperial Crown: The Multiple Kingdoms of Seventeenth-Century Britain," University of Illinois, Urbana, 1990.

109. *Her Appeal* (1646), 20–21.

110. *Her Appeal* (1646), 20, 24. Neither the portions of Dean Young's diary in print, edited by F. R. Gordon, nor the manuscript (Winchester Cathedral Library) give evidence about the Dean's opinion of Lady Eleanor. I am grateful to Canon Keith Walker, librarian, and his staff at Winchester Cathedral Library for allowing me to examine the manuscript diary.

111. *Her Appeal* (1646), 27.

112. Dr. John Young, Dean of Winchester, was not enthusiastic about the

ceremonialism of the Caroline church (see Gordon, *The Diary of John Young,* 89, 119–21.

113. *Her Appeal* (1646), 17, 22, 29–30.

114. Concerning patronage, see L. Peck, "'For a King not to be bountiful were a fault': Perspectives on Court Patronage in Early Stuart England," *Journal of British Studies* 25, no. 1 (1986): 31–61.

115. W. Prynne, *Histrio Mastix* (London, 1633), 214; P.R.O., C 115/M30/8074. I am grateful to Cynthia Herrup for sharing with me and permitting me to cite the paper about this that she read at the Berkshire Conference in June 1990; cf. C. Bingham, "Seventeenth-Century Attitudes Toward Deviant Sex," *Journal of Interdisciplinary History* 1, no. 3 (1971): 447–72.

116. *The Arraignment and Conviction of Mervin Lord Audeley, earle of Castlehaven* (London, 1642). Lord Scudamore's correspondents kept him informed of the proceedings; see P.R.O., C 115/M30/8074, 8079, 8081–82, 8091; P.R.O., C 115/M31/8133. Also see M. A. E. Greene, ed., *Diary of John Rous* (London: Camden Society, 1856), 66:66.

117. *Word of God,* 11–12 (irregular pagination).

118. *Restitution of Prophecy,* 9; see also HEH, Hastings MSS, Legal Papers, box 5, folder 2.

119. See *Word of God;* see also *Crying Charge.*

120. P.R.O., SP 16/189/69. They asked for mercy for their brother and also requested that the witnesses against him be examined. Maria had died in 1611.

121. P.R.O., SP 16/190/60.

122. I am grateful to Cynthia Herrup for finding this letter (B.L., Add. MS. 69919, fol. 15) and sharing her transcript of it with me.

123. Cynthia Herrup found this petition with the letter (B.L., Add. MS 69919).

124. *Woe to the House;* also see HEH, Hastings MSS, Legal Papers, box 3, folder 2.

125. HEH, Hastings MSS, Correspondence, HA 1470. Lady Alice reports that her grandmother, the Dowager Countess of Derby, was angry. Milton's *Comus,* performed in 1634 at Ludlow in honor of the earl of Bridgewater, brother-in-law of Anne Stanley, makes an attempt to comfort the family in the wake of the Castlehaven incident. See R. K. Mundhenk, "Dark Scandal and The Sun-Clad Powers of Chastity: The Historical Milieu of Milton's *Comus,*" *Studies in English Literature* 15 (1975): 141–52; B. Breasted, *"Comus* and the Castlehaven Scandal," *Milton Studies* 3 (1971): 201–24; W. Hunter, *Milton's Comus: Family Piece* (Troy, N.Y.: Whitson Publishing, 1983). Ann Coiro has suggested that we might see Lady Eleanor in the Lady in *Comus.* But also

see J. Creaser, "Milton's *Comus:* The Irrelevance of the Castlehaven Scandal," *Notes and Queries,* n.s., 31, no. 33 (1984): 307–17.

126. *Crying Charge,* 2.

127. *Restitution of Prophecy,* 9ff. In *Word of God* she describes the Countess of Castlehaven as a "wicked woman" (7) and an "adultress" (12).

128. *Word of God,* 6–7, 9–10.

129. P.R.O., SP 16/190/60; *Acts of the Privy Council, June 1630–June 1631,* no. 957, 1127; Folger MS. V. B. 328, fols. 30–31.

130. *Her Appeal* (1646), 21–22.

131. *Her Appeal* (1646), 22–23; see M. Maclure, *The Paul's Cross Sermons, 1534–1642* (Toronto: University of Toronto Press, 1958), 15–18.

132. HLRO, Main Papers, 19, 20, and 30 April 1642.

133. *Star to the Wise,* 11.

134. *Everlasting Gospel,* 8.

Chapter 3

1. See A. F. Johnson, "J.F. Stam, Amsterdam, and English Bibles," *Library,* 5th ser., 9, no. 1 (1954): 185–93; see also A. F. Johnson, "The Exiled Church at Amsterdam and its Press," *Library.* 5th ser., 5 (1951): 219–42.

2. P.R.O., PC 2/43, fol. 57.

3. *Everlasting Gospel,* 8–9.

4. P.R.O., SP 16/255/19. Lesley Le Claire, Librarian at Worcester College, helped me obtain a photocopy of that version. See also Hindle, 12–13.

5. *All the Kings of the Earth,* sig.A1.

6. See S. Adams, "The Protestant Cause: Religious Alliance in the West European Calvinist Communities as a Political Issue in England 1585–1630" (Ph.D. thesis, Oxford University, 1972).

7. *Warning to the Dragon,* preface.

8. See B. Lewalski, "Lucy, Countess of Bedford: Images of a Jacobean Courtier and Patroness," in *Politics of Discourse,* ed. K. Sharpe and S. Zwicker (Los Angeles: University of California Press, 1987), 52–77.

9. *All the Kings of the Earth,* sig.A1v. The letter is dated 12/22 September (P.R.O., SP 16/534/47). The dates in Amsterdam would be new style, ten days after the dates in England.

10. *All the Kings of the Earth,* title page.

11. *Revelation Interpreted,* 4; see also *Before the Lords Second Coming,* 3; *Blasphemous Charge; Dragons Blasphemous Charge.*

12. See Acts 19:24–38. Diana was notorious for her resentment against those who neglected her worship. The Temple at Ephesus, one of the

seven wonders of the ancient world, was destroyed in one night by a man who wanted to become famous. Among the points charged against Prynne in connection with *Histrio Mastix* was his alleged claim that St. Paul's had been dedicated to Diana; see *S.T.* 3:566; see also W. Prynne, *Histrio Mastix* (London, 1633), 758.

13. *All the Kings of the Earth,* title page. Astronomer Thomas Digges had written a book at the time and also wrote to Lord Burghley to inform him about the star of 1572; see A. McLean, *Humanism and the Rise of Science in Tudor England* (New York: Neale Watson Academic Publishing, 1972), 146; see also *Cal. St. P., Dom. 1547–80,* 454; Jeremiah 25:11–13.

14. *All the Kings of the Earth,* Daniel 11, note B; see also Daniel 7, note G; Daniel 11, note C.

15. *All the Kings of the Earth,* Daniel 11, notes L and M; see also notes K and O.

16. *History of the World* (1614), "Preface" in W. Ralegh, *Selected Writings,* ed. G. Hammond (Hardmondsworth: Penguin Books, 1984), 133–34.

17. P.R.O., SP 16/534/47.

18. *Given to the Elector;* see Wing, 465; see also Hindle, 22–23. Worcester College has three copies, which represent two printings from 1648. One copy was presented to Fairfax by Lady Eleanor and referred to on the final page of the 1651 edition; another is the one she inscribed for Lady Fairfax.

19. *Given to the Elector* (1633 [1648]); *Amend, Amend* (1643); *Strange and Wonderfull Prophesies* (1649); see also *Star to the Wise,* 14–15; *Her Blessing,* 7–8.

20. See W. Chappell, *Popular Music of the Olden Time* (London, 1893), 1:144–45. There were at least two tunes for the ballad, only one of which Chappell found. That, he admitted, would not fit the words. The second tune is probably that for which the first few notes appear on two of the 1648 printings of Lady Eleanor's tract (Worcester College copies). Both her words and those Chappell cites fit. I owe special thanks to Pamela Starr for the reference to Chappell and to her and Carole Goebes for help in interpreting the music on the tract.

21. *Given to the Elector,* 9.

22. See the case of Edmond Coppinger, who was cited for treason in 1590 (R. Bancroft, *Dangerous Positions,* [London, 1640]).

23. P.R.O., SP 16/255/20; see Daniel 7; Revelation 11:7; Revelation 13.

24. See J. LeNeve, *Fasti Ecclesiae Anglicanae* (London, 1716), 1:27.

25. See *As not Unknowne;* see also *Great Brittains Visitation,* 31.

26. *And without Proving,* 4.

27. P.R.O., SP 16/248/93.

28. See also her account of those events in *And without Proving*, 4.

29. *Cal. St.P. Dom.*, *1633–34*, 213. See W. Prynne, *Canterburies Doome* (London, 1646), 181. The Holland correspondence in the P.R.O. shows that this scrutiny predated Laud's translation to Canterbury (e.g., P.R.O., SP 84/147, fols. 103–105v).

30. See *Samsons Legacie*, 18–19; see also *Star to the Wise*, 19.

31. See *Blasphemous Charge against Her* (1649), Folger copy; see also HEH, Hastings MSS, Legal Papers, box 6, folder 1; R. G. Usher, *The Rise and Fall of the High Commission* (Oxford: Clarendon Press, 1913), 259.

32. See her marginal note, *Blasphemous Charge*, 5 (Folger copy); see also *Everlasting Gospel*, 12–13; *Her Appeal* (1646), 34. "The Irish Massacre" was observed on 23 October although it actually began on 22 October.

33. *Restitution of Prophecy*, 27–28.

34. *Samsons Legacie*, 18–21. See *Bill of Excommunication*, 5–6, 11–12; *Her Appeal* (1646), 34; *And without Proving*, 4–5; *Everlasting Gospel*, 12.

35. This is a thought I owe to discussion in the Folger seminar and, specifically, to John Pocock.

36. See *Everlasting Gospel*, 9; see also *Her Appeal* (1646), 34; cf. HLRO, Main Papers, 22 September 1647; see also Sarah Jones, who asked Dr. Gouge to father a book (*To Sions Lovers* [1644]).

37. *Restitution of Prophecy*, "To the Reader."

38. See *New Jerusalem*, 5ff.; see also *Her Jubilee*, 2–4.

39. *Before the Lords Second Coming*, 6.

40. *Apoc.*, chap. 11, 2; see also *Her Appeal* (1646), 34.

41. See *Everlasting Gospel*, 6–10; also *Apoc.*, chap. 11, 2.

42. *Dragons Blasphemous Charge*, 8.

43. Cf. Alexander Leighton, *An Epitome or Briefe Discoverie* (London, 1646), 19; see also the conduct of Prynne, Burton, and Bastwick at their trial in the Star Chamber in 1637 (*S.T.* 3:711–70); Lilburne objected that the oath given him in the Star Chamber was the High Commission oath (*S.T.* 3:1323–26).

44. *Cal. St. P. Dom.*, *1633–34*, 536; see also *Cal. St. P. Dom.*, *1634–35*, 176; HEH, Hastings MSS, Legal Papers, box 2, folder 12.

45. Cf. Cottington's remarks when Prynne was tried in Star Chamber for *Histrio Mastix* (*S.T.* 3:576).

46. HEH, Hastings MSS, Legal Papers, box 6, folder 1 (a transcript with her annotations from the court's register); see also *Blasphemous Charge*.

47. P. Heylyn, *Cyprianus Anglicus* (London, 1688), pt. 2, 266; see, for example, Sir Francis Cheynell's remark about being called before Lambe and his agents (Univ. of Nottingham, Clifton MSS Cl C 78; see also P.R.O., SP 16/335/19. Heylyn followed his remarks about Lady

Eleanor with an account of Lady Purbeck's denunciation of Laud [*Cyprianus Anglicus*, 266]).

48. See *Hells Destruction*, 12, concerning what befell the Lord Mayor of London and Payne, "the perfidious Printer."

49. *Blasphemous Charge*, 7.

50. *Blasphemous Charge*, 7.

51. P.R.O., SP 84/147, fols. 155–56v.

52. P.R.O., SP 16/255/21.

53. See T. Longueville, *The Curious Case of Lady Purbeck* (London: Longmans, Green, 1909); L. Norsworthy, *The Lady of Bleeding Heart Yard: Lady Elizabeth Hatton, 1576–1646* (1935; London: John Murray, 1938); also W. Knowler, ed., *The Earl of Strafford's Letters and Despatches* (London, 1739), 1:389–90, 422–23.

54. Concerning Sarah Jones, see C. Burrage, *The Early English Dissenters* (Cambridge, 1912), 1:322–25; S. R. Gardiner, ed., *Reports of Cases in the Court of Star Chamber and High Commission*, Camden Society, n.s., vol. 39 (London, 1886), 285–86.

55. For example, Thomas Blomfield (*Cal. St. P. Dom., 1633–34*, 535); Benjamin Pratt (*Cal. St. P. Dom., 1634–35*, 116). Lady Eleanor is the only woman to appear on Douglas Bush's "partial list of [early seventeenth-century] writers who suffered imprisonment, civil or political" (*English Literature in the Earlier Seventeenth Century 1600–1660* [Oxford: Clarendon Press, 1945], 29–30).

56. For example, Francis Abbott (*Cal. St. P. Dom., 1634–35*, 319–20); Richard Walker (*Cal St. P. Dom., 1634–35*, 544); Bastwick (*Cal. St. P. Dom., 1634–35*, 548).

57. *Blasphemous Charge*, 10.

58. *Cal. St. P. Dom., 1633–34*, 480–81, 535–36, 579–84; *Cal. St. P. Dom., 1634–35*, 49–54, 108–27, 175–77, 222, 258–78, 314–37; 378–79, 489–96, 532–54. R. G. Usher notes £12,000 as the highest fine (Usher, *Rise and Fall*, 266, 281–82). Star Chamber fines were apparently heavier; e.g. Leighton's of £10,000 or Prynne's of £5,000 (*DNB*, s.v. "Leighton," "Prynne").

59. Amy Green was also referred to as Amy Holland (*Cal. St. P. Dom., 1633–34*, 481). Viscountess Purbeck had been fined only £500 (Norsworthy, *Lady*, 188).

60. He claimed that Saturday was the sabbath. See *Cal. St. P. Dom., 1634–35*, 126, 549; *Cal. St. P. Dom., 1635–36*, 495; also *DNB*, s.v. "Brabourne."

61. *Cal. St. P. Dom., 1634–35*, 176.

62. *Cal. St. P. Dom., 1634–35*, 547–58, 550.

63. *Cal. St. P. Dom., 1634–35*, 269.

64. For example, Gardiner, *Reports of Cases,* 310.

65. J. Stow, *Survey of London* (1598; London: Dent, 1956), 420. See also E. Carpenter, ed., *A House of Kings: The History of Westminster Abbey* (New York: John Day, 1966).

66. See, for example, *Cal. St. P. Dom., 1634–35,* 112, 113, 124, 270, 278, 316, 378, 494, 544. Sir John Eliot and John Selden both spent some time in the Gatehouse, though on orders from the Privy Council, not the High Commission (*DNB,* s.v. "Eliot," "Selden"). Viscountess Purbeck fled to avoid the imprisonment which would have followed her refusal to pay her fine and do penance (Norsworthy, *Lady,* 188ff.).

67. *Cal. St. P. Dom., 1634–35,* 273, 493, 533, 542.

68. See C. Gillett, *Burned Books: Neglected Chapters in British History and Literature* (New York: Columbia University Press, 1932), vol. 1.

69. *Cal. St. P. Dom., 1640,* 398; cf. the refusal of the Viscountess Purbeck to submit and, in 1635, to appear in court.

70. P.R.O., C 115/M30/8114; see also *Cal. St. P. Dom., 1634–35,* 176.

71. W. Scott and J. Bliss, eds., *The Works of William Laud* (Oxford: Parker Society, 1857), 6:333–34; Knowler, *Strafford Letters* 1:155–56 and 171–74 (Wentworth's reply); *And without Proving,* 4. It is not explicitly a part of "Handwriteing October 1633," but she may have communicated that to him orally (P.R.O., SP 16/248/93).

72. HEH, Hastings MSS, Legal Papers, box 6, folder 1.

73. *Her Appeal* (1646), 34; HLRO, Main Papers, 22 September 1647; *Before the Lords Second Coming,* 14; *Her Blessing,* 35; *Star to the Wise,* 14–15.

74. Psalm 138:4; HEH, Hastings MSS, Legal Papers, box 6, folder 1.

75. See *Everlasting Gospel,* 9–10.

76. *Blasphemous Charge* (Wing D1981).

77. Wing D1980; the Folger copy is an exemplum.

78. This copy lacks a title page and is bound at the front of the Folger's volume of Lady Eleanor's tracts.

79. *Her Appeal* (1646), 31–34.

80. See J. T. Cliffe, *The Puritan Gentry* (London: Routledge and Kegan Paul, 1984), 21, 25–26; P. Mack, "Women as Prophets during the English Civil War," *Feminist Studies* 8 (1982): 19–45; E. Hobby, *Virtue of Necessity: English Women's Writing 1649–88* (Ann Arbor: University of Michigan Press, 1989); also D. Ludlow, "'Arise and Be Doing': English 'Preaching' Women, 1640–1660" (Ph.D. thesis, Indiana University, 1978); E. Huber, *Women and the Authority of Inspiration* (Lanham, Md.: University Press of America, 1985).

81. E. Petroff, "Medieval Women Visionaries: Seven Stages to Power," *Frontiers* 3, no. 1 (1978): 38–39.

82. P.R.O., SP 16/283/114.
83. P.R.O., SP 16/255/21. The petition is undated.
84. HLRO, Main Papers, 22 September 1647; see also the marginal note in *Dragons Blasphemous Charge,* 13.
85. P.R.O., SP 16/280/20.
86. For example, *Dragons Blasphemous Charge,* 13, printed gloss; *Before the Lords Second Coming,* 10 (annotation in Folger copy).
87. J. Bastwick, *The Letany* (London, 1637), 12; see also W. Prynne, *A New Discovery* (London, 1641); H. Burton, *A Narrative of the Life of Mr. Henry Burton* (London, 1643).
88. W. Waller, *Divine Meditations* (London, 1680), "Upon my imprisonment" (a reference I owe to Barbara Donagan). Richard Lovelace was imprisoned in the Gatehouse when he wrote "To Althea from Prison" in 1642 (*DNB,* s.v. "Lovelace").
89. For example, *Je le Tien,* 25; also see *Day of Judgment,* 13; *Restitution of Reprobates,* 4, but cf. *Gatehouse Salutation,* 5–7.
90. See *Bill of Excommunication,* 34.
91. P.R.O., C 115/M36/8451.
92. P.R.O., SP 16/283/114; *Ezekiel the Prophet,* 5–6; cf. Ezekiel 1: 27–2:2.
93. P.R.O., C 115/M36/8451. There had been a fire on London Bridge the preceding February. In fact, a heavy snow fell upon the city; see P. Seaver, *Wallington's World: A Puritan Artisan in Seventeenth-Century London* (Stanford, Calif.: Stanford University Press, 1983), 48–49; see also *Cal. St. P. Dom., 1633–34,* 384 where the paper is filed under 1633.
94. P.R.O., SP 16/283/114; *Ezekiel the Prophet,* 5–6; cf. Ezekiel 1:27–2:2.
95. *Cal. St. P. Dom., 1635,* 230; HLRO, Main Papers, 22 September 1647.
96. HEH, Hastings MSS, Correspondence, box 15, HA 1470. The Countess of Huntingdon had died 26 January 1634. Lucy and Ferdinando had left Ashby to live with the earl at Donnington shortly before Alice wrote; also see *Woe to the House.*
97. HEH, Hastings MSS, Correspondence, box 15, HA 1471.

Chapter 4

1. HEH, Hastings MSS, Correspondence, box 11, HA 2332. The letter's reference to Lucy's children suggests that it should be dated 1635, not 1625. In 1625, 7 September was a Wednesday, but it was Monday in 1635. (C. R. Cheyney, *Handbook of Dates* [London: Royal Historical Society, 1945], tables 8 and 27). Her reference to Elstree raises questions about her route. Concerning Elstree, see VCH, *Hertfordshire*

2:349–51. *Adulvestre* is one old variant of Elstree. See also J. S. Burn, *The High Commission* (London: J. Russell Smith, 1865), 32.

2. HEH, Hastings MSS, Religious Papers, box 1, folder 28. The tract is in her hand; to my knowledge, it was never printed.

3. I have not been able to identify Clarknes Downe.

4. P.R.O., SP 16/380/94; HEH, Hastings MSS, Correspondence, box 11, HA 2332.

5. See *DNB* s.v. "Wright"; see also *The Works of William Laud* (Oxford: Parker Society, 1853), 5:346.

6. *Cosin Correspondence* (Durham: Surtees Society, 1868), 1:217–19.

7. L. G. Wickham Legg, ed., *A Relation of A Short Survey of 26 Counties Observed in a seven weeks Journey begun on August 11, 1634, By a Captain, a lieutenant, and an Ancient* (London: F. E. Robinson, 1904), 57; J. A. Langford, *Staffordshire and Warwickshire, Past and Present* (London: William Mackenzie, n.d.), 1:430.

8. Birch, *Charles I* 2:259.

9. P.R.O., SP 16/380/94.

10. P.R.O., SP 16/380/94; *Warning to the Dragon*, 34.

11. P.R.O., SP 16/380/94; see also *Restitution of Prophecy*, 35–6; *Bethlehem*, 4–6; T. Birch, *Charles I* 2:259.

12. See K. Carroll, "Early Quakers and 'Going Naked as a Sign,'" *Quaker History* 67 (1978): 69–87.

13. See E. Macek, "The Emergence of a Feminine Spirituality in *The Book of Martyrs*," *Sixteenth Century Journal* 19, no. 1 (1988): 63–80; E. Petroff, "Medieval Women Visionaries: Seven Stages to Power," *Frontiers* 3, no. 1 (1978): 35; S. Williams, *Divine Rebel: The Life of Anne Marbury Hutchinson* (New York: Holt, Rinehart and Winston, 1981); M. M. Dunn, "Women of Light," in *Women of America*, ed. C. R. Berkin and M. B. Norton (Boston: Houghton Mifflin, 1979), 114–36.

14. P.R.O., SP 16/380/94; see also SP 16/351/18.

15. P.R.O., SP 16/380/94; cf. York, where the Dean's wife allowed a conventicle in her home (R. Marchant, *The Puritans and the Church Courts in the Diocese of York, 1560–1642* [London: Longmans, 1960], 81).

16. *Restitution of Prophecy*, 35–37; see Matthew 25:14–30.

17. *Restitution of Prophecy*, 36; *Bethlehem*, 4; Matthew 26:54.

18. P.R.O., PC 2/47, 26–27; J. Stow, *Survey of London* (1598; London, Dent, 1956), 148–49; see also P. Allderidge, "Management and Mismanagement at Bedlam, 1547–1633," in *Health, Medicine, and Mortality in the Sixteenth Century*, ed. C. Webster (Cambridge: Cambridge University Press, 1979), 141–64.

19. Allderidge, "Management and Mismanagement," 157–58, 163.

20. P.R.O., SP 16/237/5; see also Allderidge, "Management and Misman-agement," 160–64. The Minutebook of the Court of Governors shows a serious dispute between the steward and the porter and questions about dishonesty in the handling of provisions in 1637. I am grateful to Dr. Patricia Allderidge, Archivist, Bethlehem Royal Hospital, for welcoming me there and assisting me in finding relevant material in the Minutebooks.

21. P.R.O., PC 2/47, 26–27. One contemporary described William Dowsing, who was one of those appointed by a parliamentary warrant in 1643 and 1644 to destroy images in Suffolk, as "a Bedlam" (C. H. Evelyn-White, ed., *The Journal of William Dowsing of Stratford, Parliamentary Visitor* [Ipswich: Pawsey and Hayes, 1885], 7).

22. See R. Porter, *Mind-Forg'd Manacles: A History of Madness in England from the Restoration to the Regency* (London: Athlone Press, 1987); Dorothy Osborne described passion as a "refined degree of madnesse" (K. Parker, ed., *Letters to Sir William Temple* [London: Penguin Books, 1987], letter 48); cf. modern views in M. Siegler and H. Osmond, *Models of Madness, Models of Medicine* (New York: Macmillan, 1974); see also W. R. Walter, "Mental Illness and Psychiatric Treatment among Women" in *The Psychology of Women: Ongoing Debates*, ed. M. R. Walsh (New Haven: Yale University Press, 1987), 102–18.

23. R. Burton, *Anatomy of Melancholy*, (London, 1638), esp. 161ff., 213, 538, 632ff.; see also T. Adams, *Mystical Bedlam, or the World of Mad-Men* (London, 1615). See also Timothy Rogers's plea for better under-standing of the mentally ill in T. Rogers, *A Discourse Concerning Trouble of Mind* (London, 1691), a reference I owe to Barbara Donagan.

24. M. MacDonald, *Mystical Bedlam: Madness, Anxiety and Healing in Seven-teenth-Century England* (Cambridge: Cambridge University Press, 1981), esp. 120ff.

25. See R. Reed, *Bedlam on the Jacobean Stage* (Cambridge, Mass.: Harvard University Press, 1952); see also "New Mad Tom of Bedlam," in *Roxburgh Ballads* (Hertford: Ballad Society, 1873), 2:8; see also J. Wiltenburg, "Madness and Society in the Street Ballads of Early Mod-ern England," *Journal of Popular Culture* 21, no. 4 (1988): 101–27. In Thomas Middleton's *The Changeling* (1622), we hear of "but two sorts of people" in Bedlam, "fools and madmen; the one has not wit enough to be knaves, and the other not knavery enough to be fools" (T. Middleton, *The Changeling*, ed. P. Thomson [London: Ernest Benn, 1964], act I, sc. 2, line 45).

26. Burton, *Melancholy*, title page. Burton exhorted his readers to observe the madman and see themselves in him.

27. R. Porter, *A Social History of Madness: The World Through the Eyes of the*

Insane (New York: Weidenfeld and Nicolson, 1987), 104–5. All-deridge quotes from lists of Bedlamites in "Management and Mismanagement," 159–60. S. Gilman (*Seeing the Insane* [New York: John Wiley and Sons, 1982]) points out the seventeenth-century Dutch sculpture, "The Woman from the Mad House" who was a manic figure (19). "Mad Bessie" in the ballads was mad from disappointment in love (Wiltenburg, "Madness and Society," 118). I am grateful to facilitators and participants in the workshop on Reading Women and Madness in Medical, Dramatic, and Visual Texts at the conference on Attending to Women in Early Modern England, November 1990.

28. H. E. Bell, *An Introduction to the History and Records of the Court of Wards and Liveries* (Cambridge: Cambridge University Press, 1953), 128–32; see also R. Neugebauer, "Treatment of the Mentally Ill in Medieval and Early Modern England: A Reappraisal," *Journal of the History of the Behavioral Sciences* 14, no. 2 (1978): 158–69; MacDonald, *Mystical Bedlam,* 3ff.

29. A. Fessler, "The Management of Lunacy in Seventeenth-Century England," *Proceedings of the Royal Society of Medicine* 49 (1956): 901–7; see M. Hale, *The History of the Pleas of the Crown* (London, 1726), 1: chap. 4.

30. M. Dalton, *The Countrey Justice* (London, 1635), chap. 68; see also chap. 70 and 72.

31. E. Pagitt, *The Mystical Wolfe* (London, 1645), 11–12.

32. Dalton, *Countrey Justice,* chap. 42. Statutes dealing with prophecy include: 5 Eliz., c. 15; 23 Eliz., c.2; 3&4 Ed. VI, c. 15; 33 Hen. VIII, c.14. Sir Francis Bacon, who declined to discuss divine prophecies, recommended that the others not be believed, "for they have done much Mischiefe: Ane I see many severe Lawes made to suppresse them" (F. Bacon, *The Essayes or Counsels, Civill and Morall,* ed. by M. Kiernan [Oxford: Clarendon Press, 1985], 114).

33. See P. Mack, "Women as Prophets," *Feminist Studies* 8, no. 1 (1982): 19–45.

34. W. Perkins, *Works* (London, 1613), 2: chap. 1.

35. A. Evans, *An Echo to the Book called A Voyce from Heaven* (London, 1653), 29–30. See C. Hill, "Arise Evans: Welshman in London," in *Change and Continuity in Seventeenth-Century England* (Cambridge, Mass.: Harvard University Press, 1975), 48–77; C. Hill and M. Shepherd, "The Case of Arise Evans: a Historio-Psychiatric Study," *Psychological Medicine* 6 (1976): 351–58.

36. *An Echo,* 43.

37. See E. Cope, *Politics without Parliaments* (London: Allen and Unwin, 1986), 50–54.

38. See P. Studley, *The Looking-Glasse of Schisme,* 2d ed. (London, 1635). Peter Lake brought this case to my attention.

39. T. Birch, *Court and Times of James I* (London: Henry Colburn, 1849) 2:159–60.

40. *Cal. St. P. Dom.,* 1636–37, 459–60, 487–88, 507. See T. Heywood, *A True Discourse of the Two infamous upstart Prophets, Richard Farnham, Weaver of White-Chapell, and John Bull, Weaver of St. Botolphs Aldgate, now Prisoners, the one in Newgate and the other in Bridewell* (London, 1636). Writing before Farnham's commitment to Bedlam, Heywood, though he discusses the weaver's "stupidity or madnesse" (5), does not mention Bedlam. See *DNB,* s.v. "Farnham"; also see K. Thomas, *Religion and the Decline of Magic* (Harmondsworth, Penguin, 1971), 159.

41. *Registers of the Privy Council* (facsimile), 2:537; also *Cal. St. P. Dom.,* 1637–38, 188–89, 606. It is not clear whether the initial order refers to the removal of chains or indicates that the mad were restrained in ways other "prisoners" were not.

42. Concerning the release of Bedlamites, see P. Allderidge, "Bedlam: Fact or Fantasy?" in *The Anatomy of Madness: Essays in the History of Psychiatry,* ed. W. F. Bynum, R. Porter, and M. Shepherd (London: Tavistock Publications, 1985), 2:17–33.

43. Petroff, "Stages," 39–40.

44. P.R.O., SP 16/345/104, "Spirituall Antheme."

45. See *Bethelehem,* 5; see also P.R.O., SP 16/380/94.

46. *Works of William Laud* 5:346. Laud's diary and letters contain a number of references to libels and other attacks upon him. In neither his letter of 26 December 1636 or that of 18 January 1637 to Wentworth, with whom he often discussed libels, did he mention the events at Lichfield, nor does he refer to them in his letter to Lambe on 23 December 1636. He was at Croydon on 14 and 15 December and at Hampton Court on 26 December. See his *Works* 6:472, 7:302–11.

47. *Bethelehem,* 6.

48. P.R.O., SP 16/351/18. Latham supposed the problem arose because he had sent the articles to Edward Mottershed, Registrar of the High Commission, who he wrongly thought had died. This portion of the letter is marked with a note, "omit this" which may indicate that Latham heard action had been taken before he had the letter ready. Latham is identified as official to the Dean in the articles (P.R.O., SP 15/380/94). Mottershed's service as Commissary to the Dean and Chapter of York in 1637 and advocate in High Commission proceedings at Durham in the same year may explain Latham's confusion and the delayed investigation (B. Levack, *The Civil Lawyers in England, 1603–1641* [Oxford: Clarendon Press, 1973], 257).

49. P.R.O., PC 2/47, 26–27.
50. P.R.O., PC 2/47, 49.
51. P.R.O., PC 2/47, 175–76.
52. P.R.O., P C2/47, 175–76.
53. P.R.O., PC 2/47, 335.
54. Minutebook of the Court of Governors of Bridewell and Bethlehem, 3 January 1637[8], fol. 154r; *Registers of the Privy Council* (facs.), 2:619.
55. Minutebook of the Court of Governors of Bethlehem and Bridewell, 16 August 1637, fol. 133v.
56. Minutebook of the Court of Governors of Bethlehem and Bridewell, 16 August 1637, fol. 133v.
57. *Registers of the Privy Council* (facs.), 2:619.
58. Minutebook of the Court of Governors of Bethlehem and Bridewell, 28 February 1637[8], fol. 165r.
59. The Minutebooks of the Court of Governors show that Langley probably deserved the penalty they imposed upon him in February 1638.
60. HEH, Hastings MSS, Correspondence, HA 2335. She may be thinking of Matthew 8:20 with her reference to birds.
61. See the description in Lupton, *London and the Countrey Carbonadoed* (London, 1632), 75–76. See also Arise Evans' statement that those who were trying to have him committed to Bedlam told his wife that "in *Bedlam* I should have good warme meate every meale, and good usage" (Evans, *An Echo,* 43).
62. HLRO, Main Papers, 22 September 1647.
63. *Bethlehem,* 6.
64. HLRO, Main Papers, 22 September 1647.
65. *Apoc. cap. 11,* 2–3.
66. *For the States,* 6; see also *Star to the Wise,* 11.
67. *For Gerbier,* 5; Birch, *Charles I* 2:244. Concerning visitors, see also Allderidge, "Bedlam: Fact or Fantasy," 21–22.
68. *Registers of the Privy Council* (facs.), 3:123.
69. *Bride's Preparation,* 7 (irregular pagination).
70. HLRO, Main Papers, 22 September 1647.
71. HEH, Hastings Correspondence, HA 2336.
72. HEH, Hastings Correspondence, HA 2336; see also HEH, Hastings Correspondence, HA 2337.
73. See HEH, Hastings Correspondence, HA 2344; *New Jerusalem,* 13–23; concerning Sibbald, see J. Venn, *Alumni Cantabrigiensis* (Cambridge: Cambridge University Press, 1924); W. J. Pinks, *The History of Clerkenwell* (London: Charles Herbert, 1881), 67–68.
74. HEH, Hastings Correspondence, HA 2337.
75. P.R.O., SP 16/415/61.

76. See *Cal. St. P. Dom., 1640–41,* 8.
77. HEH, Hastings Correspondence, HA 4276; *Registers of the Privy Council* (facs.), 11:717.
78. The earl of Huntingdon, but not Ferdinando, traveled to York later in September for the Council of Peers. See HEH, Hastings Correspondence, HA 5553; G. E. Cokayne, *The Complete Peerage,* ed. V. Gibbs (London: St. Catherine Press, 1910).

Chapter 5

1. See *C.J.* 2:22, 24, 25, 71, 90, 92, 95, 102, 112, 120, 123–25, 134.
2. *Her Appeale* (1641), preface. This was probably the Angel Inn (later the Crown) in Kensington High Street (London County Council, *Survey of London: vol. 38: Northern Kensington* [London: Athlone Press, 1973], 26).
3. *Restitution of Prophecy,* 25.
4. The practice of monthly fasts for Parliament and the nation did not begin until February 1641/2; see J. Wilson, *Pulpit in Parliament: Puritanism during the English Civil Wars 1640–1648* (Princeton: Princeton University Press, 1969), 43–53, 63, 275–80.
5. *Her Appeal* (1641), 8–9.
6. Daniel 6; *Her Appeal* (1641), 13.
7. *Her Appeal* (1641), esp. 10–14. She still talks here about "the Elect" (15 [irregular pagination]). See Katherine Chidley's account of her sufferings in the hands of bishops and others (K. Chidley, *A New Yeares Gift* [London, 1644]).
8. *Her Appeal* (1641).
9. HLRO, Main Papers, 29 January 1641/2. P.R.O., C 2/Chas I/H69/19; see also P.R.O., C 2/Chas I/D9/55. There was no allegation of usury against Poulton, although Douglas's original arrangements with him were probably a device to obtain a loan; see N. Jones, *God and The Money Lenders: Usury and Law in Early Modern England* (Oxford: Basil Blackwell, 1989), 125.
10. HEH, Hastings MSS, Deeds, HAD 2417.
11. See HLRO, Main Papers, catalogued with material from 29 January 1641[2] and 24 May 1642; see also HEH, Hastings MSS, Correspondence, HA 4825; Personal Papers, box 18, folder 22; Legal Papers, box 9, folder 4. None of the accounts and financial records preserved among the Hastings MSS at the Huntington Library show how much assistance Lady Eleanor received from her daughter and son-in-law.
12. HLRO, Main Papers, 29 January 1641[2].
13. *L.J.* 4:548–49.

14. *L.J.* 4:602. Concerning Littleton, see E. R. Foster, *The House of Lords, 1603–1649* (Chapel Hill: University of North Carolina Press, 1983), 41–43.

15. *L.J.* 4:669, 685, 700.

16. HLRO, Main Papers, 29 January 1642 [*sic*].

17. HLRO, Main Papers, 24 May 1642.

18. HLRO, Main Papers, catalogued with material from 29 January 1641[2].

19. *Her Appeal* (1646), 22.

20. HLRO, Main Papers, 30 April 1642.

21. HEH, Hastings MSS, Correspondence, HA 2344.

22. HLRO, Main Papers, 24 May 1642.

23. P.R.O., PROB 11/189; *L.J.* 5:80.

24. HEH, Hastings MSS, Correspondence, HA 6853, HA 2342.

25. HLRO, Main Papers, April and 19 July 1642. Benyon, who was imprisoned in the Tower of London, was called to testify before the Lords in March. Oliver Lord St. John had petitioned against him for conduct while King's Receiver-General for Northamptonshire and Rutland (*L.J.* 4:669–70, 672–73, 700–701; 5:12, 30).

26. HLRO, Main Papers, 30 June, 11 July, and 23 September 1642; *L.J.* 5:168, 200, 341, 353, 367, 370. George Benyon testified about the mortgage he held of the premises; Kenrick's statement is dated 14 March 1641[2].

27. HLRO, Main Papers, 23 September 1642.

28. *L.J.* 5:370.

29. HEH, Hastings MSS, Correspondence, HA 2338; HLRO, Main Papers, 30 September 1644.

30. *Everlasting Gospel*, 12.

31. *Samsons Fall*, 4.

32. *Samsons Fall*, 4.

33. *Samsons Fall*, 4–5, 7, 10.

34. *Samsons Fall*, 6–7.

35. Thomas Taylor, *Christ Revealed* (London, 1635), 60.

36. J. Milton, *The Reason of Church-government* [1641], in *Complete Prose Works of John Milton*, ed. D. M. Wolfe (New Haven: Yale University Press, 1953), 1:858–59. I am grateful to John Steadman for this reference.

37. *The Life and Death of King Charles, or the Pseudo Martyr* (1650) quoted in L. Potter, *Secret Rites and Secret Writing: Royalist Literature 1641–1660* (Cambridge: Cambridge University Press, 1989), 80.

38. The Folger's copy shows this in continuing pagination with *Samsons Fall*, but a different version of the petition (without the gloss) appears

as a preface to Thomason's copy of *Samsons Legacie.* Thomason dates the petition 14 April 1643. Her marginal gloss on p. 13 (Folger copy) about Lord Brooke's death, "about Candlemas 1642," suggests that even that version of the petition was reprinted with the gloss. At the conclusion of the petition, she dates it 3 January 1642[3], and calls it *"The Holy Ghosts* New-Years-Gift" (Folger, p. 16; Thomason, p. 4).

39. *Samsons Fall,* 13.

40. *Samsons Fall,* 13–16. The division of king from kingdom is a theme that she would take up again and again; see also the satirical print, *Magna Britannia Divisa,* cited by Erica Veevers (*Images of Love and Religion: Queen Henrietta Maria and Court Entertainments* [Cambridge: Cambridge University Press, 1989], 205–9); R. Cotton, *A Treatise, shewing That the soveraignes Person is required in the great Councells or Assemblies of the State, as well at the consultations* (1641), cited in G. Aylmer, "Collective Mentalities in Mid Seventeenth-Century England: II. Royalist Attitudes," *Transactions of the Royal Historical Society,* 5th ser., 37 (1987): 10.

41. See E. MacArthur, "Women Petitioners and the Long Parliament," *English Historical Review* 24 (1909): 698–709; see also P. Higgins, "The Reactions of Women with special reference to Women Petitioners," in *Politics, Religion, and the English Civil War,* ed. Brian Manning (London: Edward Arnold, 1973), 179–222.

42. Cf. F. Woodcock, *The Two Witnesses . . . ,* sermons preached at Lawrence-Jewry in London and printed by order of the House of Commons, 27 April 1643.

43. Compare the first two pages of *Samsons Legacie* and *Samsons Fall.*

44. *Samsons Legacie,* 10–11.

45. *Samsons Legacie,* 4, 7, 8.

46. *Samsons Legacie,* 6, 7–8. See 1 Samuel 8. She makes this point again in *The New Jerusalem* (1649).

47. *Samsons Legacie,* 15. She refers to Genesis 6 when God tells Noah to build an ark to escape the destruction that would come to the wicked world; the word "tyrants" is hers.

48. *Samsons Legacie,* 21–24.

49. *Amend, Amend,* stanza 26; *Appeal from Court to Camp,* 6; *Warning to the Dragon,* 84.

50. *Amend, Amend,* stanzas 25, 28.

51. HEH, Hastings MSS, Correspondence, HA 2338; *C.J.* 3:280.

52. HEH, Hastings MSS, Deeds, HAD 2070.

53. HEH, Hastings MSS, Correspondence, HA 2338; see *L.J.* 5:370.

54. Concerning printing in the early seventeenth century, see P. Blayney, *The Texts of King Lear and their Origins,* vol. 1, *Nicholas Okes and the First*

Quarto (Cambridge: Cambridge University Press, 1982). For examples of her crowded last pages, see *Her Appeal* (1646) and *Day of Judgement.* For examples of missing signatures, see *For the States* and *Remonstrance;* see also *Discovery.*

55. HEH, Hastings MSS, Correspondence, HA 2338.

56. HEH, Hastings MSS, Correspondence, HA 2339.

57. HEH, Hastings MSS, Correspondence, HA 2339; also see Lady Eleanor's letter to Lucy, 13 September 1643 (HEH, Hastings MSS, Correspondence, HA 2340).

58. *Her Blessing,* 38.

59. Concerning mothers and daughters, see R. Houlbrooke, *The English Family 1450–1700* (London: Longman, 1984), 187–88; see also D. Willen, "Women and Religion in Early Modern England," in *Women in Reformation and Counter-Reformation Europe,* ed. S. Marshall (Bloomington: Indiana University Press, 1989), 151–52. We need to ask whether available evidence conceals conflict.

60. HEH, Hastings MSS, Correspondence, HA 2340; see also HA 2339. The quotation comes from the Geneva Bible, whose notes indicate that the reference in verse 10 to ten days of tribulation should be understood as ten years.

61. Thomason dates *Star to the Wise* as 25 November 1643. I have been unsuccessful in my attempts to verify her claim about the Assembly. The Assembly's minutes for this period have not been published, and I was not able to look at the original manuscript in Dr. Williams's Library.

62. *Star to the Wise,* 3–4.

63. *Star to the Wise,* 11–12. See J. T. Cliffe, *The Puritan Gentry* (London: Routledge and Kegan Paul, 1984), 21–22.

64. *Star to the Wise,* 12–13; see 2 John; Revelation 1:9; Matthew 28:1–7.

65. *Star to the Wise,* 6.

66. *Star to the Wise,* 5, 17.

67. *The Revelation Interpreted,* 5. On page 3 of *Great Brittains Visitation* she used the subtitle, "The Revelation of Jesus Christ Interpreted."

68. *Star to the Wise,* 6–8, 10, 14.

69. *Star to the Wise,* 15.

70. In addition to the account in *S.T.* 4:330–600; see H.M.C., *The MSS of the House of Lords,* vol. 11 (n.s.) *Addenda 1514–1714,* 364–467.

71. HEH, Hastings MSS, Correspondence, HA 2341. The letter should be dated 1644, not 1643 as suggested.

72. *Restitution of Reprobates,* 3, 12, 21–22, 26 [irregular pagination].

73. *Restitution of Reprobates,* 30, 32; see also 17–18, 27–28, 34.

74. HLRO, Main Papers, 22 September 1647.

75. HEH, Hastings MSS, Personal Papers, box 19, folder 1 (22 August 1644).
76. P.R.O., PROB 11/192. Kenrick is presumably the man mentioned as Douglas's lessee in a deposition of 23 June 1629 (HEH, Hastings MSS, Legal Papers, box 2, folder 12).
77. P.R.O., C 2/Chas I/D/9/60.
78. *The third part of the Reports of Sir George Croke Kt* (London, 1683), 343–47.
79. HEH, Hastings MSS, Legal Papers, box 4, folder 6.
80. *L.J.* 6:718; 7:3; HLRO, Main Papers, 30 September 1644. The answer is erroneously filed among the Main Papers under 19 July 1642.
81. P.R.O., C 2/Chas I/D/9/60, C 2/Chas I/D/5/39, C 2/Chas I/D/18/36, C 2/Chas I/D/28/6; HLRO, Main Papers, 19 July 1642.
82. P.R.O., C 7/102/39, C 7/103/30, C 7/103/38, C 7/103/98, C 7/412/34. This is not the Nathaniel Ward who went to Massachusetts and then returned to England and gave a controversial sermon to the Commons in 1647.
83. *Apoc. J.C.*, 2.
84. *Apoc. J.C.*, 11–14.
85. *Apoc. J.C.*, 31–32.
86. *Her Blessing*, 38.
87. *Her Blessing*, 3.
88. *Her Blessing*, 9–13.
89. *Her Blessing*, 10–11.
90. *Her Blessing*, 14.
91. *Her Blessing*, 17; see Acts 8:23.
92. *Her Blessing*, 12, 22–23.
93. *Her Blessing*, 35.
94. *Her Blessing*, 35; cf. *Restitution of Reprobates*, 18.
95. Both the Folger and the Worcester College copy are apparently reprints from 1649; both have appended another prayer dated in the latter year.
96. *Prayer* (1644), 4–5. A comparison with the Prayerbook shows that her wording is her own; cf. also William Lilly, *The Starry Messenger, or An Interpretation of that strange Apparition of three Suns seene in London, 19 1644, being the Birthday of King Charles.* . . . (London, 1645). Lady Eleanor does not mention the three suns.
97. *Prayer* (1644), 6; see 2 Kings 2:24.
98. *Prayer* (1644), 6–7 (Folger copy).
99. The surviving copies of these tracts are from 1649. The tracts have the same text for their first nine pages, thereafter they differ.
100. I have found only an initial fragment of the English edition; it appears to follow very closely the corresponding pages of the Latin text.

101. "Legato Lusitaniae in Anglia residenti." She may have meant Lusitania, an ancient term for Portugal, as a pun to invoke light in contrast to the darkness of Lucifer.
102. *Her Blessing* contains a number of Latin passages; for Latin marginalia, see *Before the Lords Second Coming*, title page. James McCarthy, who looked at *Prophetia*, was struck by how classical its Latin was.
103. *Her Blessing*, 25.
104. *For the Blessed Feast*, 9. The wording of the Prayerbook concerning the interpretation of the Eucharist had been a matter of dispute since the Reformation; see A. G. Dickens, *The English Reformation*, rev. ed. (Glasgow: Fontana/Collins, 1967), 347–48; 413–15.

Chapter 6

1. *Word of God*, 10–6 [*sic*] (pagination irregular).
2. *Word of God*, 9 (pagination irregular).
3. Cf. Matthew 25; *Word of God*, 5.
4. *As not Unknowne.*
5. *Brides Preparation*, 9 (irregular pagination); see Revelation 21:2, 9; cf. R. Sibbes, *The Brides Longing for her Bridegroomes second coming* (London, 1639). I am grateful to Stephen Baskerville for bringing Sibbes's work to my attention.
6. *Brides Preparation*, 7 (irregular pagination); see Revelation 21:10–27.
7. HEH, Hastings MSS, Correspondence, HA 2342. The suggested date of 1643 seems too early.
8. HEH, Hastings MSS, Correspondence, HA 2342. She signed the letter of 10 June 1644 as Eleanor D.D. (HEH, Hastings MSS, Correspondence, HA 2341).
9. HEH, Hastings MSS, Correspondence, HA 2342. It is tempting to wonder whether Lady Eleanor and Lady Elizabeth Hatton talked of difficult times with their attorney-husbands, Davies and Coke, and the problems with their daughters' in-laws, the Hastings and Villiers. Although Lady Eleanor makes no previous mention of Lady Elizabeth Hatton, the two may have known each other earlier. See also L. Norsworthy, *The Lady of Bleeding Heart Yard: Lady Elizabeth Hatton* (1935; London: John Murray, 1938).
10. *Great Brittains Visitation*, prologue.
11. *Great Brittains Visitation*, 3, 5, 7–8, 18–21, 39 (irregular pagination); see Revelation 4:7–8.
12. *Great Brittains Visitation*, 31–33.
13. *For Whitsontyds Last Feast: the Present*, 1645.
14. *For Whitsontyds*, 3.

15. For example, *Elijah the Tishbite* (1651) or *Before the Lords Second Coming* (1650).
16. T. Edwards, *Gangraena* (London, 1645). Edwards condemned women preachers (error 124). Among the individuals he named were Katherine Chidley, Mrs. Attaway, John Goodwin, and John Lilburne.
17. *For Whitsontyds,* 5.
18. *For Whitsontyds,* 9.
19. The title page of the *Second Coming* is damaged, so only part of the title remains. The inside title is "The Revealing of our Lords Second Coming" (3). See *Second Coming,* 18–19; cf. *For Whitsontyds,* 10.
20. *Second Coming,* 14, 16–17.
21. *Second Coming,* 22.
22. *And without Proving,* 5; see also *Appearance,* 12; G. N. Godwin, *The Civil War in Hampshire, (1642–45) and the Story of Basing House* (London: Elliot Stock, 1882).
23. *Prayer or Petition 1645,* 4; *Prayer or Petition 1644,* 4.
24. *For the Blessed Feast,* 4, 10, see also 7.
25. *For the Blessed Feast,* 10, 11.
26. *For the Blessed Feast,* 12, see also 7–8.
27. *Day of Judgement,* 4.
28. *Day of Judgement,* 5, see also 7.
29. *Day of Judgement,* 9, 12; see Revelation 19:11–14.
30. *Day of Judgement,* 6–7, see also 5, 8; see Revelation 4:4.
31. *Day of Judgment,* 15. See G. Yule, "The Puritan Piety of Members of the Long Parliament," in *Popular Belief and Practice,* ed G. Cuming and D. Baker (Cambridge: Cambridge University Press, 1972), 189.
32. *Her Appeal* (1646), 39–40. See *DNB,* s.v. "May, Thomas."
33. *Her Appeal* (1646), 3–4, 35–36.
34. *Revelation Interpreted,* 3, 7–8; *Excommunication out of Paradice* (1647), 10–12; see Revelation 13:18.
35. *Revelation Interpreted,* 5–6, also 8 (irregular pagination); *All the Kings of the Earth,* Revelation xi, note q.
36. *Revelation Interpreted,* 5, 8 (irregular pagination). Others shared Lady Eleanor's objection to Juxon as treasurer; see Edward, earl of Clarendon, *The History of the Rebellion and Civil Wars in England,* ed. W. D. Macray (Oxford: Clarendon Press, 1888) 1:206.
37. *Je le tien,* 14.
38. *Je le tien,* 34. The strictures against reading the Book of Revelation were not a part of *A Directory of Public Worship* in the form it was published in 1645.
39. *Je le tien,* 36, 38. See Daniel 12:8–13 and 2 Peter 3:16–18.
40. *Je le tien,* 5, 10, 11, also 44–45.

41. See *Appearance,* 9.
42. HEH, Hastings MSS, Correspondence, HA 2343.
43. *Hells Destruction,* 6. She says the warrant was dated 17 July. Her petition to the House of Lords on 22 September 1647 makes it sound as if she was first in the Gatehouse, then moved to the Compter, and then to the Kings Bench, but she was apparently in the Gatehouse in February 1647 when she wrote *The Gatehouse Salutation* (HLRO, Main Papers, 22 September 1647). Stow describes the Wood Street Compter as "one of the prison houses pertaining to the sheriffs of London" (J. Stow, *Survey of London* [1598; London: Dent, 1956], 265).
44. Paine was a printer in Goldsmith's Alley, and he printed several of Walwyn's tracts and did work for the Council of State during the Commonwealth; see H. Plomer, *A Dictionary of the Booksellers and Printers who were at work in England, Scotland and Ireland from 1641 to 1667* (London: Bibliographical Society, 1907), 146; see also J. McMichael and B. Taft, eds., *The Writings of William Walwyn* (Athens, Ga.: University of Georgia Press, 1989).
45. *Hells Destruction,* 9.
46. *Hells Destruction,* 10–11. The text of the Harvard copy varies slightly and lacks the accusation that they wanted a tip.
47. *Hells Destruction,* 12–13.
48. *Gatehouse Salutation,* 5–7; see Luke 1:46–55.
49. B.L., 1480.b.5 [Four Fragments of Works] (1646–48). This fragment is pages 9–11. The extant edition of *Gatehouse Salutation* is a work of seven pages. "FINIS" appears at the bottom of the final page (Folger copy).
50. B.L., 1480.b.5; see Revelation 11:14; see also Revelation 19–20. The reason for her reference to five months is not clear.
51. *Mystery of General Redemption,* 17. The tract has thirty-two pages.
52. *Mystery,* 25; see *DNB,* s.v. "Richardson."
53. *Mystery,* 25.
54. *Mystery,* 8. Both the Geneva and the Authorized Version of 1611 use "for ever." She cites the text as "Ages and Ages" on the title page of *Of Times and Seasons.* The Latin in the Beza-Junius Bible confirms her argument.
55. *Mystery,* 11–12.
56. *Mystery,* 13–14.
57. *Appearance,* 15; her reference is to Ezekiel 12:2.
58. *Appearance,* 16.
59. The dated annotation appears on the Folger copy. Other copies include the same words, "His writ served of Rebellion Lamentation Mourning and Woe," without the date. See Ezekiel 2:10.

60. *Ezekiel the Prophet*, 7; *Ezekiel, cap.* 2, 12–14. See also *Gatehouse Salutation*, 5.
61. Ezekiel 2:3; *Ezekiel, cap.* 2, 3, 8.
62. *Excommunication out of Paradice*, 3–7.
63. *Excommunication out of Paradice*, 12.
64. *Excommunication out of Paradice*, 10.
65. *Excommunication out of Paradice*, 13–14. Phyllis Mack first brought Lady Eleanor's many water images to my attention.
66. *Excommunication out of Paradice*, 16.
67. HLRO, Main Papers, 22 September 1647.
68. *Reader*, 2.
69. See *Reader*, 3; see also *DNB*, s.v. "Percy, Algernon."
70. See *Revelation Interpreted*, 4ff.
71. *Reader*, 3; see Isaiah 10:5; see also Ezekiel 31.
72. *Reader*, 2–3. She draws heavily upon Isaiah (see, for example, Isaiah 38:8, 60:20). The Percy family badge did include a crescent (W. Berry, ed., *Encylcopedia Heraldica* [London: Sherwood, Gilbert and Piper, n.d.], s.v. "Northumberland, Duke of").
73. *And without Proving*, 4. In all but a few instances, *And without Proving* provides a fuller text; it elaborates upon that of *Wherefore to Prove;* cf. Elizabeth Avery's comment, "though I may be counted mad to the world, I shall speak the words of sobernesse: and if I am mad, as the Apostle saith it is to God; and if I am in my right mind it is for the benefit of others" (E. Avery, *Scripture-Prophecies opened* [London, 1647], To the Reader).
74. *And without Proving*, 2, 5.
75. *And without Proving*, 3; see Jude 1:9.
76. *Writ of Restitution*, 4–7. The sheriff, Pomfret, had formerly been undersheriff; Massingale was the undersheriff. See Hertfordshire County Records, *Calendar to the Sessions Books*, ed. W. Le Hardy (Hertford, 1928), 5:369, 373, 388, 391.
77. *Writ of Restitution*, 5, 7. See also HEH, Hastings MSS, Correspondence, HA 2572 and HA 10395.
78. *Writ of Restitution*, 5–7; see also *Appearance*, 13. Charles had touched for the king's evil. See C. Levin, "'Would I Could Give You Help and Succour': Elizabeth I and the Politics of Touch," *Albion* 21, no. 2 (1989): 191–205.
79. *Writ of Restitution*, 8–9; see also 4–5.
80. *Apoc. Chap. 11*, 1–2. Her inscription, to "Sir," appears on the first page of the Harvard copy. She gives no further clues to the identity of her addressee.
81. *Apoc. Chap. 11*, 2–3.

82. *Remonstrance*, 5–6.

83. *Of the Great Days*, 3.

84. Two pages (9–10) are missing. The Folger's volume includes one copy of pp. 3–8 and another copy with pp. 3–8 and 11–20.

85. *Given to the Elector*, 12 (Worcester College copy); cf. the royalist use of Belshazzar's feast in 1649, *Epulae Thyestae, or the Thanksgiving Dinner*, a reference I owe to Lois Potter.

86. This copy is preserved in the Library of Worcester College, Oxford.

87. *Given to the Elector* (B.L.), 10.

88. This is another copy from the library of Worcester College, Oxford.

89. *Restitution of Prophecy*, 27; see Mark 4:21.

90. *Given to the Elector* (B.L.), 10.

91. *Appeal from Court to Camp*, 2–3.

92. *Appeal from Court to Camp*, 4–6.

93. *Appeal from Court to Camp*, 6; see Genesis 19:26; Luke 17:32.

94. See E. Poole, *A Vision: wherein is manifested the disease and cure of the kingdome. Being The Summe of what was delivered to the Generall Councel of the Army, Decemb. 29.1648* (London, 1648).

95. See Clarendon, *History* 11:235.

96. *Blasphemous Charge*, 3 (Folger copy).

97. This later edition has the same title, but *HER* is capitalized (*The Blasphemous Charge against HER*). The earlier edition is *The Blasphemous Charge against her*.

98. *The Blasphemous Charge against HER*, 2. This page also appears as a preface to *Dragons Blasphemous Charge* (1651).

99. *Blasphemous Charge Against HER*, 14–16. The text on these pages is crossed out in the Folger copy.

100. *Calendar of the Proceedings of the Committee for Compounding . . . 1643–1660*, 146; *DNB*, s.v. "Bradshaw."

101. *Crying Charge*, 2.

102. *Crying Charge*, 6, 7–8.

103. *Given to the Elector* (B.L.), 6, stanza 11. This does not, for example, appear in Nalson's *The Trial of Charles the First* (London, 1740), but it does appear in Henry Leslie's sermon preached June 3/13, 1649, *The Martyrdom of King Charles* (a reference I owe to Nancy McGuire); see also N. McGuire, "The Theatrical Mask/Masque of Politics: The Case of Charles I," *Journal of British Studies* 28, no. 1 (1989): 1–22.

Chapter 7

1. *New Jerusalem*, 3; see 1 Samuel 7–10. She dated the tract "February 1648," although the title page shows 1649 as the year of publication.

2. *New Jerusalem*, 4; see also 3; 1 Samuel 10:2. The example had apparently been part of a debate about monarchy among parliament and army in 1648 (see Ludlow, *Memoirs*, ed. C. H. Firth [Oxford: Clarendon Press, 1894], 1:185).

3. *New Jerusalem*, 4–5; see 1 Samuel 7:5–7.

4. *New Jerusalem*, 6–7.

5. *New Jerusalem*, 10–22.

6. *Prayer* (1644) (Folger copy).

7. *Prayer* (1644), 9, 10 (Folger copy).

8. *Prayer* (1644), 9–16 (Worcester College copy). A third version of the letter, dated, like the second, in November 1649, is bound after *Discovery* in the Folger's volume of Lady Eleanor's tracts, but there is no evidence that it was actually printed with *Discovery* (though both *Discovery* and *Sign* were reissued "with some words of addition" in 1649).

9. *Lachrymae Musarum* (1650). Several of the elegies are in Latin and at least one is in Greek.

10. *Sions Lamentation*, 1–2.

11. *Sions Lamentation*, 4.

12. *Sions Lamentation*, 6. (2 Esdras 9–10).

13. *Sions Lamentation*, 6–7; see HEH, Hastings MSS, Genealogy, box 1, folder 12.

14. *Sions Lamentation*, 8.

15. The imprimatur is dated 25 August 1649. Someone may have found her work a useful response to a royalist tract that makes Belshazzar's feast parliament's attack upon Laud (*Epulae Thyestae, or the Thanksgiving Dinner* (1649), cited in L. Potter, *Secret Rites and Secret Writing: Royalist Literature 1641–1660* [Cambridge: Cambridge University Press, 1989], 32).

16. See H. Plomer, *A Dictionary of the Booksellers and Printers . . . 1641–1667* (London: Bibliographical Society, 1907).

17. She called her tract *For the Right Noble, Sir Balthazer Gerbier Knight*. He described the academy in *To the Right Honourable the Parliament and the Councill of State of England* (1649).

18. *For Gerbier*, 2.

19. *For Gerbier*, 3, 5; see *DNB*, s.v. "Gerbier."

20. *For the States*, esp 4, 6, 7 (only the first eight pages of the tract are extant). See *DNB*, s.v. "Maurice" and "Rupert."

21. Thomason's collections drop following the act; see Potter, *Secret Rites*, 18–19.

22. The two tracts may have both been called *Sign*. Only the lower part of the title page of one survives; thus, the following page, which begins "Discovery," shows through. Its final pages are missing too (p. 12 is

the last page). The two tracts are virtually the same until p. 9; thereafter there are more variations in them.

23. *Everlasting Gospel,* 11.

24. *Everlasting Gospel,* 5–6.

25. *Everlasting Gospel,* 13.

26. *New Proclamation,* 6.

27. *Bill of Excommunication,* 3–4, 11; *Gatehouse Salutation,* 6; see also *Samsons Legacie,* 18–21.

28. *Bill of Excommunication,* 5–6. It seems as if she must have been using "Isles" to mean kingdoms.

29. *Bill of Excommunication,* 6–8.

30. *Bill of Excommunication,* 28–29; see Revelation 3:11–12.

31. *Bill of Excommunication,* 14–32, 33–40.

32. *Arraignment,* 3–4; see also Matthew 18:8; *DNB,* s.v. "Fairfax, Ferdinando"; C. Markham, *A Life of the Great Lord Fairfax* (London: Macmillan, 1870), 302–3.

33. *Appearance,* 3–4.

34. *Appearance,* 5, 7; cf. Revelation 1:10–11, 21:6.

35. *Appearance,* 8.

36. *Appearance,* 8–9; see Revelation 2:25.

37. *Appearance,* 10–15.

38. *Appearance,* 16.

39. See *Memoirs of the Life of that learned Antiquary, Elias Ashmole,* published by Charles Burman (London, 1717), 16–17, see also 29–30.

40. *Appearance,* 16. The pages following 16 are not extant.

41. *Cal. of the Committee for Compounding* 4:2533; see *C.J.* 6:290, 296.

42. *Cal. of the Committee for Compounding,* 4:2631.

43. See Revelation 19:7; cf. Ranter Mary Gadbury, who referred to herself as "the Bride of the Lamb" (*Biographical Dictionary of British Radicals in the Seventeenth Century,* s.v. "Gadbury").

44. *Before the Lords Second Coming,* 14.

45. *Before the Lords Second Coming,* 4, 12; see Jude 1:13.

46. *Before the Lords Second Coming,* 3–4, 5, 13; see Mark 3:29.

47. *Before the Lords Second Coming,* 6; Revelation 11:3.

48. A note on the title page of the Folger's copy also mentions September 3.

49. Thomason dated his copy 22 November.

50. *Elijah the Tishbite,* 6, 8; see also 1 Kings 17:9–24.

51. *Elijah the Tishbite,* 4. Her marginal note at the top of that page suggests that she may have thought the authorities were going too far in prosecuting Christopher Love; see *DNB,* s.v. "Love"; see also C. Love, *A Cleare and Necessary Vindication* (London, 1651).

52. *Her Jubilee,* 1. Concerning Stawell, see *DNB,* s.v. "Stawell"; D. Under-

down, *Somerset in the Civil War and Interregnum* (Newton Abbot: David and Charles, 1973), 128.

53. *Her Jubilee,* 2.

54. *Her Jubilee,* 3; see G. D. Stawell, *A Quantock Family* (Taunton: Barnicott and Pearce, The Wessex Press, 1910), 71–78.

55. See Stawell, *Quantock Family,* 79–80; VCH, *Somerset* 3:61–71.

56. There is a draft of her petition in Bodl., MS Carte 289, fol. 61. I have found no other record of it. The records of the Committee for Compounding make no mention of Lady Eleanor in connection with Stawell's case (*Cal. Committee for Compounding,* 1425–30, 3280).

57. J.D. Alsop, "Ethics in the Marketplace: Gerrard Winstanley's London Bankruptcy, 1643," *Journal of British Studies* 28, no. 2 (1989): 117–18.

58. See P. Mack, "The Prophet and Her Audience: Gender and Knowledge in the World Turned Upside Down," in *Reviving the Revolution,* ed. G. Eley and W. Hunt (London: Verso Books, 1988), 142–49; see also T. W. Hayes, *Winstanley the Digger: A Literary Analysis of Radical Ideas in the English Revolution* (Cambridge, Mass.: Harvard University Press, 1979).

59. Folger's copy, 7; see Genesis 14:18; Hebrews 7:1.

60. HEH, Hastings MSS, Correspondence HA 13814; see P. Hardacre, "Gerrard Winstanley in 1650," *Huntington Library Quarterly* 22 (1959): 345–49.

61. HEH, Hastings MSS, Correspondence HA 13814.

62. P.R.O., C 7/103/38.

63. She describes herself as being of Pirton in the suit; see P.R.O., C 7/103/98; see also P.R.O., C 7/412/34.

64. Lambeth Palace Library, MS Comm XIIa/10. Two dates appear with this evidence: 1 May and 26 July 1650.

65. See P.R.O., E 134/27/Chas 2/Mich 5/Hertfords.

66. HEH, Hastings Correspondence, HA 4616.

67. *Hells Destruction,* 5.

68. *Hells Destruction,* 6.

69. *Hells Destruction,* 8, 12–13.

70. *Hells Destruction;* see also 13–14.

71. *Hells Destruction,* 14; cf. *For the Blessed Feast* (1646); *Brides Preparation* (1644).

72. *Of Times,* 12.

73. *Of Times,* 3–4.

74. Rubens, *St. George and the Dragon* (1629); cf. also Carew's *Coelum Britannicum* (1634), which suggests that the nation needed a Divine St. George; see A. Patterson, *Censorship and Interpretation: The Conditions of*

Writing and Reading in Early Modern England (Madison: University of Wisconsin Press, 1984), 168–70; also E. Veevers, *Images of Love and Religion: Queen Henrietta Maria and Court Entertainments* (Cambridge: Cambridge University Press, 1989), 185–91; K. Sharpe, "The Image of Virtu: The Court and Household of Charles I, 1625–1642," in *The English Court from the Wars of the Roses to the Civil War*, ed. D. Starkey (London: Longman, 1987), 241–42.

75. *Of Times*, 6–11; cf. *Star to the Wise*, 16.
76. *Serpents Excommunication*, 7.
77. *Serpents Excommunication*, 8; see *DNB*, s.v. "Tuke, Brian."
78. She dated the letter 28 October 1651. Another edition has "Benidiction" rather than "Benediction" for its title, but shows no other variants.
79. Her citation from Isaiah 63 is not verbatim from either the Geneva or the Authorized Version of the Bible.
80. Compare the gloss about St. Paul's (7) and the Caldeans (9) with the Folger copy of *Blasphemous Charge*, 7, 9. The gloss (5) concerning the woman from Revelation 12 is similar to what she wrote in *Of Times* (June 1651).
81. On p. 3 she noted the killing of Dorislaus and Ascham, the two English ambassadors, which she had cited in the margin of one of her copies of *Before the Lords Second Coming* (1650).
82. The date printed at the conclusion of the preface is December 25; that at the end of the tract is Candlemas.
83. *Restitution of Prophecy*, To the Reader.
84. *Restitution of Prophecy*, 6–17, 40, 42. See 2 Kings 9; Revelation 17.
85. *Restitution of Prophecy*, 12–19.
86. *Restitution of Prophecy*, 20–21; see *DNB*, s.v. "Digby, Kenelm."
87. *Restitution of Prophecy*, 47; see A. Macfarlane, ed., *The Diary of Ralph Josselin, 1616–1683*, (London: British Academy, 1976), 255.
88. *Restitution of Prophecy*, 5.
89. *Restitution of Prophecy*, 25.
90. *Restitution of Prophecy*, 29–36; see Matthew 25:24–26.
91. *Restitution of Prophecy*, 26–27.
92. *Restitution of Prophecy*, To the Reader, 41, 51, 52.
93. See W. Prynne, *Histrio Mastix* (London, 1633), 758.
94. Tobit 5:7–8, 6:15–17.
95. "Touching the healing of the present Evil" is her subtitle (*Bethlehem*, 2). See also *Bethlehem*, 5–6; John 6:51.
96. *Bethlehem*, 3, 6, 8, 10; cf. *Restitution of Prophecy*, 29–30.
97. *Bethlehem*, 11–12.
98. HEH, Hastings MSS, Accounts and Financial Papers, box 16, folder 39.

99. *Abstracts of Probate Acts in the PCC,* Ed. J. and G. F. Matthews (Godalming: G. F. Matthews, 1911), 51.

100. Quoted in *The Complete Poems of Sir John Davies,* ed. A. B. Grosart (London: Chatto and Windus, 1876), 1:lv–lvi. Grosart dismisses Lady Eleanor's epitaph as "golden lies." Neither her monument nor that of Davies survived the rebuilding of St. Martin's.

101. R. Baker, *A Chronicle of the Kings of England* (London, 1670), 635.

102. HEH, Hastings MSS, Correspondence, HA 9465. The letter dates from just over two years after Lady Eleanor's death (see *DNB,* s.v. "Moulin, Peter du").

103. Jean R. Brink cites L'Estrange's response in "Sir John Davies: His Life and Major Works" (Ph.D. diss., University of Wisconsin, 1972), 64. I am grateful to Mary Robertson of the Huntington Library for providing me with a photocopy of the letter. L'Estrange told Lucy it was too late to intervene in the 1674 edition. That edition (the sixth) and the seventh, in 1679, maintained the text that appeared in the 1670 (fifth) edition.

Selected Bibliography

Manuscripts

Bethlehem Royal Hospital
    Minutebook of the Court of Governors of Bethlehem and Bridewell
      (1636–1638)
Bodleian Library
    MS. Carte 61
    MS. Carte 62
    MS. Carte 289
British Library
    Add. MS. 23212, Conway Papers concerning Eliz. Bourne
    Add. MS. 63941, Boswell Papers
    Add. MS. 69919, Coke Papers
Corporation of London Records Office
    Repertories of the Court of Aldermen
Folger Shakespeare Library
    MS. V.a.399, Commonplace Book
    MS. V.b.48, Law Reports
    MS. V.b.50, Misc. Discourses
    MS. V.b.328, Castlehaven Trial
Henry E. Huntington Library
    Ellesmere MSS (Derby Papers: letters and accounts; domestic and personal)
    Hastings MSS, Accounts and Financial Papers, boxes 8–17
    Hastings MSS, Correspondence, boxes 6–20
    Hastings MSS, Deeds
    Hastings MSS, Genealogy, box 1
    Hastings MSS, Inventories, box 2
    Hastings MSS, Irish Papers
    Hastings MSS, Legal Papers, boxes 2–6, 9

Hastings MSS, Manorial, box 59
Hastings MSS, Miscellaneous, boxes 1, 11–12
Hastings MSS, Personal Papers, boxes 17–19
Hastings MSS, Religious Papers, boxes 1–3
House of Lords Record Office
    Main Papers, House of Lords, 1640–48
Kent Archives Office
    Dering MSS
Lambeth Palace Library
    MS. Comm. xiia/10 (Parliamentary Survey of 1650)
Public Record Office
    Chancery Proceedings, Bills and answers (C 2/Chas I; C 7)
    Close Rolls (C 54)
    Patent Rolls (C 66)
    Inquisitions post mortem (C 142)
    Scudamore MSS (C 115/ M30–M31)
    Depositions taken by commission (E 134)
    Sheriff's accounts of seizures (E 379)
    Privy Council Registers (PC 2/41–47)
    State Papers (SP 12, 14, 16, 28, 46, 84)
    Wills (PROB)
Winchester Cathedral Library
    Diary of Dean John Young

Printed Works

Primary Sources

Acts of the Privy Council of England 1613–1631.
Adams, T. *Mystical Bedlam, or the World of Mad-Men.* 1615.
Annotations Upon All the Books of the Old and New Testament. 1645.
Archer, J. *The Personal Reign of Christ upon Earth.* 5th ed. 1661.
The Arraingment and Conviction of Mervin Lord Audeley, earl of Castlehaven. 1641.
Ashmole, E. *The Antiquities of Berkshire.* 3 vols. 1719.
Ashmole, E. *Memoirs of the Life of that Learned Antiquary, Elias Ashmole.* 1717.
Avery, E. *Scripture-Prophecies opened.* 1647.
Bacon, F. "Of Prophecies." In *The Essays or Counsels, Civill and Moral.* 1625.
Baddeley, R. *The Boy of Bilson.* 1622.
Baker, R. *A Chronicle of the Kings of England.* 5th ed. 1670.
Bale, John. *Select Works.* Edited by H. Christmas. Parker Society, 1899.
Bancroft, R. *Dangerous Positions.* 1640.

Barrington Family Letters, 1628–1632. Edited by A. Searle. 4th ser. no.38. London: Camden Society, 1983.

Bastwick, J. *The Answer of John Bastwick*. 1637.

Bastwick, J. *The Letany of John Bastwick*. 1637.

Bastwick, J. *A More Full Answer*. 1637.

Beard, T. *Antichrist the Pope of Rome*. 1625.

Beard, T. *The Theatre of Gods Judgements*. 1597.

Beaumont, F., and J. Fletcher. *The Prophetess*. 1647.

Bennet, Isaac. *Good and True Intelligence from Reading*. 1643.

Birch, T., ed. *The Court and Times of James the First*. 2 vols. 1849.

Brathwaite, R. *The English Gentlewoman*. 1631.

A Briefe Relation of certain speciall and most material passages and speeches in the Star Chamber. 1637.

Brightman, T. *A Revelation of the Revelation that is*. 1615.

Brightman, T. *Works*. 1644.

Burton, H. *A Narration of the Life of Mr. Henry Burton*. 1643.

Burton, H. *The Seven Vials*. 1628.

Burton, H. *The Sounding of the two last Trumpets*. 1641.

Burton, R. *The Anatomy of Melancholy*. 1624.

Calendar of State Papers, Domestic Series, 1558–1660.

Calendar of State Papers, relating to Ireland, 1599–1619.

Cary, M. *The Resurrection of the Witnesses and Englands fall from (the mystical Babylon) Rome*. 1648.

Cheeke, W. *Anagrammata, et Chron-anagrammata Regia*. 1613.

Chidley, K. *A New Yeares Gift*. 1644.

Clarendon, Edward, Earl of. *The History of the Rebellion and Civil Wars in England*. Edited by W. Dunn Macray. 1888.

The Complete Poems of Sir John Davies. Edited by A. B. Grosart. 2 vols. 1876.

Coppe, A. *A Fiery Flying Roll*. 1649.

Coppe, A. *Sweet Sips of Some Spirituell Wine*. 1649.

Cotton, J. *The Powring out of the Seven Vials*. 1642.

Croke, G. *The Third Part of the Reports*. 1683.

A Curb for Sectaries and Bold Propheciers. 1641.

Dalton, M. *The Countrey Justice*. 1635.

The Diary of John Young, S.T.P. Edited by F. Remington Gordon. London: SPCK, 1928.

The Diary of the Lady Anne Clifford. Introduction by V. Sackville West. London: William Heinemann, 1923.

A Directory for the Publique Worship of God. 1645.

Diodati, G. *Pious Annotations upon the Holy Bible*. 1643.

A Discoverie of Six Women preachers. 1641.

Duncon, J. *The Returnes of Spiritual Comfort and Grief in a Devout Soul*. 1648.

Edwards, T. *Gangraena*. 1645.

Ellis, H. *Pseudochristus*. 1650.

Englands Alarm to War against the Beast. 1643.

Epulae Thyestae, or the Thanksgiving Dinner. 1649.

E., T. *The Lawes Resolutions of Womens Rights*. 1632.

Evans, A. *An Echo to the Book Called A Voyce from Heaven*. 1653.

Evans, A. *The Great and Bloody Visions*. 1653.

Fage, M. *Fames Roule*. 1637.

False Prophecies Discovered. 1642.

Ferguson, M., ed. *First Feminists*. Bloomington: Indiana University Press, 1985.

Firth, C. H., and R. S. Rait, eds. *Acts and Ordinances of the Interregnum, 1642–1660*. 3 vols. London: H.M.S.O., 1911.

Foxe, J. *Acts and Monuments*. 1597.

Fuller, T. *The Holy State*. 1642.

Gardiner, S. R., ed. *Reports of Cases in the Court of Star Chamber and High Commission*. Camden Society, n. s. 17. 1880.

Gerbier, B. *To the Right Honorable the Parliament and the Council of State*. 1649.

Her Own Life: Autobiographical Writings by Seventeenth-Century Englishwomen. Edited by E. Graham, H. Hinds, E. Hobby, and H. Wilcox. London: Routledge, 1989.

Hakewill, G. *An Apologie or Declaration of the Power and Providence of God in the Government of the World*. 1630.

Heylyn, P. *Cyrianus Anglicus*. 1668.

Heywood, T. *A True Discourse of the Two infamous Upstart Prophets*. 1636.

H. M. C. *Report on MSS of Reginald Rawdon Hastings*. Vols. 1–4. 1928–1947.

Hoskins, J. *Directions for Speech and Style*. Edited by H. H. Hudson. Princeton: Princeton University Press, 1935.

Howell, T. B., ed. *Complete Collection of State Trials*. 1816.

James, King of Great Britain. *Ane Fruitfull Meditatioun contening Ane plane and facill expositioun of ye 7. 8. 9. and 10 Versis of the 20 chap. of the Revelatioun*. Edinburgh, 1588.

Jessey, H. *The Exceeding Riches of Grace*. 1647.

Joceline, E. *The Mothers Legacie to her unborne Childe*. 3d ed. 1625.

Jones, S. *To Sions Lovers*. 1644.

Journals of the House of Commons.

Journals of the House of Lords.

Krueger, R., ed. *The Poems of Sir John Davies*. Oxford: Clarendon Press, 1975.

Laud, W. *The Works of William Laud*. Parker Society, 1847–60.

Leighton, A. *An Appeal to the Parliament*. 2d ed. Amsterdam, 1629.

Leighton, A. *An Epitome or Briefe Discoverie from the Beginning to the Ending of the Many and great Troubles that Dr. Leighton suffered in his Body Estate and Family.* 1646.

Lenton, F. *Great Britains Beauties.* 1638.

Leslie, H. *The Martyrdome of King Charles.* 1649.

Leveller Manifestoes of the Puritan Revolution. Edited by D. M. Wolfe. London: Thomas Nelson and Sons, 1944.

The Life and Death of King Charles, or the Pseudo-Martyr Discovered. 1650.

A Light for the Ignorant. 1638.

Lilburne, J. *The Poore Mans Cry.* 1639.

Lilburne, J. *The Prisoners Plea for a Heabeas Corpus.* 1648.

Lilburne, J. *A Worke of the Beast.* 1638.

Lilly, W. *Monarchy or No Monarchy.* 1651.

Lilly, W. *A Prophecy of the White King.* 1644.

Lilly, W. *The Starry Messenger.* 1645.

Loftis, J., ed. *The Memoirs of Anne, Lady Halkett and Ann, Lady Fanshawe.* Oxford: Clarendon Press, 1979.

A Looking-Glasse for Women. 1644.

Love, C. *A Cleare and Necessary Vindication.* 1651.

McClure, N. E. *The Letters of John Chamberlain.* 2 vols. Philadelphia: American Philosophical Society, 1939.

Marshall, S. *Meroz Cursed.* 1641.

Mayer, J. *A Commentary upon all the Prophets both Great and Small.* 1652.

Memoirs of William Cavendish, Duke of Newcastle and Margaret his Wife. Edited by C. H. Firth. 1886.

Mercurius Propheticus. 1643.

Milton, J. *Comus.* 1637.

Milton, J. *The Doctrine and Discipline of Divorce.* 1643.

Milton, J. *The Reason of Church-Government.* 1641.

Milton, J. *Of Reformation.* 1641.

Morton, T. *Ezekiels Wheels: A Treatise concerning Divine Providence.* 1653.

Napier, J. *A Plaine Discovery of the Whole Revelation of Saint John.* 1593.

A Parliament of Ladies. 1647.

Pagitt, E. *The Mysticall Wolfe.* 1645.

Papisto-Mastix, or Deborahs Prayer against Gods Enemies. 1642.

Pennington, M. *A Brief Account of my Exercises from Childhood.* 1848.

Perkins, W. "The Art or Facultie of Prophecying." In *Works.* 1613.

Poole, E. *A Vision.* 1649.

Potter, F. *An Interpretation of the number 666.* 1642.

Privy Council Registers Published in Facsimile 1637–41.

A Prophecy of the Life, Reigne, and Death of William Laud. 1644.

The Prophesie of Mother Shipton. 1641.

Prynne, W. *Canterburies Doome.* 1646.

Prynne, W. *Histrio Mastix.* 1633.

Prynne, W. *A New Discovery of the Prelates Tyranny.* 1641.

S., G. *Sacrae Heptades or Seven Problems concerning antichrist.* 1625.

Sampsons Foxes: Agreed to Fire a Kingdom. 1644.

Smart, P. *Canterburies Cruelty.* 1643.

The Spirituall Courts Epitomized. 1641.

The Star-Chamber Epitomized. 1641.

Stow, J. *Survey of London.* 1598. Edited by H. B. Wheatley. London: Dent, 1956.

Studley, P. *The Looking-Glasse of Schisme.* 1635.

Swan, J. *Speculum Mundi.* 1635.

Taylor, J. *A Discourse of the Liberty of Prophesying.* 1647.

Taylor, T. *Christ Revealed.* Delmar, N.Y.: Scholars Facsimiles and Reprints, 1979.

Thomason, G. *Catalogue of the Pamphlets, Books, Newspapers, and Manuscripts Relating to the Civil War, the Commonwealth, and Restoration.* London: Trustees of the British Museum, 1908.

Toxander, T. P. *Vox Coeli to England.* 1646.

Trapnel, A. *Anna Trapnel's Report and Plea.* 1654.

Trapnel, A. *The Cry of a Stone.* 1654.

Trapnel, A. *Strange and Wonderful Newes from White Hall.* 1654.

Vicars, J. *Prodigies and Apparitions.* 1642.

Wall, A., ed. *Two Elizabethan Women: Correspondence of Joan and Maria Thynne.* Wiltshire Record Society, no. 38. Devizes: Wiltshire Record Society, 1983.

Walwyn, W. *The Writings of William Walwyn.* Edited by J. R. McMichael and B. Taft. Athens, Ga.: University of Georgia Press, 1989.

Wilson, T. *Arte of Rhetorique.* Edited by T. J. Derrick. New York: Garland Publishing, 1982.

Woodcock, F. *Christs Warning-piece.* 1644.

Woodcock, F. *The Two Witnesses Discovered.* 1643.

Secondary Sources

Allderidge, P. "Bedlam: Fact or Fantasy?" In *The Anatomy of Madness: Essays in the History of Psychiatry.* Edited by W. F. Bynum, R. Porter, and M. Shepherd, 1:17–23. London: Tavistock Publications, 1985.

Allderidge, P. "Management and Mismanagement at Bedlam, 1547–1633." *Health, Medicine, and Mortality in the Sixteenth Century.* Edited by C. Webster, 141–64. Cambridge University Press, 1979.

Alsop, J. D. "Ethics in the Marketplace: Gerrard Winstanley's London Bankruptcy, 1643." *Journal of British Studies* 38, no. 2 (1989): 97–119.

Amussen, S. *An Ordered Society: Gender and Class in Early Modern England.* Oxford: Basil Blackwell, 1988.

Aylmer, G. E. "Collective Mentalities in Mid Seventeenth-Century England: III. Varieties of Radicalism." *Transactions of the Royal Historical Society* 5th ser. 38 (1988): 1–25.

Ballard, G. *Memoirs of British Ladies.* 1775.

Barbour, H. "Quaker Prophetesses and Mothers in Israel." In *Seeking the Light,* edited by J. W. Frost and J. M. Moore, 41–60. Wallingford and Haverford, Pa: Pendle Hill Publications and Friends Historical Association, 1986.

Beilin, E. *Redeeming Eve: Women Writers of the English Renaissance.* Princeton: Princeton University Press, 1987.

Bell, H. E. *An Introduction to the History and Records of the Court of Wards and Liveries.* Cambridge: Cambridge University Press, 1953.

Bingham, C. "Seventeenth-Century Attitudes Toward Deviant Sex." *Journal of Interdisciplinary History* 1, no. 3 (1971): 447–72.

Blayney, P. W. M. *The Texts of King Lear and their Origins.* Vol. 1. Cambridge: Cambridge University Press, 1982.

Bone, Q. *Henrietta Maria: Queen of the Cavaliers.* Urbana: University of Illinois Press, 1972.

Bray, A. "Homosexuality and the Signs of Male Friendship in Elizabethan England." *History Workshop Journal* 29 (1990): 1–19.

Brink, J. R. "Sir John Davies: His Life and Major Works." Ph.D. diss. University of Wisconsin, 1972.

Burrage, C. "Anna Trapnel's Prophecies." *English Historical Review* 26, no. 103 (1911): 526–35.

Bynum, C. W. "Religious Women in the Later Middle Ages." In *Christian Spirituality,* ed. by J. Raitt, 121–37. New York: Crossroad, 1987.

Byrne, F. I. M. "Sir John Davies: an English Intellectual in Ireland, 1603–1619." M.A. thesis, National University of Ireland, University College, Galway, 1985.

Capp., B. S. *The Fifth Monarchy Men: A Study in Seventeenth-Century English Millenarianism.* London: Faber and Faber, 1972.

Christianson, P. *Reformers and Babylon.* Toronto: University of Toronto Press, 1978.

Cioni, M. L. *Women and Law in Elizabethan England.* New York: Garland Publishing, 1985.

Cohn, N. *The Pursuit of the Millenium.* Rev. and exp. ed. Oxford: Oxford University Press, 1970.

Cope, E. S. "Dame Eleanor Davies Never Soe Mad a Ladie?" *Huntington Library Quarterly* 50, no. 2 (1987): 133–44.

Cross, C. "'He goats before the flocks': A Note on the Part Played by Women in the Founding of Some Civil War Churches." In *Popular Belief and Practice,* edited by G. Coming and D. Baker, 195–202. Cambridge: Cambridge University Press, 1972.

Cust, R., and A. Hughes, eds. *Conflict in Early Stuart England.* London: Longman, 1989.

Dickson, D. R. "The Complexities of Biblical Typology in the Seventeenth Century." *Renaissance and Reformation,* n.s. 11, no. 3 (1987): 253–72.

Dobin, H. *Merlin's Disciples: Prophecy, Poetry, and Power in Renaissance England.* Stanford, Calif.: Stanford University Press, 1990.

Durston, C. "Signs and Wonders and the English Civil War." *History Today* 27 (1987): 22–28.

Eales, J. *Puritans and Roundheads: The Harleys of Brampton Bryan and the Outbreak of the English Civil War.* Cambridge: Cambridge University Press, 1990.

Ezell, M. *The Patriarch's Wife.* Chapel Hill: University of North Carolina Press, 1987.

Fessler, A. "The Management of Lunacy in Seventeenth-Century England." *Proceedings of the Royal Society of Medicine* 49 (1956): 15–21.

Fildes, V., ed. *Women as Mothers in Pre-Industrial England.* London: Routledge, 1990.

Findley, S., and E. Hobby. "Seventeenth Century Women's Autobiography." In *1642: Literature and Power in the Seventeenth Century,* edited by F. Barker, J. Bernstein, J. Coombes, P. Hulme, J. Stone, and J. Stratton, 11–36. Colchester: University of Essex, 1981.

Firth, K. *The Apocalyptic Tradition in Reformation Britain.* Oxford: Oxford University Press, 1979.

Foucault, M. *Madness and Civilization,* trans. by R. Howard. New York: Random House, 1973.

Fraser, A. *The Weaker Vessel.* London: Weidenfield and Nicolson, 1984.

Frost, K. *Holy Delight: Typology, Numerology, and Autobiography in Donne's Devotions upon Emergent Occasions.* Princeton: Princeton University Press, 1990.

Fullerton, G. *The Life of Elisabeth Lady Falkland.* 1883.

Gardiner, S. R. *History of the Commonwealth and Protectorate.* London: Longmans, Green, 1903.

Gardiner, S. R. *The History of England.* 1884.

Gardiner, S. R. *The History of the Great Civil War.* 1893.

George, M. *Women in the First Capitalist Society.* Urbana: University of Illinois Press, 1988.

Gilman, S. *Seeing the Insane.* New York: John Wiley and Sons, 1982.

Grant, D. *Margaret the First.* London: Rupert Hart-Davies, 1957.

Greaves, R., ed. *Triumph over Silence: Women in Protestant History.* Westport, Conn.: Greenwood Press, 1985.

Greaves, R., and R. Zaller, eds. *Biographical Dictionary of British Radicals in the Seventeenth Century.* Brighton: Harvester, 1982.

Greenberg, S. J. "Dating Civil War Pamphlets, 1641–44." *Albion* 20, no. 3 (1988): 387–401.

Greenblatt, S. *Renaissance Self-Fashioning.* Chicago: University of Chicago Press, 1980.

Hannay, M. P. *Philip's Pheonix: Mary Sidney, Countess of Pembroke.* Oxford: Oxford University Press, 1990.

Hannay, M. P., ed. *Silent But for the Word.* Kent, Ohio: Kent State University Press, 1985.

Hardacre, P. "Gerrard Winstanley in 1650." *Huntington Library Quarterly* 22, no. 4 (1959): 345–49.

Hayes, T. W. *Winstanley the Digger: A Literary Analysis of Radical Ideas in the English Revolution.* Cambridge, Mass.: Harvard University Press, 1979.

Henderson, K. U., and B. F. McManus. *Half Humankind: Contexts and Texts of the Controversy about Women in England, 1540–1640.* Urbana: University of Illinois Press, 1985.

Hibbard, C. *Charles I and the Popish Plot.* Chapell Hill: University of North Carolina Press, 1983.

Higgins, P. "The Reactions of Women, with Special Reference to Women Petitioners." In *Politics, Religion, and the English Civil War,* edited by R. B. Manning, 179–22. London: Edward Arnold, 1973.

Hill, C. *Antichrist in Seventeenth-Century England.* Oxford: Oxford University Press, 1971.

Hill, C. "Arise Evans: Welshman in London." In *Change and Continuity in Seventeenth-Century England,* 48–77. Cambridge, Mass.: Harvard University Press, 1975.

Hill, C. *The World Turned Upside Down.* New York: Viking Press, 1972.

Hill, C., and M. Shepherd. "The case of Arise Evans: a Historico-Psychiatric Study." *Psychological Medicine* 6 (1976): 351–58.

Hindle, C. J. *A Bibliography of the Printed Pamphlets and Broadsides of Lady Eleanor Douglas, the 17th Century Prophetess.* Edinburgh: Bibliographical Society, 1936.

Hobby, E. *Virtue of Necessity: English Women's Writing, 1649–88.* Ann Arbor: University of Michigan Press, 1989.

Houlbrooke, R. *The English Family, 1450–1700.* London: Longman, 1984.

Huber, E. *Women and the Authority of Inspiration.* Lanham, Md.: University Press of America, 1985.

Ingram, M. *The Church Courts, Sex, and Marriage in England, 1570–1640.* Cambridge: Cambridge University Press, 1987.

Jackson, J. E. "The Eminent Ladies of Wiltshire History." *Wiltshire Magazine* 20 (1882): 26–45.

Jardine, L. *Still Harping on Daughters.* Brighton: Harvester Press, 1983.

Jelinek, E. C. *The Tradition of Women's Autobiography.* Boston: Twayne Publishers, 1986.

King, J. N. "The Godly Woman in Elizabethan Iconography." *Renaissance Quarterly* 28, no. 1 (1985): 41–84.

Kingston, A. *Hertfordshire during the Great Civil War and the Long Parliament.* 1894.

Lake, P. "Calvinism and the English Church." *Past and Present* 114 (1987): 32–76.

Lake, P. "Feminine Piety and Personal Potency: The 'Emancipation' of Mrs. Jane Ratcliffe." *Seventeenth Century* 2 (1987): 143–65.

Lamont, W. *Godly Rule: Politics and Religion, 1603–1660.* London: Macmillan, 1969.

Lewalski, B. *Protestant Poetics and the Seventeenth-Century Religious Lyric.* Princeton: Princeton University Press, 1979.

Lossky, N. *Lancelot Andrewes the Preacher.* Oxford: Clarendon Press, 1991.

Ludlow, D. "Arise and Be Doing: English Preaching Women, 1640–1660." Ph.D. diss., Indiana University, 1978.

MacDonald, M. *Mystical Bedlam: Madness, Anxiety, and Healing in Seventeenth-Century England.* Cambridge University Press, 1981.

Macek, E. "The Emergence of a Feminine Spirituality in *The Book of Martyrs.*" *Sixteenth Century Journal* 19, no. 1 (1988): 63–80.

Mack, P. "Feminine Behavior and Radical Action: Franciscans, Quakers, and the Followers of Ghandi." *Signs* 11, no. 3 (1986): 457–77.

Mack, P. "The Prophet and Her Audience: Gender and Knowledge in the World Turned Upside Down." In *Reviving the Revolution,* edited by G. Eley and W. Hunt, 139–52. London: Verso Books, 1988.

Mack, P. "Women as Prophets during the English Civil War." *Feminist Studies* 8 (1982): 19–45.

Maclean, I. *The Renaissance Notion of Woman.* Cambridge: Cambridge University Press, 1980.

Maguire, N. K. "The Theatrical Mask/Masque of Politics: The Case of Charles I." *Journal of British Studies* 28 (1989): 1–22.

Manners, E. *Elizabeth Hooten: First Quaker Woman Preacher.* London: Headley Bros., 1914.

Marcus, L. *The Politics of Mirth.* Chicago: University of Chicago Press, 1986.

Mendelson, S. H. *The Mental World of Stuart Women.* Amherst: University of Massachusetts Press, 1987.

Moody, T. W., F. X. Martin, and F. J. Byrne. *A New History of Ireland.* Vol. 3. Oxford: Clarendon Press, 1976.

Morgan, J. *Godly Learning*. Cambridge: Cambridge University Press, 1986.

Morrill, J. "The Religious Context of the English Civil War." *Transactions of the Royal Historical Society,* 5th ser. 24 (1984): 155–78.

Nelson, B. "Lady Elinor Davies: The Prophet as Publisher." *Women's Studies International Forum* 8, no. 5 (1985): 403–9.

Norsworthy, L. *The Lady of Bleeding Heart Yard: Lady Elizabeth Hatton.* 1935. London: John Murray, 1938.

Patterson, A. *Censorship and Interpretation.* Madison: University of Wisconsin Press, 1984.

Pawlisch, H. *Sir John Davies and the Conquest of Ireland.* Cambridge: Cambridge University Press, 1985.

Petroff, E. A. "Medieval Women Visionaries: Seven Stages to Power." *Frontiers* 3, no. 1 (1978): 34–45.

Petroff, E. A. *Medieval Women's Visionary Literature.* Oxford: Oxford University Press, 1986.

Plomer, H. R. *A Dictionary of the Booksellers and Printers.* London: Bibliographical Society, 1907.

Pollock, L. *Forgotten Children: Parent-Child Relations from 1500–1900.* Cambridge: Cambridge University Press, 1983.

Porter, R. *Mind-Forged Manacles.* London: Athlone Press, 1987.

Porter, R. *A Social History of Madness.* New York: Weidenfeld and Nicolson, 1987.

Potter, L. *Secret Rites and Secret Writing: Royalist Literature 1641–1660.* Cambridge: Cambridge University Press, 1989.

Russell, C. *The Causes of the English Civil War.* Oxford: Clarendon Press, 1990.

Russell, C. *The Fall of the British Monarchies, 1637–1642.* Oxford: Clarendon Press, 1991.

Scheffler, J. "Prison Writings of Early Quaker Women." *Quaker History* 73, no. 2 (1984): 25–37.

Seaver, P. *Wallington's World.* Stanford, Calif.: Stanford University Press, 1985.

Smith, C. F. "Jane Lead: The Feminist Mind and Art of a Seventeenth-Century Protestant Mystic." In *Women of Spirit,* edited by R. R. Ruether and E. McLaughlin, 183–203. New York: Simon and Schuster, 1979.

Smith, C. F. "Jane Lead: Mysticism and the Woman Cloathed with the Sun." In *Shakespeare's Sisters: Feminist Essays on Women Poets.* Edited by S. Gilbert and S. Gubar, 3–18. Bloomington: Indiana University Press, 1979,

Smith, H. *Reason's Disciples: Seventeenth-Century English Feminists.* Urbana: University of Illinois Press, 1983.

Smith, N. *Perfection Proclaimed: Language and Literature in English Radical Religion 1640–1660.* Oxford: Clarendon Press, 1989.

Sommerville, J. P. *Politics and Ideology in England 1603–1640*. London: Longman, 1986.

Spencer, T. "The History of an Unfortunate Lady." *Harvard Studies and Notes in Philology and Literature* 20 (1938): 43–59.

Stallybrass, P. "Patriarchal Territories: The Body Enclosed." In *Rewriting the Renaissance,* edited by M. W. Ferguson, M. Quilligan, and N. J. Vickers, 123–42. Chicago: University of Chicago Press, 1986.

Stone, L. *Crisis of the Aristocracy, 1558–1641*. Oxford: Oxford University Press, 1965.

Stone, L. *The Family, Sex, and Marriage in England 1500–1800*. New York: Harper and Row, 1977.

Thomas, K. V. *Religion and the Decline of Magic*. Harmondsworth: Penguin, 1971.

Thomas, K. V. "Women and the Civil War Sects." In *Crisis in Europe, 1560–1660*, edited by T. Aston, 317–40. New York: Basic Books, 1965.

Todd, B. J. "The Remarrying Widow: A Stereotype Reconsidered." In *Women in English Society, 1500–1800*, edited by M. Prior, 54–92. London: Methuen, 1985.

Todd, M. "Humanists, Puritans, and the Spiritualized Household." *Church History* 49, no. 1 (1980): 18–34.

Underdown, D. "The Taming of the Scold." In *Order and Disorder,* edited by A. Fletcher and J. Stevenson, 116–36. Cambridge: Cambridge University Press, 1985.

Usher, R. G. *The Rise and Fall of the High Commission*. Oxford: Clarendon Press, 1913.

Wright, S. G. "Dougle Fooleries." *Bodleian Quarterly Record* 8 (1932): 95–98.

Wall, A. "Elizabethan Precept and Feminine Practice: The Thynne Family of Longleat." *History* 75, no. 243 (1990): 23–38.

Wall, A. "Faction in Local Politics 1580–1620: Struggles for Supremacy in Wiltshire." *Wiltshire Archaeological Magazine* 72/73 (1980): 119–33.

Wall, A. "The Feud and Shakespeare's *Romeo and Juliet:* A Reconsideration." *Sydney Studies in English* 5 (1979–80): 84–95.

Weigall, R. "An Elizabethan Gentlewoman." *Quarterly Review* 215 (1911): 119–138.

Wheatley, H. B. *Of Anagrams*. 1863.

Willen, D. "Women and Religion in Early Modern England." In *Women in Reformation and Counter-Reformation Europe,* edited by S. Marshall, 140–65. Bloomington: Indiana University Press, 1989.

Williamson, G. C. *Lady Anne Clifford: Countess of Dorset, Pembroke and Montgomery*. 2d ed. Wakefield: S. R. Publishers, 1967.

Wilson, J. *Pulpit in Parliament: Puritanism during the English Civil Wars.* Princeton: Princeton University Press, 1969.

Wiltenburg, J. "Madness and Society in the Street Ballads of Early Modern England." *Journal of Popular Culture* 21, no. 4 (1988): 101–27.

Woodbridge, L. *Women and the English Renaissance.* Urbana: University of Illinois Press, 1984.

Woolrych, A. *Soldiers and Statesmen: The General Council of the Army and its Debates, 1647–1648.* Oxford: Clarendon Press, 1987.

Index

The main entry for Lady Eleanor is: Davies, Eleanor. In subheadings her name is abbreviated ED; Sir John Davies is JD; Sir Archibald Douglas is AD; and Lucy Hastings (née Davis) is LH. Except for members of Lady Eleanor's immediate family who appear under their family names instead of titles, e.g., Touchet or Hastings instead of Audeley, Castlehaven, or Huntingdon, members of the nobility appear under their titles. Most are referred to by title in the text. The same abbreviations for the titles of Lady Eleanor's tracts that appear in the text are used in the index.